Crosscurrents / Modern Critiques
Third Series
Edited by Jerome Klinkowitz

Jerzy Kutnik

(THE NOVEL as PERFORMANCE)
The Fiction of Ronald Sukenick and Raymond Federman

Southern Illinois University Press
CARBONDALE AND EDWARDSVILLE

Printed in the United States of America
Edited by Carol Burns
Designed by Design for Publishing, Inc.
Production supervised by Kathleen Giencke

89 88 87 86 4 3 2 1

Library of Congress Cataloging-in-Publication Data

Kutnik, Jerzy, 1953–
    The novel as performance.

  (Crosscurrents/modern critiques. Third series)
    Bibliography: p.
    Includes index.
    1. American fiction—20th century—History and
criticism.   2. Literature, Experimental—History and
criticism.   3. Sukenick, Ronald—Criticism and interpretation.   4. Federman, Raymond—Criticism and interpretation.   I. Title.   II. Series.
PS379.K88   1986   813'.54'09   85-22280
ISBN 0-8093-1249-2

Contents

Crosscurrents/
Modern Critiques/
Third Series

I N THE EARLY 1960s, when the Crosscurrents/Modern Critiques series was developed by Harry T. Moore, the contemporary period was still a controversial one for scholarship. Even today the elusive sense of the present dares critics to rise above mere impressionism and to approach their subject with the same rigors of discipline expected in more traditional areas of study. As the first two series of Crosscurrents books demonstrated, critiquing contemporary culture often means that the writer must be historian, philosopher, sociologist, and bibliographer as well as literary critic, for in many cases these essential preliminary tasks are yet undone.

To the challenges that faced the initial Crosscurrents project have been added those unique to the past two decades: the disruption of conventional techniques by the great surge in innovative writing in the American 1960s just when social and political conditions were being radically transformed, the new worldwide interest in the Magic

Realism of South American novelists, the startling experiments of textual and aural poetry from Europe, the emergence of Third World authors, the rising cause of feminism in life and literature, and, most dramatically, the introduction of Continental theory into the previously staid world of Anglo-American literary scholarship. These transformations demand that many traditional treatments be rethought, and part of the new responsibility for Crosscurrents will be to provide such studies.

Contributions to Crosscurrents/Modern Critiques/Third Series will be distinguished by their fresh approaches to established topics and by their opening up of new territories for discourse. When a single author is studied, we hope to present the first book on his or her work or to explore a previously untreated aspect based on new research. Writers who have been critiqued well elsewhere will be studied in comparison with lesser-known figures, sometimes from other cultures, in an effort to broaden our base of understanding. Critical and theoretical works by leading novelists, poets, and dramatists will have a home in Crosscurrents/Modern Critiques/Third Series, as will sampler-introductions to the best in new Americanist criticism written abroad.

The excitement of contemporary studies is that all of its critical practitioners and most of their subjects are alive and working at the same time. One work influences another, bringing to the field a spirit of competition and cooperation that reaches an intensity rarely found in other disciplines. Above all, this third series of Crosscurrents/Modern Critiques will be collegial—a mutual interest in the present moment that can be shared by writer, subject, and reader alike.

Jerome Klinkowitz

Foreword

Larry McCaffery

There is a telling but predictable irony that the first book-length study of the fiction of Ronald Sukenick and Raymond Federman to be published in the United States—Jerzy Kutnik's fine analysis, *The Novel as Performance*, which follows—has been written by a young Polish professor who teaches American history at the Uniwersytet Marii Curie–Skłodowskiej in Lublin. The "telling" aspect of the irony has to do with the seemingly ingrained conservatism which continues to mark the American critical and popular reaction to our own artistic innovators. As Ronald Sukenick recently pointed out during a panel discussion dealing with the influence of Latin American literature on North American writing (at the 1984 MLA Convention in Washington, D.C.), publishers, scholars, and even the reading public in the United States seem far more willing to accept experimentalism in foreign writers than they are in works by our own authors. The "predictable" part of this irony, however, evolves from the more encouraging fact that the most significant American avant-garde art is indeed appreciated and talked about in Europe—so much so that we have numerous examples of American artists gaining attention in the United States only after they have received the "legitimization" of European approval. This peculiar phenomenon has always been true to some extent (one thinks of the enthusiasm in France for Faulkner during the 1940s, while in the United States his books were being allowed to go out of print), and recent examples abound: only after Lauri Anderson's "O Superman" became a huge hit in Europe did it occur to the American music industry than an avant-garde performance artist could actually sell records; it requires the winning of the Cannes Film Festival Grand Prize before *Stranger than Paradise* finds its way into our movie theaters; similarly, European audiences are much more likely than their American counterparts to be familiar with Phillip Glass or Robert Wilson, with Francis Coppola's recent experimental Zoetrope productions, or with the fiction of Kathy Acker, Walter Abish, Gilbert Sorrentino, Edmund White, Ronald Sukenick, and Raymond Federman.

Certainly if my own experiences in Poland are any indication (I was there for two weeks during July 1984), the postmodern American novel is alive and flourishing within the Polish literary community. Indeed, during the past decade, there has emerged in Poland a growing number of scholars, translators, and editors (not to mention a supportive reading public) who have focused considerable interest on contemporary American innovative fiction. These are mostly young men and women from cities such as Warsaw, Lublin, Poznań, and Kraków, and they include such figures as Jerzy Kutnik and Jerzy Durczak (Lublin); Zbigniew Lewicki, Tomasz Mirkowicz, Julita Wroniak, and Anna Kołyszko (Warsaw); and Janusz Semrau, Marek Wilzsyński, and Andrzej Kopcewicz (Poznań). Although not yet widely recognized in the United States, their collective accomplishments are already impressive. They have organized major international literary conferences dealing with postmodern American fiction. They publish journals like *Studia Anglica Posnaniensia,* which often contains essays about recent American fiction, and magazines such as *Literatura na Świecie,* which specializes in contemporary world literature (a recent copy, sent to me by Tomasz Mirkowicz, includes translations of a half-dozen Donald Barthelme stories; other fiction by Robert Coover, Walter Abish, Thomas Berger, and William Gaddis; essays on related topics; poems; and even an interview with Barthelme). They have invited and met with dozens of major American writers and critics (Jerzy Kutnik alone has arranged recent visits by Stephen Dixon, Harry Mathews, Sukenick, Federman, Jerry Klinkowitz, Clarence Major, myself, and several others), and they have produced a body of criticism dealing with contemporary fiction that rivals our own, if not yet in quantity (which is growing), then certainly in quality. They are working under conditions that are almost unimaginably difficult by our standards: their chief difficulty is obtaining primary and secondary sources (books from the United States are not imported at all, and because of the currency exchange, the price of used American books is prohibitively high, sometimes as much as a week's salary). Thus, they must rely on friends to send them books and magazines, but they also lack photocopying facilities, secretarial assistance, and even essential writing supplies. But despite such difficulties, they have managed to initiate a lively, sophisticated dialogue with postmodern American fiction. It is out of this context that Jerzy Kutnik's *The Novel as Performance* has emerged—and out of which more significant scholarship is sure to follow.

There are, of course, complex reasons why so many scholars and readers in Poland have found the disruptive experimental works of postmodern American fiction to be so compelling—complexities which I can't claim to understand fully. Part of their enthusiasm can probably be traced to Poland's own long and distinguished tradition of avant-garde art. This tradition remains a strong and vital part of the Polish art scene today, as I discovered when I attended the Polish National Theater in Warsaw and witnessed an astonishingly original theater piece that mixed dance, drama, painting, voice, poetry, mime, and music (such combinations, incidentally, are typical of the performance art examined by Kutnik). Poles also appear to be avid, even voracious readers. There are bookstores everywhere in the major cities, and although the availability of Western titles is naturally limited to used copies, translations of contemporary American authors like Coover, Abish, Gaddis, Steve Katz, John Barth, and Paul Theroux are excerpted in magazines or appear in editions that quickly sell out. My sense is that Polish readers respond appreciatively to postmodernism's playfulness, its delight in disrupting conventions, its implicit undercutting of notions like objectivity, final truths, and authority. One thing I can say with absolute conviction is that Poles have a respect for, even love of, language itself which would make them naturally receptive to postmodernism's foregrounding of language, its shaping and reshaping of words into new shapes within surprising contexts.

As to the present study at hand, Jerzy Kutnik presents a lucid and penetrating discussion of Sukenick and Federman, who are two of postmodern fiction's most important and original practitioners of and theoreticians about the antirealist, antitraditional novel. There are a number of reasons to recommend *The Novel as Performance*, not the least of which are Kutnik's individual discussions of each major work by Sukenick and Federman—works whose self-reflexiveness, playfulness, and formal oddities have resisted book-length analysis until now. Equally important, however, is Kutnik's formulation of a theory of performance art which allows him to deal with these works from a perspective which is focused and illuminating but also open-ended enough to allow for individual treatment. Kutnik's thesis, presented in an opening chapter which skillfully brings together a wide range of aesthetic, philosophical, scientific and artistic viewpoints, is that performance art engages the artist and the audience in a process whose function is fundamentally different from the great mimetic tradition that Erich Auerbach identifies as *the* central tradition of Western art; that is, rather than aiming at *representing* some preexisting state of affairs, performance art seeks to *be an experience for its own sake*, an experience which is ultimately to be recognized as continuous with reality and not merely an occasion for interpretation and analysis. What is highlighted in such performance-oriented art is the artistic process itself, the ways in which the artist uses the materials of his or her medium to produce an imaginative structure; freed from its suspension of disbelief and illusionist presuppositions, the audience of such art is encouraged to see that this artistic process is basically analogous to the process through which we compose our daily reality.

In developing this notion, Kutnik summarizes some of the intellectual and aesthetic forces which brought about the shift from mimetic to performance-oriented presentations. His conclusion is that the conception of the world implicit in mimetic art is no longer ours. Such areas of investigation as quantum physics, linguistic analysis, anthropology, information theory, and poststructuralism have all helped to undermine our faith in the basic ordering principles built into mimetic art (principles such as causality, chronological time, the existence of an irreducible individual psyche, objectivity, the concrete reality of things—in short, the principles of Western rationalism). Since, as Sukenick has observed, it is always art's fundamental struggle to "rescue the truth of our experience" from outmoded forms of interpretations, it was therefore necessary that art discover a means to reflect more accurately the textures and conceptions of contemporary existence. As Kutnik shows, during the 1950s and 1960s, artists in various fields began to explore a conception of art based on performance. The results were obvious in such fields as music (in the works of John Cage and Steve Reich, for instance), painting (abstract expressionism, Action Painting, pop art), poetry (the Beats, projectivist verse), and in multimedia hybrid forms (Happenings, rock operas). This complex swirl of interactions was also having direct effects on fiction writers in general and on the aesthetic principles of Sukenick and Federman specifically. Both authors, for example, were obviously influenced by the improvisational methods that were very much in the air during the 1950s due to the prominence of the Beat writers (much admired by Sukenick) and jazz musicians (of near obsessional interest to Federman). These related improvisional methods became essential features of the aesthetic developed by Sukenick and Federman, which brought to forefront the dynamics of the consciousness's confrontation with the writing process itself. Just as the Beats and jazz musicians broke with classical notions of structure in order to free themselves to respond and react to individual moods, the flow of the present, so too have Federman's and Sukenick's fiction emphasized spontaneity and the ability of the art to render, as concretely as possible, the ongoing processes of the imagination transforming experience into language. This emphasis makes their works resistant to convenient paraphrase (which may partly account for the distrust that many academic critics have for them), for they are intent on creating a literature of surfaces, fiction which cancels meaning and logic, which denies its referentiality to anything other than to their ongoing play with words. Such play prevents any single notion of truth from emerging from their texts and encourages readers to bring forth their own imaginative powers. Their works can thus be seen as a collective demolition of absolute meanings—but also as a free construction of provisional ones. The exhilaration of reading Federman or Sukenick is the same exhilaration we experience when we respond to a great Charlie Parker saxophone solo or a Springsteen guitar solo: it's the joy of being in the presence of an artist bringing into being *real* passions, *real* emotions, which are then shared with us.

That Sukenick and Federman share certain key literary affinities should not obscure the fact that their works are also idiosyncratic and very different in exe-

cution. Some of these differences, of course, result from
the unique circumstances which shaped their personal
lives and their literary careers. Of the two of them, Sukenick has led the more normal-seeming life. A Brook-
lyn native (b. 1932), Sukenick made frequent excursions
as a teenager into Manhattan, where his sister first introduced him to the excitement of the New York City
art scene. He began writing as an undergraduate at Cornell in the 1950s during a period in which that university
was a hotbed of literary activity: Nabokov was teaching
there, and so were young writers like Steve Katz, William
Gass, Richard Farina, and Thomas Pynchon (Sukenick
met Pynchon briefly after Pynchon had submitted a story
to the campus literary magazine, which Sukenick was
editing). He went on to do graduate work at Brandeis
University, from which he received an M.A. in 1957 and
a Ph.D. in 1962. His Ph.D. thesis examined Wallace Stevens, who probably had the most important literary influence on Sukenick's work and thought (other literary
influences include Laurence Sterne, James Joyce, Samuel Beckett, and Henry Miller, all of whom explored
alternatives to mimetic norms and whose specific un-
derminings of the notion of character were of special
interest to Sukenick). But as Kutnik's study demonstrates, it was Stevens' investigations into the relationship
between the imagination and reality that were crucial in
helping to shape the direction that Sukenick's own work
would take. "Adequate adjustment to the present can
only be achieved," Sukenick argued in his first public
work (based on his Ph.D dissertation), *Wallace Stevens:
Musing the Obscure* (New York: New York University Press,
1967), "through ever fresh perception of it, and this is
the effort of [Stevens'] poetry." Clearly, this is the prin-

cipal effort of Sukenick's fiction as well, which has included *Up* (1968), *The Death of the Novel and Other Stories* (1969), *Out* (1973), *98.6* (1975), and *Long Talking Bad Conditions Blues* (1979).

In addition to writing fiction, Sukenick has had a major impact on postmodern fiction in other ways as well: one of the most articulate theoreticians and proponents of experimentalism, Sukenick has published dozens of influential essays about the topic (collected as *In Form: Digressions on the Act of Fiction* [Carbondale and Edwardsville: Southern Illinois University Press, 1985]); in the early 1970s Sukenick was the driving force behind the formation of The Fiction Collective, a writers' cooperative dedicated to the publication of serious, nontraditional fiction that would otherwise be ignored by commercial houses (although its output is limited to the publication of a modest six titles each year, the Collective has published some of the most significant innovative fiction of the past decade, including works by Steve Katz, Jonathan Baumbach, Harold Jaffe, Jerry Bumpus, Fanny Howe, as well as by Federman and Sukenick); the continuing misrepresentation of such works—or, more typically, the complete lack of response to them—inspired Sukenick to found *The American Book Review*, which presents discussions (mainly by fiction writers and poets themselves) of poetry and fiction that would otherwise go unnoticed.

Since Raymond Federman has played with and fictionalized the key elements of his life from the outset of his career as a writer, readers familiar with his work are already aware of the outlines of his autobiography. Born in 1928, Federman grew up in Paris in a bohemian, lower middle class environment (his father Simon was a painter). The central event in Federman's life occurred in 1942 when the Nazis took his parents and two sisters away (they were exterminated in Auschwitz) and Federman was saved only because his mother managed to hide him successfully in a closet. It is this literally unspeakable event—typically represented in his fiction only with the typographical symbols "(X-X-X-X)"—that Federman's fiction has urgently and obsessively circled, evaded, interrogated, and denied; both womb and tomb, the closet in which Federman was placed has become a powerful, complex symbol, recurrent in all his work, drawing together many strands of his investigation of what it means to live and write in a post-Holocaust world. After spending the later years of World War II on a farm in southern France, Federman eventually came to the United States in 1947, living first in Detroit, where he attended high school, played jazz saxophone, and held a series of jobs. Inducted into the United States Army during the Korean conflict, he enrolled at Columbia University after he was released and there began writing and studying literature seriously. After receiving his B.A. from Columbia in 1957, he went on to receive a Ph.D. in French at the University of California at Los Angeles in 1963, where he wrote his thesis on Samuel Beckett that was eventually published as *Journey to Chaos: Samuel Beckett's Early Fiction* (1965). Until he began work on his first novel in 1966, Federman chiefly thought of himself as a poet, and his first significant creative publication was a collection of poems, *Among the Beasts/Parmi les monstres* in 1967. His first published novel, *Double or Nothing* (1971), pulverized the story of his arrival in the United States and his early experiences here into obsessive digressions, typographical designs, metafictional ruminations about writing a novel, and the process of finding and defining our experience. His later works include *Surfiction: Fiction Now . . . and Tomorrow* (1975), a highly influential collection of essays edited and introduced by Federman, *Take It or Leave It* (1976—a French version, considerably shorter, was published as *Amer Eldorado* in 1974), *The Voice in the Closet/La Voix dans le Cabinet de Débarras* (1979), *The Twofold Vibration* (1982), and *Smiles on Washington Square* (1985). Since 1964 Federman has been a professor of comparative literature at the State University of New York at Buffalo.

Despite these differences in personal background, Sukenick's and Federman's passionate and uncompromising dedication to a performance-based aesthetic of fiction writing has made them natural allies; indeed, since the early 1970s, they have been close personal friends and vocal public supporters of each other's works, which they read and comment upon while still in manuscript. In articulating what unites their work while identifying their individual qualities, Kutnik demonstrates what is most unique about their fiction: their unswerving commitment to what Jerome Klinkowitz has called "pure writing": writing which is self-reflexive, which explores the process of its own creation as sensory objects of visual design and sound. In pioneering a fictional approach that aims at liberating words (and the imagination) from the illusionistic presuppositions of realism, Sukenick and Federman have devised a highly original means of liberating the wisdom which exists within language. Playful, self-conscious, sexy, and full of life's sense of mystery, confusion, and excitement, their works perform themselves into being as "real fictitious" discourses. By focusing on this performatory feature of their work, Jerzy

Kutnik's *The Novel as Performance* seizes perhaps the most essential—and most misunderstood—aspect of Sukenick's and Federman's aesthetic and then explores the way each of their individual works applies this principle in unique ways. Kutnik's study will thus inevitably be the starting point for all future discussions of these two authors and of the performatory function of postmodern writing in general.

Acknowledgments

I wish to thank several persons for their interest and encouragement along the way. Foremost are Professor Andrzej Kopcewicz, who patiently directed the dissertation which preceded this work, offering professional counsel and scholarly judgment, and Professors Jerome Klinkowitz and Raymond Federman, without whose unfailing moral support and intellectual stimulation this study could not have been launched and completed. Ronald Sukenick kindly accepted my invitation to come to Lublin for a lecture tour, as did Jerome Klinkowitz and Raymond Federman before him, and submitted to formal and informal interviews. Janusz Semrau supplied many of the ideas that are developed here and Sinda Gregory, Larry McCaffery, and Tomasz Mirkowicz read substantial parts of the manuscript and offered detailed criticism. Larry McCaffery, who visited Poland in 1984, volunteered the initial editing of this manuscript, reducing it substantially from its original form. Nina Klinkowitz organized the manuscript.

Introduction

The classical Western model of art-as-aesthetics remained virtually unchanged from Aristotle and Plato's time until the beginning of the twentieth century, when the rise of modernism and the powerful dislocations of the avant-garde first shook the foundations upon which this aesthetics was based. In the years following World War II, more radical tendencies developed which further undermined the credibility of the classic model of mimetic art and eventually made a major restructuring of traditional aesthetic theory inevitable. Particularly noteworthy among such developments was the process of "theatricalization" by which certain characteristics of theatrical performance were transplanted into the conventionally defined plastic arts and a number of new, hybrid genres were invented which relied almost exclusively on performance. In the performing arts themselves, performance was also given a new emphasis, often replacing the traditional primary categories—the artist, the work of art, and the audience—as the focus of attention. The rise of Action Painting, the Happening, The Living Theatre, John Cage's experimental music and Charles Olson's "projective verse," to name only a few examples of performance-oriented works of the 1950s and 1960s, forced many aestheticians to review the underlying assumptions of classic aesthetics. Performance was now seen as a category which could be made relevant to all art forms. Indeed, for the postmodern artist, performance was shown to be an essential element of all creative activity, a fundamental value in itself, an indispensable, even unavoidable, ingredient of the work of art.

But it should also be noted that performance is not something that, as a result of certain historical developments, was added as a new element in the creative process, for it had always been there, though ignored or suppressed. What was added, rather, was the awareness that all art is always performatory, that it not so much says something *about* reality but, by its occurrence and presence, *does* something as a reality in its own right. The crucial point here is that as a *symbol of awareness* performance soon began to be identified with a broader cultural context so that the idea of the inseparability of artistic creativity from performance—represented by the new notion of the artist as primarily a performer and the work of art as primarily a performance—found numerous counterparts in current scientific and philosophical theories based on the performatory model. In linguistics, speech act theory focused attention on the performatory aspects of utterances. In sociology and psychology, the world came to be viewed as literally a stage and people as actors in the social drama, while the self was now defined as a product of one's performance in the theater of everyday life. Similarly, anthropologists discovered that in many primitive cultures there existed readily available patterns of social behavior based on participatory performance as a fundamental form of social process. And natural scientists argued that knowledge of the physical world was acquired not by detached observation or deductive logic but by active participation in the dynamic processes of the universe.

Today artists, critics, philosophers, scientists, and various kinds of social thinkers and commentators often use *performance* as a catchword to evoke a series of associations with other current, and concurrent, developments in different spheres of human thought and activity in what is variously called our postindustrial, posthumanist, postmodern, or simply postculture society. The extent to which these associative meanings have proliferated can be seen in Michel Benamou and Charles Caramello's *Performance in Postmodern Culture* (Madison: Coda Press, 1977), a collection of essays on topics ranging from philosophy, sociology, and psychology through ethnopoetics, film, music, drama, and literary criticism to culture theory and creative writing. The book's main premise is briefly and crisply stated by Michel Benamou in the introductory essay, "Presence and Play": "Performance, the unifying mode of the postmodern, is now what matters." Instances of the use of the concept of performance by the book's other contributors—for example, "The fact of performance now runs through all our arts" (Jerome Rothenberg); "Performance is not just an aesthetic act but a moral act, a community act, a celebration of what is being brought to experiential fullness through performance" (Richard Palmer); "Essen-

tially, public reflexivity takes the form of a *performance*"
(Victor Turner); "Performance is always a theoretical
statement" (Régis Durand); or "If posthumanist culture
is the matrix of contemporary performance, there is a
matrix larger still: the universe itself, everything that
was, is, and will become. What a performance!" (Ihab
Hassan)—illustrate how the meaning of the term has
been recently transformed and broadened from a secondary aesthetic category to a primary one, from a theatrical concept to a sociological and philosophical one,
from a familiar word meaning "a doing of something"
to an epitome of postmodern consciousness, a concept
encompassing "the being of everything." To put it another way, they illustrate to what extent the term has
been endowed with implicative power that extends far
beyond the original scope of its meaning, that is, to what
extent its present meaning has become *metaphorical*, fig-
urative and not literal. At the same time, performance
is now used not so much as a metaphor for various kinds
of creative activity—after all, activities performed by
painters, actors, writers, scientists, philosophers, and so
on have always been basically the same—but as a metaphor for a specific, postmodern, kind of consciousness
which makes "the emphasis on performance, whether
demystified as illusionistic or resurgent with symbolic
message," to quote Benamou again, "a pattern of all
postmodern art." The term, then, functions today as a
kind of "conceptual archetype" (Max Black's term) or
"root metaphor" (Stephen C. Pepper's term).

The present study will attempt to demonstrate the
usefulness of the performance metaphor in the study
of the contemporary novel by considering the writings

of Ronald Sukenick (part 1) and Raymond Federman (part 2), two avant-garde novelists who have successfully adapted the performatory model of art developed earlier in the plastic and performing arts as well as in poetry to the unique conditions of fiction. Accompanied by a substantial body of criticism written by both authors, their novels and stories not only reflect the vogue of performance as a dominant tendency in postmodern art, but they also reflect upon the aesthetic and ethical implications of the ongoing redefinition (demimetization/ theatricalization) of fiction and art in general as well as the broadly philosophical implications of the epistemological shift of western culture toward the postmodern turn. I hope to demonstrate that Ronald Sukenick's and Raymond Federman's repudiation of the idea of the novel as mimesis (representation) in favor of the genuinely postmodern idea of the novel as performance (presentation) not only brings fiction up-to-date with contemporary art and culture at large but also leads to a profound exploration of zones of consciousness inaccessible to the modern (realistic or modernist) writer. Preceding the discussion of Ronald Sukenick's and Raymond Federman's writings, the introductory chapter will discuss the specific context in which the performance metaphor will be defined in these pages and the ways in which its meaning will be extended in its analogical uses. The intention is to insure that the term "performance" is not used in a *loosely* metaphorical sense, with reference to unrelated or isolated phenomena, but that it functions as a clearly defined critical tool capable of bringing out all the associations that make performance fully commensurate with postmodern culture. The final

chapter will consider the more general aesthetic implications of how Ronald Sukenick's and Raymond Federman's use of the performatory model of art has
contributed to the "post-modernization" of contemporary American fiction.

The Novel as Performance

1

Aspects of Performance

APART FROM BRIEF definitions to be found in standard dictionaries, the concept of performance remains a vaguely defined aesthetic category. This haziness results partly from the fact that performance is traditionally regarded as relevant only to the conventionally defined performing arts, which automatically disqualifies it as an issue of primary importance to many critics, and even in the performing arts themselves, performance's function is defined as derivative, a form of mediation in the transmission of the original content of the work of art from the primary artist to the audience. Small wonder, then, that, as Hilde Hein observes in her essay "Performance as an Aesthetic Category," "there are significantly few discussions in the historical literature of aesthetics on the status and role of performers and performance." Typical of this reductionism are F. E. Sparshott's *The Structure of Aesthetics* and Monroe C. Beardsley's *Aesthetics: Problems in the Philosophy of Criticism*, in which performance is either mentioned only in passing with reference to the performing arts and without being defined at all or is defined so narrowly that its theoretical uniqueness is all but ignored.[1] Whether we accept Sparshott's notion of the work of art as an object possessing some physical characteristics or Beardsley's view that the aesthetic object is the primary artist's intention, it remains that, to use Sparshott's words, "we do not identify *the* work of art with any one performance even if only one should happen to exist or take place."[2]

As Hein points out, this deprecatory view of performance manifests itself in the tendency to refer to performance as interpretation,[3] which seems to be a good way of stressing its secondary function—an interpretation of something is not that something but follows it in time and value. Accordingly, performers are ideally reduced to a transparent medium while their performance becomes a largely passive, though masterly and proficient, rendition of whatever form of notation is called for (text, score, schema, and so on). As a result, regardless of the performer's skill or virtuosity, Hein observes, "the theoretical uniqueness of the concept of performance as so represented is minimal; for it is entirely subordinated to the primary aesthetic categories, the creative artist, the work of art, and the audience."[4] This is no great loss for traditional aestheticians, for they can well do without this concept at all by parceling its features between the primary categories so that it virtually disappears as an autonomous entity.

Hein also points out that the failure of classic aesthetics to assign a primary status to performance "is particularly odd from the point of view of laymen for whom the issue of performers and performance is often the central feature of art."[5] Referring to current trends in the visual and performing arts towards merging the experience of the primary artist and the spectator in a participatory performance, she stresses that the situation must not be perpetuated, or art theory will get completely out of touch with art practice. This danger, she suggests, can be averted by correcting the "category mistake"[6] of traditional aesthetics and recognizing performance as a primary category. This is an important recognition, but it is probably a mistake to believe that such a move is possible without a major restructuring of aesthetics and a redefinition of its underlying principles. In her analysis of the causes of the situation, she does not pursue the structural implications of the failure of traditional aesthetics to deal appropriately with performance, and so she does not reach the heart of the problem—the fundamental irreconcilability between the classic theory of art as mimesis and the performatory theory of art implicit in the works of an increasing number of twentieth-century artists. The difference is that between the static notion of representation and the dynamic notion of (non-re-)presentation, a difference which could never be resolved in traditional aesthetics because of its insistence that mimetic standards are the ultimate criteria of relevance.

Interestingly, there is one notable exception to these mimetic assumptions, and that is music criticism. Music is the only one of the arts which lacks any unequivocally representational dimension and is best defined in dynamic terms as process. Of course, given the bias of traditional aesthetics toward the object and the content/form dichotomy, it is not surprising that music is often deprived of its right to represent only itself by being not just described but also *interpreted*. As Beardsley asserts:

"It has often been observed that the flow of music bears striking resemblances to the flow of meaningful human discourse. Hence the temptation to speak of music as a 'language,' and to take over linguistic terms for its analysis: 'phrase,' 'sentence,' 'paragraph,' for example." This in turn leads to the view that music is something more than just sounds, that it has "a semantic dimension, like words or gestures."[7] Still, even such a traditional aesthetician as Beardsley admits that music finally "is no symbol of time or process, mental or physical, Newtonian or Bergsonian; it *is* process. And perhaps we can say it is the closest thing to pure process, to happening as such."[8] Consequently, he cannot avoid the question of performance as it is inseparable from the happening of music, though he typically depreciates its status.

The American arts of the post–World War II period offer a great number of instructive examples which illustrate how the performatory mode came to dominate such conventionally defined arts as painting, sculpture, theatre, music, dance, and poetry, causing at the same time the emergence of such hybrids as Happenings, Events, Assemblages, Environments, Intermedia, or Performances in which performance is an essential, and often the sole, ingredient. In the course of this process, a revision of traditional aesthetic principles became necessary and inevitable. Of special importance here are two specifically American contributions to postmodern art, Action Painting and the Happening, which most undermined the foundations of classic aesthetics by bringing into focus the conception of art as performance.

The American painters associated with Action Painting challenged, separately and yet simultaneously, the idea of pictorial vision which had dominated Western painting since the rise of perspective in the Renaissance. Inevitably, they also found themselves taking such earlier trends of the avant-garde as Cubism and Expressionism to their logical conclusion by substituting in their works actual physical motion, the actual movement of the artist's body, for the illusory representation of motion. The concurrence of the orientation toward abstractness, of the elimination of any identifiable subject matter, on the one hand, and the "theatricalization" of painting, on the other, has been stressed by Harold Rosenberg, who gave the Action Painters their most popular name. In his seminal *The Tradition of the New*, he observed: "The apples weren't brushed off the table in order to make room for perfect relations of space and color. They had to go so that nothing would get in the way of the act of painting. . . . Form, colors, composition, drawing, are auxiliaries, any one of which—or practically all, as has been attempted logically, with unpainted canvases—can be dispensed with. What matters always is the revelation contained in the act."[9]

The notions of the creative artist, the work of art and the spectator were immediately affected in a most profound way. The painter became an actor, the canvas a stage, and the viewer a participant in the creative act. Jackson Pollock, for example, took the canvas off the easel, tacked it to the floor, and literally performed a painting, dripping paint as he walked and danced on it. The painting itself, the material object, was but a trace of the painter's presence and told only the story of its own happening. Viewers, enveloped by the sheer immensity of the size of a Pollock painting, not only reenacted in their minds the movement of the artist's body but were forced to retrace this movement in physical motion by walking in front of the painting. The act, or performance, became a necessary condition for the creation of a painting, for its being a work of art, and for its being apprehended and experienced by the viewer. The nature of this act was best described by Pollock himself:

> When I am *in* my painting, I'm not aware of what I'm doing. It is only after a sort of "get acquainted" period that I see what I have been about. I have no fears about making changes, destroying the image, etc., because the painting has a life of its own. I try to let it come through. It is only when I lose contact with the painting that the result is a mess. Otherwise there is pure harmony, an easy give and take, and the painting comes out well.[10]

An Action Painting thus possesses a set of interrelated characteristics which follow logically from one another. First, it has an unpremeditated character since there is no preset, referential meaning to be conveyed; simply, meaning is generated in the act, and it is the painting's own existence. Nonreferentiality in turn means that a painting has "a life of its own" and needs no authority outside itself to justify and evaluate its existence. Being its own subject matter, a record of its own occurrence, such a painting also automatically moves away from the idea of masterpiece and becomes value free: it cannot be judged for its success or failure in reaching some goal, for it has no goal beyond its own happening.

This may suggest that Action Painting stands for the idea of art for art's sake and is completely detached from life. It does have, however, a profoundly human dimension which follows from its experiential nature: an Action Painting is not a picture of or response to some past experience, but it is itself an experience. For the artist, painting is a way of breaking down the barrier between art and life, a mode of being in the world, as Pollock's "When I am *in* my painting" suggests. As part of the artist's life, painting is for him the most immediate way of articulating his view of the world. Most naturally, his is a dynamic vision in which the world is conceived of in terms of energy flow, an idea typically represented by Hans Hofmann's "push-and-pull" principle. According to it, everything—the surface of the canvas, the paint, the brush, the space around the painter and the model— is, as Rosenberg observes, "a vital substance quivering with energies which it constantly [draws] in and [sends] forth." The pulsation that permeates the material world finds its counterpart in the painter's intellectual and emotional energy which is discharged in painting in an uncontrolled and unpremeditated manner. The effect is that, as Clement Greenberg notes, "[Hofmann's] paint surfaces *breathe* as no others do, opening up to animate the air around them."[11] Ultimately, it is not the lifelike quality (illusion) but the actual life of and in painting that matters.

By focusing attention on the act/action of painting, Action Painting creates an entirely new situation in which all basic elements of the classic model are transformed. The traditional primary categories lose their primary status as the underlying principle, mimesis, is abandoned. Consequently, the traditional view of art and life as separate realms becomes indefensible. Similarly, critical judgment in the conventional sense is rendered superfluous or even impossible, for the only set of definable characteristics which could be evaluated concerns the canvas and the paint as material substances. Other than that, there is only the "lucid drama"[12] of painting which can only be participated in, not contemplated from a detached perspective and judged.

The theatricalization of painting described above demonstrates that the concept of performance emerging from the strategies of Action Painting had little to do with the traditional notion of performance as execution of the creative artist's will retained in a script, score, or schema. This fact became spectacularly obvious when the ideas of the Action Painters were transplanted directly into theater. The marriage of painting and theater resulted in the creation of a new genre, the Happening, which was often called simply the painters' theater. As Allan Kaprow, the "instigator" of the first Happenings, admits, they "have come directly out of the rites of American Action Painting."[13] (Actually, the inspiration for Kaprow and his followers came from many other sources as well, such as Schwitters' collage, the Dada, the Bauhaus, Surrealism, Artaud's theater, and other earlier avant-garde and popular arts.) John Cage, central to virtually all experimental arts in the United States since World War II, also developed important precursors of the Happening. In the summer of 1952, Cage presented at Black Mountain College an early form of the Happening, which he called a "simultaneous lecture" that involved several performances of various artists (an actor, a poet, a musician, a painter, and a dancer). It was, however, only after Kaprow's first Happening, entitled *18 Happenings in 6 Parts*, soon followed by other Happenings as well as by his theoretical statements, that more painters—Jim Dine, Claes Oldenburg, and Red Grooms, to name a few—and other artists took to organizing performances which they variously labeled Happenings, Activities, or Events.

Originally, the idea behind Kaprow's decision to give up painting for the Happening was a desire to establish "organic connections between art and its environment" so that "the line between art and life should be kept as fluid, and perhaps as indistinct, as possible."[14] The collapse of these barriers was achieved by creating theatrical situations in which real life activities of various people were paired with painting, sculpture, music (sound), films, lights, objects, and so on. The separation between audience and play virtually disappeared since most Happenings were, as Kaprow asserts, "spawned in old lofts, basements, vacant stores, in natural surroundings and in the street, where very small audiences, or groups of visitors, [were] commingled in some way with the event, flowing in and among its parts."[15]

The orientation of the Happening toward creating experience, as opposed to reproducing it, manifested itself in various ways. For one thing, in many Happenings, no distinction was made between the "acting" and the physical aspects of the production. This emphasized the truth of the medium, its concrete and nonreferential status. Similarly, the function of the actor was changed in the Happening from role playing to task performing, which was often assigned at random to members of the audience as well; thus, performers and audience were joined in a communal, ritualized ceremony in which people were vital but impersonal, even self-less, elements of the performance. Likewise, the distinction between material objects and persons was also frequently abolished. Persons, as Susan Sontag notes, were treated "as material objects rather than characters" and were "often made to look like objects, by enclosing them in burlap sacks, elaborate wrappings, shrouds, and masks."[16] The self, then was given up almost completely.

On a different level, the Happening abolishes the text and relies heavily on improvization, often resorting to chance. It has no preset meaning, for it does not develop according to a script but, at best, according to a loose scenario which typically produces a free and open-ended form. Since many Happenings, as Kaprow observes, "have no structured beginning, middle, or end," they "appear to go nowhere."[17] Naturally, he adds, they have no plot and, consequently, no development of the action in any strict sense—"The action leads itself any way it wishes."[18] In the process of dissolving the attributes of traditional theatrical performance, the Happening not only dispenses with the text and the actor, but also with the temporal dimension of drama, becoming essentially an art of the moment. Susan Sontag points out:

As the name itself suggests, Happenings are always in the present tense. The same words, if there are any, are said over and over; speech is reduced to a stutter. The same actions, too, are frequently repeated throughout a single Happening—a kind of gestural stutter, or done in slow motion, to convey a sense of the arrest of time. Occasionally the entire Happening takes a circular form, opening and concluding with the same act or gesture.[19]

With no sense of direction and time attached to it, a Happening does not aim at any goal beyond its own happening. When it is finished, it disappears without any product, or even trace, left. If it is an instance of "art for art's sake," it is an instance of "experience for experience's sake" as well.

The Happening brought together representatives of many different arts. Largely through personal contacts of its practitioners, it adopted ideas from other arts and influenced them at the same time—so much so, that it is sometimes quite difficult to determine what the exact nature and direction of the exchange between the Happening and such arts as painting, sculpture, dance, theater, music, and poetry was. Yet, although the Happening epitomized the features of the model of art as performance more completely than any other form, it did not exhaust the potential of performance as an artistic mode and diminish its adaptability to the specific conditions of other arts at all. Both the visual and the performing arts continued to develop in the direction pointed to first by Action Painting and then by the Happening, finding new, though essentially parallel, applications for the performatory model. The process of the theatricalization of the plastic arts started by Action Painting was continued by later artists who, going beyond its gestural techniques, developed other forms of movement in painting and sculpture. Their works subordinated the object to the act of the artist and relied on the viewer's active participation in the creation and presence of the work of art. A good example of this kind of work was Jim Dine's famous paint-construction—a big hatchet on a chain attached to a canvas divided down the center by a rough beam of wood. As Jill Johnston observes, "Jim Dine's hatchet-canvas did not require participation by the observer to be complete; but if the observer did attack the wood with the hatchet, it became a performance."[20]

Many ideas of the Action Painters were also transplanted into sculpture, via such hybrid forms as Rauschenberg's "combines" (which made use of ready-made objects that retained their identity as real and not representational objects). Starting with Oldenburg's "soft scuplture" and Op Art, which relied for their effect on the viewer's motion or, conversely, on the motion of the object, through sculptures which were conditioned by location (for example, Tony Smith's room-filling sculptures), sculpture moved outside the museum and into the environment.

As should be clear by now, the introduction of performance into the plastic, nonperforming arts did not mean merely adding an ingredient which had previously been absent, or at least suppressed, in those arts. Not only were the boundaries between the various arts and art forms effectively blurred or even abolished completely, but the distinctions between the creative artist, the work of art, the performer, and the audience—and ultimately the distinction between art and life, too— became quite problematic as the work of art was made part of experience and the environment. By abandoning the object completely (as in Conceptual Art), a new emphasis was placed on the immediacy and ultimate autonomy of the act of creation, whether physical or mental, and by using ready-made objects and materials of art as materials (paint as paint), the nonrepresentational quality of painting and sculpture became their central feature. The creative artist's performance was no longer seen as merely a necessary phase in the production of the work of art, in the process of the objectification of his vision, but it became itself the aesthetic object and the most effective strategy of nonmimetism.

The aspiration of so much of contemporary art to the condition of an act could not leave the performing arts themselves unaffected. It might seem that the impact of the focus on performance should be of much smaller significance in music, theater, and dance than it was in painting and sculpture since performance was not a new element in the performing arts. However, as already noted, the concept of performance associated with non-mimetism and theatricalization is utterly different from the traditional notion of performance as a secondary category subordinated to the activities of the creative artist, the work of art, and the audience. This new concept which evolved from the strategies of Action Painting and the Happening was indeed equally new to the visual arts and to theater, music, and dance, eventually producing results comparable to those in the former.

In music, Cage has been the most forceful proponent of the inherently nonmimetic character of the performatory model. Experimental music, he says, is by definition nonmimetic and theatrical, providing that the term "experimental" "is understood not as descriptive of an act to be later judged in terms of success or failure, but simply as of an act the outcome of which is unknown."[21] The nonmimetism is in experimental music's unpremeditated character, in its being "intentionally purposeless," and in its repudiation of the idea of masterpiece—"A sound accomplishes nothing." Its theatricality is in its being an act—"Relevant action is theatrical."[22]

The implications of this doctrine are essentially parallel to the results of the theatricalization of painting and sculpture sketched above. First of all, having been freed from the need to imitate or represent, experimental music becomes self-reflexive—it tells its own story, that is, the story of its material. Just as Action Painting is about canvas and paint, so is Cage's experimental music about its sounds and silences—"an identification has been made with the material, and actions are then those relevant to its nature." The story music has to tell is described by Cage in the following words: "A sound does not view itself as a thought, as ought, as needing another sound for its elucidation, as etc.; it has no time for any consideration—it is occupied with the performance of its characteristics: before it has died away it must have made perfectly exact its frequency, its loudness, its overtone structure, the precise morphology of these and of itself."[23]

The story of music, of "the performance of its characteristics," has the form of a flow of energy. It is one of many kinds of energy that permeates the universe, eternally intermingling and interacting with one another. Cage's holistic, or organismic, conception of music as inseparable from other phenomena in the universe—"Without it life would not last out the instant"—is in fact a logical consequence of its nonmimetism. Because it is "intentionally purposeless" and "meaningless," experimental music makes the distinction between object and intention fundamental to the interpretation of music in traditional aesthetics totally irrelevant. This in turn leads to the breakdown of other dichotomies resulting from it—"If, at this point, one says, 'Yes! I do not discriminate between intention and non-intention,' the splits, subject-object, art-life, etc., disappear."[24]

In terms of the standard aesthetic classification, this breakdown means the virtual disappearance of the traditional primary categories. First, with the sounds of music being part of the eternal discourse of sound and silence, it does not make much sense to talk about the work of art, for music *is* always, everywhere, and in whatever form—"It can appear when- where- as whatever (rose, nail, constellation, 487.73482 cycles per second, piece of string)."[25] Second, since no intentional action on man's part is necessary for music's happening or existence, the concept of the composer as conscious creator, or manipulator, becomes simply useless—sounds do not have to be intentionally arranged, they are music without, or despite, man's intervention. Third, the listener becomes indistinguishable from the primary artist and the performer ("getting up in the morning and discovering oneself a musician") or even from the work of art (music "is you yourself in the form you have that instant taken").[26] And fourth, the critic as interpreter becomes superfluous since, as Cage asserts, "you will never be able to give a satisfactory report even to yourself of just what happened."[27]

The best-known example of a work that eliminates the composer as conscious creator, the work as the composer's intention and/or score, the performer as interpreter of the composer's intention, and the listener as merely appreciator is Cage's famous piece entitled *4'33"*. It consists of four minutes and thirty-three seconds of silence, or rather of the noises made ("performed") by the audience during the (non-)performance of this "composition." It illustrates but one, possibly the most radical, way of eliminating the traditional aesthetic categories by chance methods.

Cage's ideas about music found an easy way into dance as a result of the close cooperation of the composer with America's leading avant-garde dancer and choreographer, Merce Cunningham. The two introduced the principle of indeterminacy into dance, first of time structure—

they worked independently to fill an arbitrary time structure with movement and sound—and then of the order of the parts of a dance—Cunningham tossed coins to determine the sequence. In effect, the dancer's impersonal concentration on the material at hand was determined by chance and coherence became completely linked to performance. The dance, as Cunningham puts it, "is free to act as it chooses, as is the music,"[28] which means that it naturally abandons the idea of meaning, intentionality, interpretation, and so on and approaches the idea of superficiality. Like paint on canvas in Action Painting and sounds transmitted through space in Cage's "experimental music," in Cunningham's dance "that which is seen, is what it is." In other words, the emphasis is on movement as movement. Dance as pure movement freed from the necessity to represent tears down the boundary between art and life and becomes a part, and not a picture, of reality. Merce Cunningham says:

What the dancer does is the most realistic of all possible things, and to pretend that a man standing on a hill could be doing everything except just standing is simply divorce—divorce from life, from the sun coming up and going down, from clouds in front of the sun, from the rain that comes from the clouds and sends you into the drugstore for a cup of coffee, from each thing that succeeds each thing. Dancing is a visible action of life.[29]

With many other dancers, like Ann Halprin, Judith Dunn, and Simone Morris, dance indeed got very close to the Happening and its meaning was extended to include any kind of activity at all. This in turn led to the disappearance of any recognizable distinction between the primary artist (choreographer), the performers (dancers), and the audience (nondancers), the latter being often drawn into the "action" and thus becoming inseparable from the performance. Exploring the affinities between dance and the visual arts,[30] some artists moved in the direction of the complete obliteration of the self in action. In *Colorado Plateau*, for instance, the painter Alex Hay dragged and carried six actors around the arena of performance which, as Jill Johnston observes, "became a changing sculpture of diagonals, verticals and horizontals. The performers were neutral objects in this visual exercise."[31] The dance thus became literally to an equal extent the mind and the body's domain.

Coming to the third of the conventionally defined performing arts, theater, it should be stressed once again that the concepts of theatricality and performance that evolved in the context of other nonmimetic "action" arts have little to do with traditional theater, whether in the Aristotelian or Stanislavskian sense. Rather, they spring from the tradition of Artaud's antitheater. Artaud abandoned mimesis and set before art the task of closing the gap between art and life. As Susan Sontag observes, "Once the leading criterion for art becomes its merger with life (that is, everything, including other arts), the existence of separate art forms ceases to be defensible."[32] Therefore Artaud dreamed of a total art which, Sontag goes on to say, "had to be, to feel large; it had to be a multivoiced performance."[33] It was to be theatrical, but not theater in the traditional sense:[34] it was to be "pure" theater based on "true action" and immediacy. Artaud said: "Objects, accessories, sets on the stage must be apprehended directly . . . not for what they represent but for what they are."[35] In the United States, from the 1950s onward, the line originated by Artaud was continued and developed by several "theatres of non-actors" (as Richard Gilman calls them). Writing in 1968 about the American scene, Gilman thus described the situation:

> In America, where we've produced no significant body of formal dramatic works, there is an increasing interest in theatres of improvisation and games, testimony to the dissatisfaction with the stage as a place for the conjuring up of images. The desire that it become an arena for new, original gestures, performed by actors who are no longer executors, *stand-ins*, but instigators and makers, lies behind the growing repudiation of formal texts as well as increasing currency of words like "ritual," "myth" and "play" (the verb). A vocabulary with a potential for self-deception and indulgence of adolescent ambitions, it nevertheless also expresses an appetite for theatre as an actuality rather than a reflection, an original gesture rather than an interpretive one—for theatre, in other words, to stop being illusion.[36]

This appetite has been forcefully articulated in the work of several American experimental theaters during the last twenty-five years or so, the most distinguished among them being The Living Theatre, The Open Theatre, and Richard Schechner's The Performance Group, all of which abandoned representation in art in favor of original presentation. But in theater a new element borrowed from primitive cultures was added: ritual. Its introduction into theater was a crucial moment in the development of "performance theater" for at least two reasons. One, it added an entirely new, extraartistic and broadly cultural, or anthropological, dimension to the concept of postmodern performance; two, it initiated the process of going back to the roots of modern theater in order to show that the idea of performance inherited from the primitive world and now revived in postmodern theater is essentially foreign, and indeed contradictory, to modern, mimetic theater.

Richard Schechner's writings on the subject are particularly illuminating. Giving the kind of theatrical performance based on ritual characteristic of primitive cultures the name "actual," he defines it as a "special way of handling experience and jumping the gaps between past and present, individual and group, inner and outer."[37] Actualizing is very different from conventional acting; in fact, one is the opposite of the other. "The goal of conventional acting and the basis of Stanislavsky's great work is to enable the actor to 'really live' his character. Nature ought to be so skillfully imitated that it seems to be represented on stage. The tendency of an actual is the opposite."[38] As Schechner explains: "The play and *mise-en-scène* have a quality of having-been-lived, while the performance has the quality of living-now."[39] One is a representation/communication of a drama, the other is a presentation/manifestation of an actuality; one stresses structure and sequence, the other process and presence, the "there and then" of traditional theatre as opposed to the "here and now" of performance theater.

The tendency is typically represented by the productions of The Living Theatre, which get the closest to the idea of pure process plays. *Paradise Now*, for example, is made up of eight Rungs, each of which consists of a Rite, a Vision, and an Action. At each Rung is a "stumbling block" which is to be overcome by dynamic action, called "Impetus." The audience is given a chart of the entire event but the play develops basically in a random, disorderly manner. Or so it seems, for, as Schechner contends, "*Paradise Now* is very well organized if one recognizes diversion, disruption and side-tripping as part of that organization."[40] Guiding the audience from "The Rite of Guerilla Theatre" toward "The Street," the actors move toward a complete breakdown of the barrier between art and life, which for The Living Theatre means chiefly the barrier between art and politics. The performance approaches, then, the ideal of a communal ceremony in which fragmentation and separation are overcome through actual group interaction.

A study of the development of recent American arts demonstrates that the current drive toward performance, or theatricalization, has been inseparable from what Susan Sontag calls the "flight from interpretation,"[41] that is, the movement away from the notion of content-oriented, mimetic art. The application of the performatory model to literature, however, may seem quite problematic as it apparently poses special difficulties following from the unique conditions of literature as an art form. Logically, a literature which orients itself toward performance should eventually also approach the condition of a nonmimetic art. But within the framework of classic aesthetics, the notion of nonmimetic literature is a contradiction in terms, for according to the traditional view, literature is necessarily mimetic or representational. This view is rooted in the assumption common to all major philosophical systems from Descartes to Husserl that language, the medium of literature, is also inherently representational because its meaning depends utterly on its referentiality, that is, on the existence of a correspondence between secular facts and statements about those facts.

But in modern and postmodern epistemology, language is regarded as a human-invented, hence artibrary, system of signs which can be changed at will; thus, the modern writer, critic, or philosopher tends to see words as naturally inferior to secular facts which they name because, unlike words, facts are recognized as objective, that is, as existing irrespective of people's perception and naming of them. In fact, both the modern rationalist and the modern phenomenologist believe that it is exactly because facts are objective that we can eventually come to know them by describing and explaining them in words, that is, by inventing names for them. Consequently, language is seen as merely a tool with which people subordinate and win control of the world, an instrument of communication and scientific notation. Viewed in this way, it is automatically deprived of the sacred and mystic power that it holds for premodern people, for whom, as Richard Palmer notes, the word "is a mark of what it names; it retains a mysterious link or connection with what it names."[42] The modern dividing mind breaks this link, detaches the word from being, and interposes arbitrary reference between them. For modern people, then, language does not articulate what *is* but what *means*. And modern people, of course, conceitedly assume that it is exclusively in them, in their minds, that all meaning takes origin.

In the twentieth century, the modern reductive view of language was first questioned and eventually rejected by the precursor of a truly postmodern philosophy of language, Ludwig Wittgenstein, who discovered that if people controlled their language, they were to an equal extent prisoners of it, too. In his famous dictum "The limits of my language are the limits of my world."[43] he acknowledged that people's perceptions and knowledge of both physical and psychic phenomena are determined by the possibilities of language to articulate experience, a view that contradicts the Cartesian confidence in the unlimited possibilities of the human mind and the belief that language obediently serves people as a perfect, or at least perfectible, system for recording experience.

Wittgenstein's inferences about the autonomy of language were soon confirmed by other logicians and, notably, mathematicians, who showed that formal systems—and language is just such a system—after reaching a certain level of complexity become self-referential. This condition has been explored by Douglas R. Hofstadter in *Gödel, Escher, Bach*, where he demonstrates how dualisms are overcome in such formal systems as computer language, logic, and musical structure. Thus, for example, he states that "a statement of number theory is not *about* a statement of number theory; it just *is* a statement of number theory" and calls this phenomenon "Strange Loopiness," which is simply the mathematician's version of nonmimetism. Formally speaking, every work of literature, indeed every utterance, states a more or less complex "number theory" in general language, and so it may also reach a level at which the statement and the fact stated will become one and the same thing. In such a situation, the work will no longer be *about* reality but will become itself a self-contained reality. It is in such a situation that language becomes, as Richard Palmer puts it, "a medium of ontological disclosure in which things take on being through words."[44]

The consequences for literature of recognizing language as potentially autonomous, as capable not only of stating facts but also of itself being a fact, of literally bringing new things, or new meanings, into being, are fairly obvious: literary works are freed from the obligation to describe or express something other than themselves and become potentially autonomous entities to be approached on their own terms; no longer windows that open to or mirrors that reflect or lamps that illuminate reality, they are surfaces which are realities in their own right. The tradition of such works is predominantly poetic (as opposed to novelistic), probably because poems are more immediately recognizable as autonomous aesthetic facts and not as pictures or imitations of objects and phenomena. Simply, most works of poetry are shorter than novels and less dependent for their impact on logical discourse; they do not rely exclusively, as most novels do, on language's semantic dimension but make use of its concrete (visual and auditory) aspects as well.

The first modern poet who broke with the tradition of Romantic and Symbolic poetry and thus took poetry toward the postmodern turn was, as Marjorie Perloff argues in her *The Poetics of Indeterminacy*, Arthur Rimbaud, who "discovered language in its autonomous (dis)functioning, freed from its obligation to express and to represent, a language in which the initiative is truly surrendered to the words."[45] In the first half of the twentieth century, the line originated by Rimbaud, or as Perloff has it, "the 'anti-Symbolist' mode of indeterminacy or 'undecidability,' of literalness and free play,"[46] was continued by such American poets as Gertrude Stein, Ezra Pound, and William Carlos Williams. They were all profoundly influenced by contemporary avant-garde visual artists, who, Perloff contends,

from the early days of Cubism in 1910 through Vorticism and Futurism, Dada and Surrealism, down to the Abstract Expressionism of the fifties, and the Conceptual Art, Super-Realism, assemblages, and performance art of the present . . . have consistently resisted the Symbolist model in favor of the creation of a world in which forms can exist "littéralement et dans tous les sens," an oscillation between representational reference and compositional game.[47]

The eventual drifting of anti-Symbolist poetry toward performance could already be seen as an inevitable development in the works of Gertrude Stein, whose "Accents in Alsace" Perloff describes as a text that "allows for free play, constructing a way of happening rather than a description of how things look,"[48] and of Ezra Pound, who, the critic notes, admired Rimbaud for his "directness of presentation" and advocated a new nonmimetic art which he called Vorticism, defining the "vortex" as "the point of maximum energy."[49] The merger of the anti-Symbolist and the performatory modes became a fact with the American poets associated with the artistic avant-gardes gathered around Black Mountain College and New York's Action Painters. Significantly, both groupings produced several first-rate poets but not a single novelist of similar stature. Two of these poets, Charles Olson and Frank O'Hara, have played a fundamental role in establishing the performatory as the dominant mode of postmodern American poetry.

Charles Olson, the more theoretically minded of the two, expounded his views about poetry in a considerable number of critical works, the most important among them being his poetic manifesto "Projective Verse," which discusses the nature of poetry conceived in terms of energy transference. Projective verse is defined by Olson as an art in which "the *kinetics* of the thing" is the crucial aspect of what he calls composition by field: "A poem is energy transferred from where the poet got it (he will have some several causations) by way of the poem itself to, all the way over to, the reader. Okay. Then the poem itself must, at all points, be a high-energy construct and, at all points, an energy-discharge."[50] As a verbal structure, such a poem is constantly in motion keeping track of its own composition. Thus, it is not about anything existing outside itself but is a record of its own occurrence. It also has an unpremeditated character, for the poet "can go by no track other than the one the poem under hand declares for itself."[51] By the same token, a projective poem frees itself from "the lyrical interference of the individual as ego, of the 'subject' and his soul,"[52] so the poet's role is merely "to get on with it, keep moving. . . . USE USE USE the process at all points."[53] Indeed, the self in projective verse is placed on equal footing with "those other creations of nature which we may, with no derogation, call objects. For a man himself is an object, whatever he may take to be his advantages."[54]

Defining man's place in the world in terms of how he conceives his relation to nature, Olson points out that the right relation is participation through action, for only "if he is contained within his nature as he is participant in the larger force, he will be able to listen, and his hearing through himself will give him secrets objects share." Here the poet has a special role to play: if he listens to and participates in the process of nature, nature will share its secrets with him, and both will profit. By giving "his work his seriousness, a seriousness sufficient to cause the thing he makes to try to take its place alongside the things of nature,"[55] he will partake of the ultimate act of communion of man and world, art and life. He will make his performance as a poet continuous with his presence in the world. Olson's projective verse displays other features of postmodern performance besides its dynamic holism. The seriousness he has in mind does not preclude the playfulness so characteristic of today's performance-oriented art. Replacing the modern "I think, therefore I am" with "I play, therefore I am," the poet asks, "Is it not the PLAY of a mind we are after, is it not that that shows whether a mind is there at all?"[56] His poetic also emphasizes the process of composition, including the mechanics of it, here meaning the mechanics of type-writing—"It is the advantage of the type-writer that, due to its rigidity and its space precisions, it can, for a poet, indicate exactly the breath, the pauses, the suspensions even of syllables, the juxtapositions even of parts of phrases, which he intends."[57]

"Playing the typewriter" was an important aspect of Frank O'Hara's "conversational life." He considered Olson's views on poetry with some skepticism, finding the leader of the Black Mountain school too theoretical and self-consciously programmatic, but many postulates of "Projective Verse" found their way into O'Hara's "personist" poetry. Less concerned with literary theory, he took inspiration from his friendship with many New York Abstract Expressionists and his work as assistant curator at the Museum of Modern Art in New York. His ideas concerning poetry were in fact often contained in his art criticism and paralleled the ideas of the Action Painters so closely that, as Fred Moramarco suggests, it is enough to change the words "canvas," "painter," and "picture" in a description of Action Painting to get a statement on O'Hara's poetry. O'Hara himself often used the Action Painters' vocabulary when talking about his own poems. In a letter to his frequent collaborator in poem-painting, Larry Rivers, he wrote:

Now please tell me if you think these poems are filled with disgusting self-pity, if there are "holes" in them, if the surface isn't kept "up," if there are recognizable images, if they show nostalgia for the avant-garde, or if they don't have "push" and "pull," and I'll keep working on them until each is a foot high.
Yours in action at,
Frank[58]

Like Action Painters, O'Hara emphasized the autonomous nature of his poems, not as representations of reality but as integral objects existing in reality. He said, "I hope the poem to *be* the subject, not just about it."[59] Paraphrasing his statement on the art of Jackson Pollock, one may say of O'Hara's own poetry that "It is the physical reality of the poet and his activity of expressing it, united with the spiritual reality of the poet in a oneness which has no need for the mediation of metaphor or symbol. It is Action Poetry."[60] O'Hara's collaborators, the painters Larry Rivers and Norman Bluhm, have often stressed the importance of the event more than the final product, comparing their work with the poet to a Happening.

The element of play, or playfulness, also manifested itself on the level of the mechanics of writing. As it was for Olson, the typewriter was for O'Hara the essential instrument in conveying the speed and spontaneity of the verse act. As Marjorie Perloff observes about O'Hara's work, "'Playing the type-writer' rather than writing in longhand inevitably leads the poet to emphasize visual prosody,"[61] which in turn calls attention to the material of poetry as printed text—letters and words filling the white space of the page. Typing a poem the poet creates visual patterns that later request physical involvement from the reader, who not only reads the words but actually scans the surface of the page the way the viewer of a painting does. As Jerome Klinkowitz notes: "The chief components of Frank O'Hara's poetry are the author and the reader—all of his techniques lead to this conclusion. It was the dual principle he admired most in Abstract Expressionist painting, that a good work of art 'engages the viewer in its meaning rather than declaring it.' Equal parts of perception and participation were the sum of Frank O'Hara's poetry."[62]

A further analogy between Abstract Expressionism and O'Hara's poetry concerns its superficial character: both Action Painters and O'Hara are artists of the surface, regarded as a field upon which the artist discharges his physical and spiritual energy. This quality is powerfully conveyed in those of O'Hara's poems in which the poet is physically present, walking as he talks. These poems are casual sidewalk conversations skimming the surface of life in a big city. There is, however, a depth to such superficiality, for, as Anthony Libby observes, "as Pollock flattened the field of his painting only to discover the depths of their surfaces, O'Hara's flat recording of mundane existence only reveals the depths of his perception."[63]

Olson's and O'Hara's emphasis on the immediacy of thought and perception, their desire to convey the living flow of experience as opposed to the analysis and explanation of it, is accepted as a matter of course by contemporary American poets working within the tradition of what Perloff calls "the poetry of indeterminacy," that is, nonmimetism. In the case of John Ashbery, the most distinguished representative of this "other tradition," this means writing "stories that tell only of themselves" and which make one aware of the poem "as an open field of narrative possibilities."[64] A typical Ashbery poem is thus, in the poet's own words, a "reality which you dreamed and which is therefore real."[65] In fact, the relation between the poet and his work is reciprocal—one gives authority to the other—for, as Ashbery observes, "it is you who made it, therefore you are true."[66]

Ultimately, the reality of the poem, the truth that it conveys, is not determined by *what* it says but *how*. In "The System," Ashbery explains his approach to writing in this way: "I think that the question of *how* we are going to use the reality of our revelation, as well as to *what* end, has not been resolved. First of all we see that these two aspects of our question are actually *one and the same*, that there is only one aspect as well as only one question, that *to wonder how is the same as beginning to know why*. For no choice is possible."[67] In other words, Ashbery suggests that people come to know the world not by dividing and classifying the content of their experience but by concentrating on the process of thought and perception, which they regard as a unified flow of their intellectual and physical energy and as part of the external flux of life. In fact, the poet declares, people cannot choose to do otherwise, for the *what* of human experience is inscrutable—it always escapes us, or, rather, we always escape it. Even though the physical world may exist objectively and eternally, it never enters our life as a permanent, stable factor because our perception of it changes constantly—"The phenomena have not changed / But a new way of being seen convinces them they have."[68]

John Ashbery's version of the performatory mode represents the idea of poetry as primarily mental process. His poems exploring the reality of dreams, or rather the reality of dreaming, are performances of and for the imagination. Poets like David Antin, Dick Higgins, Jackson Mac Low, and Jerome Rothenberg practice language art whose principal means of coherence is not syntax or semantics but sound and/or "word image." Notwithstanding the idiosyncracies of these "visual" and "sound" poets, they all start from the assumption that poetry involves not just mental activity but physical activity as well, of the poet and of the reader. For them, poetry is not so much to be read and contemplated, that is, understood and interpreted; rather, it is to be enacted and participated in, first in writing and then in reading (which with these poets means increasingly watching and listening or even performing). The words of the poem, they claim, must be made continuous with the experience of their performance, for only then does the poet achieve a sense of unity between his poetry and the environment, between art and life, which in turn will allow him to gain new insights about nature and himself. The cognitive, or even epistemological, value of such poetry is summarized by Jackson Mac Low in the following statement:

The poet creates a *situation* wherein he invites other persons and the world in general to be co-creators with him! He does not wish to be a dictator but a loyal co-initiator of action within the free society of equals which he hopes his work will help bring out.

That such works themselves may lead to new discoveries about the nature of the world and of man I have no doubt. I have learned, for instance, that it is often very difficult to tell, in many cases, what is "chance" and what is "cause." There are kinds of inner and hidden causation that are very difficult to distinguish, on the one hand, from "chance" or "coincidence," and on the other, from "synchronicity": "meaningful acausal interconnection." Also, absolutely unique situations may arise during performances of such works, and the experiences of those participating in them (whether as performers, audience or both) cannot help but be of new *aesthetic* (experiential) meanings. That is, not only do the works embody and express certain metaphysical, ethical, and political meanings, but they also bring into being new aesthetic meanings.[69]

Thus, the poem is not just the words of the text but the totality of phenomena surrounding it. It may be, as in concrete poetry, a "word image" on a page to be looked at and not just read or a material object to be handled. It may be what Jerome Rothenberg calls a "sounding," or what David Antin calls a "talk piece," or what Jackson Mac Low calls a "dance-poem." Irrespective of the forms that such poems assume in action, they are not, as John Cage observes about his own "process pieces," "preconceived objects. . . . They are occasions for experience."[70]

The poetry of performance also shares with other performance-oriented arts some features which naturally follow from the unique conditions of language art. As Perloff notes in *The Poetics of Indeterminacy*, the introduction of the performatory mode into poetry has resulted in a clearly visible movement of such poetry toward what Northrop Frye defines as the "associative rhythm" of speech. The associative rhythm is one of the three primary rhythms of verbal expression, the other two being verse and prose. Frye thus describes the relationship between them: "The irregular rhythm of ordinary speech may be conventionalized in two ways. One way is to impose a pattern of recurrence on it; the other is to impose the logical and semantic pattern of the sentence. We have verse when the arrangement of words is dominated by recurrent rhythm, prose when it is dominated by the syntactical relations of subject and predicate."[71]

The associative rhythm, as it happens, is more like prose than it is like verse; therefore, the name "prose poem" is frequently used in literary criticism to stress the difference between conventional verse and what is also called free verse. Much of the poetry of performance written, or one should rather say "done," today fits Frye's definition of the associative rhythm more than his definition of poetry. He defines the former in the following way: "One can see in ordinary speech . . . a unit of rhythm peculiar to it, a short phrase that contains the central word or idea aimed at, but is largely innocent of syntax. It is much more repetitive than prose, as it is in the process of working out an idea, and the repetitions are largely rhythmical filler. . . . In pursuit of its main theme, it follows the paths of private association, which gives it a somewhat meandering course."[72]

Jerome Rothenberg, characterizing the "counter-poetics" of the American poetry that came into existence in the 1950s (Black Mountain, Beats, the New York school, deep image, concrete poetry, chance poetry, to name a few), notes that in this new poetry metrics give way to measure—"not the sequence of the metronome" (Pound) but a variable succession of sounds and silences, breath- or mind-directed, a "musical line" derived from the complex movements of actual speech. The written text becomes the poem's notation or, in the formulation of visual and concrete poets, a space in which the eye reads visible shape and meaning at a single glance. Here and there too, one sees the first experiments with performance and a fusion with the other arts—toward "intermedia" and the freedom of a poetry without fixed limits, which may change at any point into something else.[73]

The deversification of contemporary poetry and its orientation toward the associative rhythm of ordinary speech is clearly one of the results of the more generalized tendency towards demimetization and theatricalization. Almost inevitably, this tendency became apparent in fiction, which moved toward associative rhythms in much the same way as poetry had been doing. As Northrop Frye observes: "Criticism does not appear to have any such term as 'free prose' to describe an associative rhythm influenced, but not quite organized, by the sentence. But that free prose exists is clear enough."[74] Indeed, as will be shown, free prose is the dominant medium in the stories and novels of Ronald Sukenick and Raymond Federman.

It seems quite natural to pair Ronald Sukenick and Raymond Federman as the leading exponents of the performatory mode in postmodern American fiction. Although their fiction has evolved from different cultural backgrounds and literary traditions, they have developed two central, essentially parallel approaches to nonmimetic writing: the more nativistic, romantic,

American approach intrinsic to the writings of Emerson, Poe, Melville, Whitman, Stevens, and Henry Miller (Sukenick) and that growing out of the European theory and the attendant, predominantly French, practice of fiction from Proust through Beckett to the *nouveau roman* (Federman). These two traditions moved the twentieth-century novel toward what can be called the metafictional turn, a historical and paradigmatic shift marking the transition from modern to postmodern literature, whether the turning point is located between *Ulysses* and *Finnegans Wake*, between Joyce and Beckett, between Proust, Céline, and Camus on the one hand and Sarraute, Robbe-Grillet, and Butor on the other, or between the great American modernists and the "fabaultors" of the 1960s.

The consolidation in the nineteenth century, both in Europe and in America, of what we call the realistic novel, or mimetic art in general, was a triumph in art of modern man's demand for objectivity, or objective verifiability. The realists' concern with what they believed was objective reality, together with a new involvement with the historical process, caused the novel to become, as William Barrett puts it, "the form of existential history par excellence . . . since the heart of the novel, its self-appointed destiny, had come to be its ability to portray the reality of everyday life more accurately than any other literary form."[75] However, the second half of the nineteenth century and the first decades of the twentieth century brought about new perceptions which could not be reconciled with the rationalistic view of the world underlying fictional realism. Simply, the notion of reality as something to be observed from a detached perspective and subordinated to reason by

being measured, described, and explained, while epit-
omizing our high estimate of ourselves as the controllers
of nature and the pinnacle of a long process of evolution,
was now proved to be unrealistic. Under the philosophical pressures of Nietzschean irrationalism, phenome-
nology, and existentialism, the concept of a single,
objective reality gave way to a new vision which acknowledged the existence of an infinite number of "realities"
individually perceived by each person. Progress in science (particularly in theoretical and atomic physics), psychology, anthropology, sociology, technology, and other
areas of exact knowledge confirmed the inferences of
philosophers and eventually led to the virtual destruc-
tion of the foundations of modern epistemology. In literature, all these developments were reflected in the
emergence of the modernist movement which responded directly to the twentieth-century person's loss
of confidence in objectivity and the ability of the human
mind to understand and explain the world.

Faced with the loss of the ego and the dissolution of
the Cartesian clockwork universe into a multiplicity of
amorphous phenomena defying description and rationalization, the moderns found nineteenth-century realism naive and simply useless—historical narration, causal
plotting, characterization, description, and verisimilitude lost their credibility as precepts of the realistic faith.
To deal with the fracture and dishevelment of contemporary experience, they invented and successfully (from
the artistic point of view) employed various new strategies. Particularly important was their use of myth as a
structuring device, for it called the writers' attention to
the place of structure in the process of composition and,
in more general terms, moved the novel from a moral

level to an aesthetic and formalistic one. The interest in the texture of the novel as an artistic form produced a revival of self-conscious fiction, practiced in the previous centuries by Cervantes, Fielding, Sterne, and Diderot as a form of epistemological, moral-intellectual, experiential, and metaphysical realism.[76] In modernist novels, self-consciousness came to manifest itself largely in the exploration of language as the material of fiction. While the realists regarded language as a transparent medium, the modernists realized that the mediation of language in the communication of one's experience to others could not be ignored.

There also emerged the notion that reality and fiction are not different at all, not because fiction is capable of creating perfect imitations of reality, but because reality, like fiction, is not given but constructed or invented. Joyce carried the awareness of the restrictions and possibilities of language and imagination to extremes in *Finnegans Wake*, where, apart from using some thirty different languages, he experimented with individual words, thus creating a completely new, self-contained code which did not describe any external reality but which presented itself as reality in its own right, or, to use Joyce's own words, as a "verbivocovisual presentment." Similarly, with Gertrude Stein, particularly in *Tender Buttons*, language became *the* subject of the novel, and with Samuel Beckett the world of fiction was effectively reduced to a single, verbal dimension. Eventually, fiction's own linguistic awareness of itself became the most powerful metaphor for, as Raymond Federman puts it, "man's obsessive need to construct artificial codes or systems with which he can conceal from himself the real lack of any code or system in life."[77]

The twentieth-century novelist's loss of faith in the fixity of reality not only meant the elevation of the medium of fiction as an independent source of interest and control but also the degradation of the narrative voice, and indeed of the notion of authorial self, as a unitary and fully autonomous interpretive center, the ultimate source of authority and truth. With the renunciation in psychology and sociology of the conception of man as a static entity of some absolute nature, in favor of the view that man's personal identity develops as a multiplicity of selves that come into existence and are then dropped as life progresses from one moment to the next, the status of the author as a discrete originator of meaning became problematic and was eventually rejected as simplistic and false. Consequently, in the absence of a fixed reality to be represented in fiction and a fixed center of narrative mediation to convey an image of the "real," the question "*What* does fiction say (mean)?" was replaced by the question "*How* is fiction constituted?" as the focus of the writer's attention.

The new kind of self-consciousness which evolved as a corollary of this transformation was not merely a technique of realism designed to show how the mind works but entailed a wholly new vision of literature. As Richard Poirier, one of the chief exponents of the new literary orientation, asserts in *The Performing Self:* "Literary works only provisionally constitute what Marcuse calls 'another dimension of reality.' They should be construed more properly as merely another dimension of action, of performance with language as its medium."[78] In Europe, the concept of literature (and art in general) conceived in terms of action or process should be traced back to the formalists, who placed the act of perception before the finished product and thus not only focused attention on the aesthetic function of the literary work as a verbal message but also recognized the experiential value of writing.

The European theory and practice of fiction originating in formalism—for example, (post)structuralism and the French (*nouveau*) *nouveau roman*—represent an approach which is essentially foreign to the American vision of the postmodern, a vision characterized first of all by a dynamic holism. Ihab Hassan's critical evaluation of French structuralism and poststructuralism pointedly articulates the opposition between the two approaches:

a. The (post)structuralist metaphysic of absence and its ideology of fracture refuse holism almost fanatically. But I want to recover my metaphoric sense of wholes. The difference between Norman O. Brown and Gilles Deleuze (who fails to acknowledge Brown) is precisely this: Brown knows that open is broken and fractured is free, but he knows also that reality is one (*Love's Body*). Subtle rhetoricians, materialists, the French only disconnect. Opposed to ontological bad faith, they cultivate an ontological brittleness. For them, the Platonic apple must remain both erotically and epistemologically split.

b. The (post)structuralist concept of literature is, as Richard Schechner has noted, entirely implosive. Everything collapses inward on language itself, on structures within/without structures. But I long for a concept of literature that is also explosive: outward into gesture and performance, outward into action, responsive to change. By textualizing existence, the new rhetoricians can safely become Heroes of Reality . But is rhetoric really the foundation of all contemporary praxis and thought? (See Frederic Jameson's *The Prison House of Language*.)

c. The structuralist idea of structure may be finally inadequate to both human history and cosmic evolution, to the reality of *process*. Physicists, biologists, information theorists now prefer to speak of systems rather than structures, "self-transcendent systems" that ensure both continuity and change (Erich Jantsch and C. H. Waddington, eds., *Evolution and Consciousness*). And some geneticists want to supplant the concept of "code" with the more dynamic concept of instruction. No life-denying formalism here.

d. The (post)structuralist temper requires too great a depersonalization of the writing/speaking subject. Writing becomes plagiarism; speaking becomes quoting. Meanwhile, we do write, we do speak. I realize that the problematic of the "subject" is exceedingly complex (from Sartre's *Critique de la raison dialectique*, 1960, and Lévi-Strauss's *La Pensée Sauvage*, 1962, the controversy continues through to Kristeva's *La Révolution du langage poétique*, 1974). Yet I know that I myself must articulate my historical voice as well as silence it, lose my life and find it. I cannot stand forever *beside* myself, nor reflexively *between* my selves.

e. The style of many (post)structuralists fascinates at first, and then—begins to repel? Consider the oblique styles of Lévi-Strauss, Barthes, Derrida, Foucault, Kristeva, Deleuze, Serres. But what does "difficult" mean here? Hegel, Heidegger, and Husserl are often more difficult to read. Is it because the (post)structuralists rightly transgress disciplines—they are not *only* philosophers *or* anthropologists *or* critics—and so must transgress certain received categories of "clarity"? Or is it because, having banished the "subject" from their epistemology, the subject returns perversely to assert its presence in idiosyncratic styles, in complex verbal ceremonies that pretend to shun the vulgarities of the signified?

f. The (post)structuralist activity, when all is said and done, does not sufficiently enhance the meaning, experience, force, value, pleasure of particular literary texts, enhance what draws *me* to literature or quickens *me* to it. For Barthes, pleasure is crucial, though it implies a process of coding and uncoding, making and unmaking, recuperation and loss—finally of "fading"—a process that is not central to my own temper (*Le Plaisir du Texte*). This touches on elusive questions: boredom, ennui.[79]

Yet, these two approaches are not entirely irreconcilable, as demonstrated by Raymond Federman's highly idiosyncratic and original theory and practice of "surfiction," which combines the natural vitality and energy of the American character with the writer's European background. What is important in the present context, though, is the fact that the performatory model central to postmodern art has an American lineage not just in the plastic and performing arts but in the novel as well.

Among recent critics who have recognized the American moderns' contribution to the rise of performance as an essential ingredient of postmodern fiction, one can mention Tony Tanner, Richard Poirier, James Mellard, and Charles Caramello, whose studies of contemporary American fiction succeed in providing a historical context for the discussion of recent trends and tendencies. Writing about his "life in American literature," Tony Tanner observes that "it is perhaps not entirely accidental that the idea of 'language as gesture' and the sense of literature as a 'performance' have originated with American critics." In his *City of Words*, he argues that American writers have always revealed an unusual degree of awareness of "the importance of verbal space as being the space in which the writer can not only arrange his perceptions of the external world in his own pattern but also allow his consciousness to have what Henry James called its 'fun.' "[80] Borrowing the term "foregrounding" from the formalists and defining it as such use of language in fiction which compels the reader "to submit to the turbulence, or share the delight, of the writer's mind working itself out in visible verbal performance," he demonstrates that "much contemporary American writing is foregrounded to a remarkable extent, and that it was precisely in such foregrounding that writers like Melville and James liberated and explored the potentialities of their own consciousness."[81]

In his own study, Tanner praises Richard Poirier's earlier book, *A World Elsewhere*, where the author concerns himself with the effort of the classic American writers to create through language an "environment of freedom," that is, "an environment in which the inner consciousness of the hero-poet can freely express itself, an environment in which he can sound publicly what he privately is." In the title chapter of *The Performing Self*, Poirier addresses some specific issues involved in the writer's performance within the verbal space of the literary work by considering three writers who, he claims, "treat any occasion as a 'scene' or a stage for dramatizing the self as a performer"[82]—Robert Frost, Norman Mailer, and Henry James. Pointing to James' profoundly personal reasons for being extremely self conscious about his performance as "a shaper of life"—especially the challenge of the real deaths in his life which he answered with "his marvelous suppleness in the management of fictional death"—Poirier hails the novelist as "the great theorist and exponent of 'composition,' both as a form of art and a mode of existence."[83]

The crucial thing about Poirier's notion of performance is that it appears as inseparable from self-consciousness or self-reflexivity. Defining performance as "any self-discovering, self-watching, finally self-pleasuring response to the pressures and difficulties"[84] of contemporary life, he stresses that, as was the case with James, "the self-consciousness isn't merely implicit in verbal mannerisms; it is also a matter of his actually referring to writing as an act barely possible against the pressures he encounters as he proceeds, the problem, literally, of holding the pen."[85] Another important point is that despite the poignancy of his themes, Poirier observes, James "probably had, at the terrible depths of creative power, 'a *hell* of a good time doing it'—there at his desk, there at the cemetery arranging the scene for the desk, there even in his room dying when he dictated his last rumination."[86]

The element of fun, or play, so central to postmodern performance and theatricalized art is also emphasized by James Mellard in *The Exploded Form*. Speaking about postmodernism, which he regards as the third, "sophisticated," stage of modernism, he makes an important distinction between "the performative term *play* and the artifactive term *game*." While both game-oriented and play-oriented writers "seek to some degree, 'explicitly or implicitly,' to represent 'the act of writing as an act of play,' " the former clearly-belong to what Mellard calls "naive modernism" (and what other critics more popularly identify as the realistic strain in modern literature), for they "take an essentially objective stance toward universe, audience, self, and work," whereas the latter reveal a genuinely postmodern disposition by assuming that "value, grace, and sanctification exist . . . in the reciprocity of the activity, in the performance itself, rather than in the work or world, author or audience alone."[87]

A traditionalist of sorts, Mellard refuses to recognize the current drive toward performance as a symptom of the advent of a new, postmodern sensibility but sees it merely as continuation of modernism. Yet his approach is valuable in pointing to the sources and origins of what otherwise might appear to be a completely disruptive and subversive development. He traces the division between the artifactive and the performatory modes back to "the contrast between the classic notion of a stable, mechanically structured universe whose secrets can be mastered in formula and diagram, and the romantic notion of a phenomenal, dynamic, emerging universe whose secrets cannot be known in anything other than the relationship of knower and known, self and object." In the most general terms, the contrast is that between the "realist, Aristoltelian premise, the major premise of traditional science" and "the more idealist, Platonic notion, the lyrical or dramatistic sense of the world-as-flux drawn into a realm of ideas or an essentialist Self."[88]

Within the modern tradition itself, Mellard points out by quoting Charles Altieri, "the argument can be summarized by distinguishing between Coleridge's recreation of the object through the subject and early Wordsworth's sense that the subject is created by means of its participation in the object."[90] Mellard goes on to observe that the contemporary play-oriented novelists writing in the performatory mode (he includes Barthelme, Brautigan, Sukenick, and Vonnegut) are direct inheritors of the Wordsworthian tradition (Sukenick has often stressed his affinity with Wordsworth)—an inheritance which is of course mediated by the "imagist experiments of Stein, Anderson, and Hemingway, experiments which have been capable of becoming lyrically expressive just as easily as dramatistically objective."[90]

As Mellard points out, this tradition has been less privileged than the "classic" modernist tradition represented by T. S. Eliot and Ezra Pound. But because of the perceptual transformation of the world in twentieth-century science, philosophy, and art, the "sophisticated" modernist authors and their critics have not only lost all faith "in the world 'out there,' physical or historical, a belief available to be given up by the early modernists," but also "in most of those modernist authorities posited for the world 'in here,' the interior worlds of man's intellect or imagination"; and since "no author (as the word suggests) can continue to write without authority," they "have begun to consider as their authority . . . the artistic performance itself."[91] The recognition of this transformation by the critics is particularly important:

> If we now reassess the "performances" of certain authors—poets like Frost, Stevens, and Williams, and novelists like Anderson, Hemingway, and Fitzgerald—we see that they can be construed in ways compatible with the peculiarities of works by very recent authors like Barth, Barthelme, Brautigan, Coover, DeLillo, Kosinski, and Vonnegut. The reason is plain: many of the naive modernists were already involved in "minimal" or even anti-art, and these late modernists, in taking them up, have taken up a particular strain of naive-modernist fiction. And as critical modernism converted into themes some of the implied bases of the early modernists, so these sophisticated modernists have transformed into themes and authority the assumptions of their predecessors, turning the very act of writing into a devotional—however playful—to the vitality of the human imagination, discovering in the process that they have linked themselves, as well, to a vastly more authoritative power in the ancient mode of narrative art."[92]

Whereas Mellard does not pursue the full aesthetic implications of this loss of artistic authority, in his recent study of postmodern American fiction entitled *Silverless Mirrors*, Charles Caramello offers a sophisticated analysis of the consequences of the disappearance of the modern authorities in terms of the "transformation of the book into Text and the attendant transformation of authorial self as shaping presence into textual self as shaped presence."[93] Significantly, the fourth element of the total artistic situation only occasionally referred to by Mellard, the audience, features prominently in Caramello's considerations. In the most general sense, this approach is valuable because it points to one of the central characteristics of postmodern performance—its orientation toward audience participation. In a more narrowly contextual sense, it also connects the nativistic, romantic or pastoral, strain of the performatory mode with which Ronald Sukenick can be readily identified with the European, more theoretical version of the performatory mode that Raymond Federman explores in his novels.

Particularly pertinent here is Roland Barthes' "pleasure of the text" thesis through which, Caramello observes, he resolves the question of the lost authority in literature by positing the writerly/readerly opposition, at the heart of which is the assumption that "the goal of literary work (of literature as work) is to make the reader no longer a consumer, but a producer of the text."[94] On the one hand, this assumption is simply a recognition of the fact that, as Caramello asserts, "whatever the style and form of the individual 'work,' the reader can never not be its coauthor and its performer (the one who executes the work)." On the other hand, however, Barthes perceives certain specific styles and forms which account for the "readerliness" of some and the "writerliness" of other literary works. It is only in the latter that

in addition to the success which can . . . be attributed to an author, there is also . . . a pleasure of performance: the feat is to sustain the *mimesis* of language (language imitating itself), the source of immense pleasures, in a fashion so radically *ambiguous* (ambiguous to the root) that the text never succumbs to the good conscience (and bad faith) of parody (of castrating laughter, of 'the comical that makes us laugh').[95]

As a precondition for experiencing "the pleasure of the text" ("bliss"), Barthes emphasizes the necessity of collapsing the modern subject/object dichotomy by conceiving of the text as a performing space, a stage where the writer and the reader join in the composition of the book as, to use Caramello's words, a "multimedia artifact." Barthes says, "On the stage of the text, no footlights; there is not, behind the text, someone active (the writer) and out front someone passive (the reader); there is not a subject and an object."[96] In his theory of the "writerly," the reader's practical collaboration with the author in the making of the book is expressed through his notion of reading as "ourselves writing"[97] and, conversely, the notion of writing as reading, of uttering, vocally, the text being written.

Though he is quite skeptical about the writer's response, Barthes' call for "vocal writing"[98] is not a theoretical proposition at all since many novels written in the performatory mode depend on what Northrop Frye has called the associative rhythm of auditory language. Ronald Sukenick's experiments with the tape recorder and his attempts to capture the rhythm of vocalized language in what he defines as "prose measure" and Raymond Federman's conception of the novel as a multivoice performance of several narrative voices *speaking* within one another, addressing the audience within the novel, and even suggesting to the reader that the text should be read aloud seem to explore a very wide spectrum of writing's auditory possibilities. Combined with their use of the visual, or the concrete, these writers' awareness of the performatory tradition in literature and of the theoretical basis for postmodern literary performance, as well as their pronounced desire to bring the novel up to date with concurrent developments in art and culture in general, make their work an ideal object for the study of the postmodern performatory sensibility.

Part I
Ronald Sukenick

2

Wallace Stevens: Musing the Obscure

R ONALD SUKENICK'S FIRST book was a critical study of the poetry of Wallace Stevens entitled *Wallace Stevens: Musing the Obscure.*[1] Although Sukenick's scholarship must be considered here chiefly for the bearing it has had on the evolution of both his theory and practice of fiction, the publication of the Stevens volume had a direct impact on his career as a fiction writer, for when his novel *Up* appeared only a year after *Musing the Obscure,* he was promptly labeled an academic novelist, with all the consequences of such a reputation. For traditionally minded critics, reviewers, and the reading public shaped by them, academicism invariably means both detachment from immediate reality and social indifference and extreme formalism or aestheticism. Only a few sympathetic critics praised the academicism of Sukenick's early fiction as an expression of a heightened level of artistic self-consciousness, a view characteristically represented by Jerome Klinkowitz in his book *Literary Disruptions,* where he observes about Ronald

Sukenick and Raymond Federman that these two novelists "have published the most straightforward academic writing and so offer the highest profile of theory behind such works."[2]

As it happens, Sukenick was well prepared to defend himself against unsympathetic criticism focusing on his concern with theoretical matters, for the critics' charges were almost identical with those which had been leveled against Stevens after the publication of his earlier volumes, notably *Harmonium* and *Ideas of Order*[3]—charges which Sukenick had answered in his own study. However, despite some similarities between their respective situations, Sukenick's position was probably worse in the 1960s than Stevens' had been back in the 1930s. First of all, Sukenick was an academic with a Ph.D. in literature, so the academicism of his fiction could, more or less justifiably, be taken for granted in an a priori manner. And if being called an academic novelist was bad enough, writing a book on Stevens that was an assault upon the academic Stevens establishment drew counterattacks from the academy itself, challenging Sukenick's credentials and making it all the harder for his writerly ambitions. The scholarly journals which had endorsed Stevens as a philosophical yet quintessentially nondiscursive modernist poet balked at Sukenick's refusal to read him didactically. Lewis Leary dismissed the book as "a useful guide to the forty-seven of the most often discussed Stevens poems" which nevertheless "must not be depended upon for critical analysis in depth,"[4] while other Stevens critics whose readings Sukenick had rejected filed their own negative reviews; significantly, within the realm of literary and academic politics, *Wallace Stevens: Musing the Obscure* had its best reviews in the

nonacademic press, earning approval from such popular critics as Irving Howe and Denis Donoghue. Such
negative comments aside, *Musing the Obscure* is still worth
considering here not just because the introductory essay,
"Wallace Stevens: Theory and Practice," offers a persuasive description of a coherent poetic but because Sukenick's alleged tendency to misrepresent Stevens sheds
considerable light on his own views about literature.
Whether what Sukenick found in Stevens' poems was
there or not is a matter of practical irrelevance here;
what matters is that his investigation of Stevens' poetic
provided him with an appropriate platform to articulate
his own general views about literature which would be
later developed into a rule-of-thumb theory of composition formulated in both his critical essays and fictional
works.

Sukenick's description of Stevens' poetic concerns the
poet's views on life, art (poetry), and the relationship
between the two. What particularly fascinates Sukenick
is that Stevens regards reality in genuinely postmodern
terms, that is, as "an entity whose chief characteristic is
flux" (5) and so recognizes change as the world's fundamental condition. His world view is typically expressed by the following lines from "Notes Toward a
Supreme Fiction" quoted by Sukenick:

It is a theatre floating through the clouds,
Itself a cloud, although of misted rock
And mountains running like water, wave on wave,

Through waves of light. It is of cloud transformed
To cloud transformed again, idly, the way
A season changes color to no end,
Except the lavishing of itself in change. (35)

Stevens' dynamic conception of reality contained in these lines parallels Sukenick's own postmodernity as a fiction writer, a fact more striking when one considers the persistence of the image of clouds in his stories and novels as a metaphor for writing and for life in general. Two crucial aspects of Stevens' worldview concern the origin of change and the nature of the process of change. As Sukenick observes, in "Notes Toward a Supreme Fiction," Stevens "describes, in a series of examples, 'the origin of change' as the intercourse of dependent opposites that produces a third thing" (147). Thus, he implies that change is a holistic agent, for through it, "the interacting opposites become one" (147). Since it has no fixed goal toward which it aspires, life does not follow any predetermined or predictable course but unfolds in a completely random manner, that is, chaotically. Stevens, Sukenick asserts, recognizes chaos as "the only order that exists" (10).

The "purposeful purposelessness" of life and the completely fortuitous character of one's experience in the world demand from people an affirmation of change if they want "to live in the health of change," which means "to live always in a present of constant change" (8). Unlike most typically modern, human-centered systems (whether objectivist or subjectivist), Stevens' vision reverses the order of the elements in the human/world, mind/body, or spirit/matter dichotomy: the second element is given priority over the first one—"Reality is recognized as the unique source of the ego's content" (11). This, of course, is a direct consequence of acknowledging fortuitous change as the fundamental principle of the world's operation. Faced with chaos in radical flux, the mind (whose main faculty, according to the modern conception of human beings, is logical thinking and rationalization) is in Stevens totally helpless and falls back on a radical, fleeting experience that, Sukenick points out, "has no definite intellectual content. The experience is fortuitous, since one does not know what objective content to seek: it is comprised of 'things that came of their own accord, / Because he desired without knowing quite what' "(29).

How does one, then, approach reality, come to know and understand it? The answer Sukenick reads in Stevens' poetry is the following: "It may be . . . that only 'the ignorant man,' whose mind works without preconception and without premeditation, thus in a way parallel to nature's operation, in a natural way—it may be that only a man with such a mind can apprehend nature in such a way as to become one with it, 'to mate his life with life,' that life of nature which is 'sensual' and beyond the mind, therefore unavailable to systematic thought or intellectual preconception" (106).

This, however, raises a further question: how does one make sense of what the senses take in? Sukenick replies: "One may . . . enjoy a pleasurable relation with reality in which the ego demands from the chaos of reality nothing but what it can give, and chaos is therefore adequate to satisfy the desires of the ego. In this state one simply enjoys the sense of one's own existence in a physical reality, beyond any meaning of that existence imposed by the ego"(10). In one phrase, Stevens' poetic, enjoying "the sense of one's own existence beyond any meaning of that existence imposed by the ego," is most naturally a function of the imagination. Unlike in the rationalization process (which Stevens defines as an imposition of "violent order" on, and therefore a falsification of, the chaos of reality), in the process of imaginative perception of reality, "one loses consciousness of the self and becomes aware of an order which is in fact that of the imagination" (29). The "ultimate good" of such perception is that "at the heart of this interchange between the ego and reality is the effort of the imagination in bringing the two into vital relation" (14); this means, Sukenick explains, "an agreement between the ego and reality in which the separation between the two disappears and they seem one harmonious entity" (31). To put it another way, the modern dualism of subject and object is resolved in the imagination, a unitary faculty in which the interacting opposites become one.

The kind of interaction that interests Stevens most is that between the external world and the poet's mind, or intellect, and the reconciliation of chaos with logic in the imagination. One of the poet's most important discoveries is that if the imagination is to bridge "the dumbfoundering abyss / Between us and the object,"[5] perception must be given priority over intellection, experience over contemplation of experience, for only in this way will a poet manage to keep up with the change of reality. When a poet exposes himself to "the pressure of reality" in this way, writing poetry becomes for him "a way of getting along" and the act of composition becomes "a way of discovering and crystallizing what [Stevens] called in one of his last poems, 'Local Objects,' 'the objects of insight, the integrations / Of feeling' " (1). In this way, poetry is made continuous with the poet's actual experience, each poem being a presence, a "crystallization" of the experience of writing it.

The poem as presence is thus not so much a description of an experience as a revelation of it, "an imaginative perception of the thing described: it is neither the thing itself, nor a pretended reproduction of the thing, not reality but a real artifice, so to speak, with its own reality that makes actual reality seem more intense than it ordinarily is" (17). As "a real artifice," it does not rely on other objects for its meaning but is a self-contained, or self-existent, entity; or as Stevens has it in "An Ordinary Evening in New Haven," "the poem is the cry of its occasion, / Part of the res itself and not about it."[6] Such a poem also naturally abandons the idea of representation as well as that of the masterpiece since these two concepts imply the existence of a fixed, static model to be imitated or represented. Reading "Notes Toward a Supreme Fiction," Sukenick observes, "The ideal and its representation, for not changing with the change of reality, have become obsolete" (147). Stevens thus emphasizes in "Notes Toward a Supreme Fiction" that if a poem is not about anything outside itself, it "must be abstract," from which he derives the notion that "poetry is the subject of the poem."[7]

Being its own subject, however, a poem is no more *about* poetry than a musical piece is *about* music or a painting is *about* painting. As an aesthetic abstractness with a reality of its own, a poem inevitably focuses attention not on its discursive meaning (Stevens says, "A poem need not have a meaning and like most things in nature often does not have"),[8] but on the concreteness of its material, that is, on words and sounds. Sukenick points out that for Stevens "it is not only written language but also its sound that gives us, in poetry, a credible sense of reality: 'words, above everything else, are, in poetry, sounds' " (19). Stevens thus affirms the autonomy of language not as a medium but as a source of meaning—"There is a sense in sounds beyond their meaning."[9]

With the poem freed from the obligation to represent, composition remains the central issue in the writing of poetry. It is in the process of composition that the poet establishes a "vital relation" between his experience of the outside world and his mind. The manner of capturing experience is not based on preconception of any kind since the "experience of ideal relation with reality is by nature fugitive," and so "there can be no formulation of it that one can repeat to summon it up; nothing avails but improvisation" (32). Improvisation is the only principle the poet can follow in keeping up with fortuitous experience; therefore, Sukenick remarks, "if [Stevens' poems] may be said to have a structure, it is fundamentally the structure of the poet's mind as it is realized in the act of improvisation" (23). One function of poetry is to provide the poet with "arbitrary forms . . . which serve as a frame within which to improvise" (23). Improvisation in turn asserts play as an important element of the process of composition, and writing a poem becomes "a game which, lacking any purposes but the playing of it, can only be played again and again" (4). And a poem that is a game in which the imagination, itself "no more than a process" (85), brings interacting opposites into a vital relation with each other prescribes a specific role for the poet and for the reader. The vital relation established in this way is that of a person who "becomes one with his environment, and is changed by it, 'The partaker partakes of that which changes him' " (147).

Sukenick's presentation of Stevens' poetic is thus essentially a theory which concentrates on the process and not on the content of the imagination, on the how and not on the what of perception and experience. As Sukenick argues, it "comprises more of a mechanics, or psychology, of belief than an assertion of particular belief" (7). In Stevens' poetic practice, "poetry is a way of saying things in which the way of saying yields the meaning and in which the way of saying is more important than, but indistinguishable from, the things said" (19). Stressing the dynamic character of nature, the change, and the necessity of "adequate adjustment to the present"—which "can only be achieved through ever fresh perception of it" (3)—Stevens' poetry "is aimed not at distinguishing the objective from the subjective, but at uniting the two" (24). It overcomes stasis and fragmentation by affirming change and recognizing the autonomy of the poet's imagination and its products, with all the consequences that follow from such a move, such as the "loss of self" and the renunciation of the primacy of logic and intentional prearranged meaning.

The dynamic holism in Stevens' poetic theory and practice was seen by Sukenick as an attractive, if not the only possible, way of revitalizing poetry and uniting the truth of experience with poetic truth. Stevens' poetic provided Sukenick with cues about how to achieve the same condition in fiction. During the decade that followed the publication of *Musing the Obscure*, he wrote not only novels and short fiction but also numerous critical and theoretical essays, book reviews, and newspaper articles in which, starting from the premises established by his book on Stevens, he developed a postmodern theory of fiction. He was motivated by a desire to bring the novel, whose "death" had just been announced, back to life and make it harmonious with both the other arts and with the experience of contemporary man by focusing on the performatory aspect of writing, on writing as a fully experiential activity.

3

In Form: Digressions on the Act of Fiction

I N SUKENICK'S OPINION, the crisis of fiction to which John Barth, among others, addressed himself in the late 1960s does not concern the novel in general but *the* novel, that is, the traditional novel, both in its realistic and modernist versions. The distinction is vital for Sukenick, for the novel as such, he observes, is inexhaustible by definition ("The novel *is* innovation—it is not called the 'novel' for nothing"[1]) whereas particular forms of it have their own life-and-death cycles. Viewed in this way, the whole "death-of-the novel" phenomenon can be explained as a "category mistake," to use Hein's term, by which one form of the novel—the modern (realistic and modernist) novel—has come to be identified as the only legitimate form, that is, as *the* novel. The persistence of the traditional model is explained by Sukenick very simply: the realistic novel sustains "a series of comforting illusions" about the world and man's place in it, among which one might include the feeling that the individual is the significant focus among the phenomena of "reality" (characterization); the sense that clock, or public time is finally the reigning form of duration for consciousness (historical narration); the notion that the locus of "reality" may be determined by empirical observation (description); the conviction that the world is logical and comprehensible (causal sequence, plot). The fairy tale of the "realistic" novel whispers its assurance that the world is not mysterious, that it is predictable—if not to the characters, then to the author, that it is available to manipulation by the individual, that it is not only under control but that one can profit from this control. The key idea is verisimilitude: one can make an image of the real thing which, though not real, is such a persuasive likeness that it can represent our control over reality. This is the voodoo at the heart of mimetic theory which helps account for its tenacity. (3–4)

However comforting, these assumptions are nonetheless representative of a worldview which no longer holds true in our age, and so "the form of the traditional novel is a metaphor for a society that no longer exists" (3). Inevitably, then, the confrontation of such beliefs with the facts of contemporary life must result in a collision in which the facts naturally get the upper hand. But it is not just that illusions lose in a contest with reality, which in turn makes readers lose faith in the novel as a medium that gets at the truth of their lives. Much worse is the fact that the traditional novel not only fails to capture our experience but falsifies this experience and thus separates us from it:

The idea of art as a mirror sustains a disconnected, emotionally dissociated attitude toward experience. Such art presents us with an image of our experience in a way that assures us it is not real: it is a reflection, only a picture, only a story. At last, a way of defining our experience in a form in which we do not have to take responsibility for it. The mode that must have been a means of meditation for Vermeer for us, as cliché, becomes a form of limited liability, a way of packaging our experience so that we can walk away from it. What we call realism saps our experience of its immediacy and authority. . . . (41)

The immediacy of experience is for Sukenick the greatest value of it. Its loss is particularly dangerous for the novel, whose uniqueness is in that, like no other medium, it "can so well deal with our strongest and often most immediate responses to the large and small facts of our daily lives. No other medium, in other words, can so well keep track of the reality of our experience" (242). But whenever one form of the novel is canonized as *the* novel, this ability is lost irrevocably because "as soon as fiction gets frozen into one particular model, it loses that responsiveness to our immediate experience that is its hallmark" (241). This is an abnormal situation for the novel to be in, for the novel is inherently "the most fluid and changing of literary forms, the one that most immediately reflects the changes in our collective consciousness" (241) and as such has "the obligation . . . to rescue experience from any system" (11). Therefore, Sukenick observes, "instead of reproducing the form of previous fiction, the form of the novel should seek to approximate the shape of experience" (207).

This shape, the writer knows, is utterly indeterminate and unpredictable, for events happen according to no a priori scheme or logic, which means that the novel, in order to accommodate the ongoing flow of experience, should not assume any predetermined form either—unless it is an arbitrary form. The structure of the arbitrary, Sukenick asserts, is "a way of moving from the meditated to the unpremeditated" (19). Another way to approximate the fortuitous character of experience is by improvisation. Here Sukenick acknowledges his indebtedness to Wallace Stevens, jazz, the Beat writers, and Laurence Sterne and explains the connection between the experiential and the improvisational in the following way: "Improvisation liberates [fiction] from any a priori order and allows it to discover new sequences and interconnections in the flow of experience" (212). Yet another method is what is called "collage linkage": "It has the virtue of generating unforeseen connections, and is particularly useful in a time when traditional causes no longer seem adequate to account for observed effects" (14).

As Sukenick's remarks about the arbitrary, improvisation, and collage linkage suggest, these three techniques not only free the novel from a predetermined, static form but also from a prearranged, referential meaning. Just as the meaning of experience comes, or is perceived, "after the fact," so the meaning of a novel is a product generated in the creative act and not something preexisting it and only reproduced in, or transmitted by, a literary form. Fiction, Sukenick argues, is "a form of invention, a way of bringing into being that which did not previously exist" (8). With the rejection of premeditation in the composition of a novel, the notions of imitation and representation are discarded and replaced with those of abstraction and opacity. "Abstraction," Sukenick explains, "frees fiction from the representational and the need to imitate some version of reality other than its own" (212), whereas opacity makes it completely nonreferential and autonomous, or autotelic. Sukenick thus defines this quality of the nonmimetic novel: "The experience [of the novel] exists in and for itself. It is opaque in the way that abstract painting is opaque in that it cannot be explained as representing some other kind of experience. You cannot look through it to reality—it is the reality in question and if you don't see it you don't see anything at all" (212). Therefore, opacity "is a good antidote for that way we have of fending off experience by explaining it" (212).

As a result of its abstractness and opacity, the kind of novel that Sukenick has in mind is neither a mirror nor a window, and not a lamp illuminating some other reality, either. As such, it resists interpretation in terms other than its own and directs our attention to its own reality as both an imaginative and a concrete structure. The technological aspect of the novel, its objecthood, is for Sukenick as important as the imaginative aspect, for it plays a crucial role in making the transaction between the author and the reader possible. A novel is most immediately apprehended as a book, a material object—pages, print, binding—"containing a record of the movements of a mind" (205). Therefore, Sukenick notes, "there is no reason why we can't go ahead in that direction and improve the technological structure to suit the purposes of our imagination" (205). As examples of such improvements, he mentions the French writer Marc Saporta, whose *Composition No. 1* is a "shuffle novel" with loose pages in a box instead of binding, and John Barth, whose "Frame-tale" is a moebius strip story. He also envisions novels printed on scrolls, on globes, "or not printed at all but produced on electronic or video tape, or acted out on a stage" (205). The purpose of all such anti-illusionistic strategies would be to prevent the reader from suspending disbelief by reminding him constantly, though ideally by ever fresh means, that there is no reality to plunge into beyond the surface of the work. The "truth of the page" does not refer narrowly to the arrangement of print against blank space but to the acknowledgment of the autonomic nature of the medium of fiction in general, whose meaning is really a matter of the experience of writing/reading the text. Besides, even though the writer may create structures which communicate by means of pattern rather than by means of sequence, the medium is still an independent source of interest, even to the extent of being given priority over the novel's discursive content. Sukenick explains: "The contemporary novelist describes things with whose appearance we are already perfectly familiar (through photography, film, travel, or simply the modern quotidian) not to make us see those things but to test language against them, to keep it alive to visual experience. The pleasure of description is the pleasure of a linguistic skill, not that of a genre painting" (30–31). Such a view is merely a recognition of the fact that literature, like any art, "after all the things it may be about, is fundamentally about its medium" (208).

The arbitrary formalism of anti-illusionistic fiction and what Sukenick calls the "pleasure of description" also make the reader aware that in the novel space and time are not merely dimensions of fictive reality but that they define both the movement of the text in the space of the page and "the time it takes to compose the work or experience it" (30). For the "truth of the page," besides the truth of the medium, also involves the writer sitting there writing the page and a reader eventually reading it. In other words, the novel comprises all the phenomena that surround it and amidst which it comes into existence and then impinges upon the reader. Such an understanding of the "truth of the page" offers a series of advantages unknown to the traditional novelist and reader:

First, one comes closer to the truth of the situation. Second, for the writer, writing becomes continuous with the rest of his experience. Third, the writer is clearly at liberty to use whatever material comes into his head as he is writing, including the data of his own experience. Fourth, he becomes, in Wordsworth's phrase, "a man speaking to men," and therefore continuous with their experience. Fifth, the reader is prevented from being hypnotized by the illusion of that make-believe so effective in the hands of nineteenth-century novelists but which by now has become a passive, escapist habit of response to a creative work—instead he is forced to recognize the reality of the reading situation as the writer points to the reality of the writing situation, and the work, instead of allowing him to escape the truth of his own life, keeps returning him to it but, one hopes, with his own imagination activated and revitalized. (25)

Sukenick's notion of experiential veracity is based on similar conceptions developed earlier by poets (Ezra Pound, William Carlos Williams, Wallace Stevens, Charles Olson, Frank O'Hara), painters (the Abstract Expressionists), sculptors (George Segal), Happening artists, and novelists (Laurence Sterne, Rabelais, Kafka, Jean Genet, Henry Miller, and Jack Kerouac) in whose works "the process of cogitation, of experiential thinking that their [creation] is constantly going through is much more important than what they happen to think at a particular time" (132). For all of them, the work of art is an element in the art/life continuum, "an event in the field of experience that, like many other events, has the power to alter that field in a significant way" (42).

The kind of "event" that Sukenick is most interested in is the experience that occurs during and because of the composition of a novel. Composition is this activity during which the text is generated "in an ongoing interchange between the mind and the page" (8), an activity for which Sukenick proposes a new theory of *fiction as generation* which considers the novel from the point of view of the actual performance of the writer in the course of the fiction-making process. The first important characteristic of writing as composition is that it unites thought and action—the thought about writing, about what one is writing, and the action of writing down this thought. Sukenick puts it this way:

Don't make up stories about yesterday or tomorrow, but write what's in your head at the moment—that's very important to me. And I want to make it clear—I'm not writing illusions—I'm not writing about a fantasy that I've had, if it's a fantasy, but I'm having a fantasy and writing it down. In fact, the act of writing it down is part of the fantasy, that is, it's like sleeping is part of dreaming—the act of writing is part of the fantasy.[2]

It follows then that the course of composition is as unpredictable as the course of one's thoughts. Writers are in control of the process of writing only so much as they can be in control of their own minds. Improvisation, collage linkage, and the arbitrary help writers to create such forms which do not allow them to plan what is going to happen next. The use of strategies which reduce the possibilities of the writer's conscious manipulation of the material at hand in turn automatically increases the autonomy of composition. Granting composition such a high degree of autonomy means that the relationship between the text and the author is not so much dissolved as it is reversed, for "as the field becomes organized, the shaping influence of personality, and of any other single element, becomes less and less until finally it is the structured field itself that becomes the organizing power, shaping personality, shaping energy, shaping language, culture, literary tradition" (14).

The above statement points to yet another element of Sukenick's poetic of composition, namely, the fact that composition creates and occurs within an open field which is a "nexus of various kinds of energy, image and experience" (11). Energy transference is for Sukenick a central issue, for "as an activity, fiction first of all involves a flow of energy" (12). This in turn implies that rather than the movement of the plot, narrative should be "the movement of the mind as it organizes the open field of the text" (13). For, Sukenick observes, "though there is not necessarily plot or story in a narrative, there is always a field of action, and in a field of action the way energy moves should be the most obvious element" (12–13).

Sukenick's differentiation between the movement of plot and the movement of energy in a field of action states the crucial difference between the modern and the postmodern standpoints. According to the modern view of reality rooted in Cartesian rationalism, movement means linear, causal, and purposive development which can be abstracted geometrically and presented in a static form as a series of dots framed by the coordinates of space and time. For Sukenick, however, "space plus time equals movement: *things in process of happening*" (9, emphasis added). His conception, then, parallels that developed, for example, by atomic physicists, who do not speak of the movement of an object (particle) in space and time but of the instantaneous presence of whatever form of energy in the space-time continuum.

As Sukenick observes about George Chambers' novel *The Bonnyclabber,* the autotelic and energetic character of composition "involves a deferral of intention" (47), which in turn raises the question of *self*-expression and of the meaning of personal identity in general. Sukenick's conception of self has little to do with the modern idea of the individual as encapsulated ego. Personality for him is by no means stable and absolute but is indefinite, changeable, and fluid, something that man invents for himself as he goes along. His dissolution of the concept of authorial self leads to shifting narrative authority from the writer to the text, or language, and is attended by a similar dissolution of the character in fiction. Sukenick explains:

I don't really believe in characterization in the old sense. A lot of my characterizations tend to take the form of a cartoon or sketch, or the characters tend to be very fluid. This represents my sense that character is much more heavily influenced from moment to moment by environment, both interior and exterior, than seemed to be the case in the traditional novel. In my fiction there is a heavier sense of the way situation can influence characterization in contemporary life. . . . I also think the interior environment of the personality has become more fluid, more subject to immediate incident and circumstance than was true in the Victorian personality as portrayed in traditional fiction. . . . My characters have some very basic minimal identity, but beyond that the changes they go through are enormous, even contradictory. I prefer the characters to be as little consistent with themselves as they can be, so that everything but that tiny, perhaps genetic, trace of identity is cancelled out. (132–33)

By dissolving character, Sukenick clearly aims at making the self an utterly performatory category, something that takes shape and exists only when man acts as a human agent of energy transference, whether in real life or within the open field of the text.

Ronald Sukenick's poetic of fiction-as-composition is a holistic ("our yen is union, not separation" [32]) and processual ("fiction concerns itself with process" [9]) theory based on the conception of the imagination as "the means of uniting the self with reality" (26). It is also expressive of the writer's general aesthetic views, according to which "the successful work of art is a discrete energy system that takes its place among the other things of our world" (29). But this poetic is not absolute and normative, or prescriptive. If anything, it is rather *post*-scriptive and constantly in the process of being worked out, that is, in the process of being adjusted to the writer's developing practice of fiction.

Appropriately enough, Sukenick included in his early works little apologies for his style of writing, hoping to capture the reader baffled by his experiments before some hostile critic did. Besides being a self-defensive and didactic measure, a novel's own criticism (like the "review" of *Up* written by Sukenick himself and included in the novel or the "critifictional" story "The Death of the Novel") also involves the reader directly in the experiential veracity which compels the writer to deal with all aspects of composition, including the theory behind it as well as possible reactions to it.

Finally, the important thing to bear in mind when considering Sukenick's short fiction and novels is that they should not be seen as artificial constructs designed to satisfy some purely theoretical and abstract requirements and, consequently, judged as mere aesthetic exercises. The fact is that Sukenick's poetic is largely of an experiential origin, just as the fiction itself is. It is a processual theory which concentrates on the meaning-*making* process and not on the transmission of some preset, referential meaning. In this theory, the discursive and the formal (including concrete) components are subordinated to the compositional one under the assumption that the medium of fiction "is neither language in general, nor speech, but writing, which has its own reality and particular power" (46) and that a work of fiction is "not only an artifact but also an activity" (6). Consequently, Sukenick argues, "if fiction may be considered an activity, . . . it does make sense to talk about what that activity is and how it generates the work" (12). At least for himself, the investigation of the nature of the generative activity called writing constitutes the raison d'être of his stories and novels to be discussed in the remaining chapters of part 1 of this study.

4

The Death of the Novel and Other Stories

A LTHOUGH PUBLISHED AFTER *Up, The Death of the Novel and Other Stories* will be considered here first for two reasons. One is that some of the stories were in fact written earlier than the novel; the other is that these stories can be considered to be (in Robert Coover's phrase) "exemplary fictions"—that is, short pieces which explore various strategies of composition. Thus, they can function as an excellent introduction to Sukenick's longer works in which different compositional strategies are combined to make the writing, and reading, of a novel a truly experiential performance.

The stories collected in the volume are often experiments in the literal sense of the word, for the writer frequently consciously only initiates the creative act and then lets his writing have its own way while he, or the tape recorder, faithfully records the unpredictable course writing declares for itself. Yet, as Jerome Klinkowitz has observed, the collection is exceptionally well structured and has the form and integration of a novel.[1] The stories are built principally around one theme, namely, the way people structure their experience. In *Musing the Obscure,* Sukenick noted: "The mind orders reality not by imposing ideas on it but by discovering significant relations with it, as the artist abstracts and composes the elements of reality in significant integrations that are works of art."[2] In his own fiction, he follows Stevens' poetic dictum by assuming that "adequate adjustment to the present can only be achieved through ever fresh perception of it," and so he tries "to find what is fresh and attractive in a reality that is frequently stale and dispiriting by way of coming to a satisfactory rapport with it."[3]

And what can be more dispiriting for a writer than the sense of a permanent crisis caused by the lack of a "satisfactory rapport" with his own experience? Such a situation is the subject of the book's first story, "The Permanent Crisis." The protagonist is a distressed husband who cannot discover any significant relation with the world, chiefly represented in the story by his wife, and therefore suffers from an emotional and intellectual paralysis. He is like "a bug caught and squirming on its own pin" or "a self that could only analyze its own consciousness, a consciousness aware only of its own muttering."[4] Since he happens to be a writer too, this "permanent crisis" manifests itself in the worst experience known in his vocation: writer's block.

According to Sukenick's approach to writing, there should not be anything wrong about such a situation, since writer's block is an experience that, like all other kinds of experience, can and should be used. The husband/writer, however, in attempting "to describe what was happening so it would stop happening" (1), begins to use writing as a way of shutting himself off from an experience that he finds unpleasant. The result is further separation from the world, further fragmentation of reality into disparate bits which cannot be put together to form a meaningful whole.

His personal and artistic plights change only when he stops trying to think his way out of the paralyzing bind and makes his predicament an object of perception only. It is then that he gains a new insight about, and thus comes to a "satisfactory rapport" with, both his life and his art—"He stopped trying to figure it out, playing it by ear, listening to himself because there was nothing else to listen to and it sounded right he wondered why, as if he were some kind of artist and knew he was right but didn't know how he knew" (7). Replacing thought with perception, instead of cutting off experience by "figuring it out," he opens himself up to it. He is saved, as a person and as a writer, when he discovers that the vital relationship with the world is sensual rather than intellectual (the senses perceive nature's order, whereas the mind imposes its own, "violent" order upon phenomena); and he learns that writing succeeds only when one describes what is happening not "so it would stop happening" but as it is happening.

This discovery inevitably raises some problems, such as the question of how to capture the living flow of experience without becoming too self-conscious about the act of recording and how to use one's past experience if one is so preoccupied with what is present at the moment of writing. The first question is largely a technical matter for Sukenick and he solves it in the second story of the collection, "Momentum," by objectifying the recording, and thus reducing the burden of self-consciousness about it to the minimum, through the use of the tape recorder, a strategy he later employs in other stories and novels as well.

"Momentum" is told on two levels. One is the level of the recording which comprises the words actually uttered by the narrator-hero, called Ronald Sukenick, in his New York apartment and recorded by a tape recorder:

okay here we go   i don't want to whisper this   i want to hear my natural speaking voice   the way it really sounds   also i can see myself in a full-length mirror as i speak   there's another mirror too   so that i can't really lose sight of myself as i sit down on my bed or lie down or walk around   i want to say this as it comes without premeditation because i want to say it before i lose it   or not so much say it as tell it   tell it to myself so i'll have it down   so that i can come back to it again and recapture it   so the speed of the tape is my form (9)

The other level is the story that is told by the narrator to the microphone, recounting the events of the past two weeks: taking a bus trip from New York to Ithaca to find an apartment for a summer's residence at Cornell University, buying a car there, meeting an old friend (the writer Steve Katz), having a brief affair with a coed, all this set against the background of campus life in the late 1960s dominated by antiwar demonstrations and civil rights turmoil.

The trip to Ithaca is in fact a revisitation, for Sukenick had studied at Cornell in the mid-1950s. It might seem, then, that the memories that seeing familiar places inevitably evokes in the narrator should introduce a third level of narration. However, nothing like that happens. Quite the contrary, Sukenick develops a unique time structure in which past experiences are integrated in and with the present. This is made possible because, as the writer says elsewhere, the tape recorder records "a continuous present" and "it makes real time coincide with medium time."[5] In the glosses appended to the text of the story printed in a column on the right-hand side of the page, the narrator explains what the reality of the present is: "Real means locating the present in terms of the past locating the self in terms of the present" (13). The past is never absolute, for it exists only in the form of memories as they return to us, and these are always in the present tense.

As the gloss just quoted also suggests, it is through the union of the present and the past in his mind that a writer discovers his own identity. Conducting an affair with a student during his brief stay in Ithaca, Sukenick is constantly aware of the interplay of past and present in his mind—"My double view, here merged through her in a single view, neither one nor the other, past and present each defining each finally finding balance" (33). When the affair comes to its end, it does not leave any physical traces in his life. Psychologically, however, its importance is a lasting one. When, back in New York with his wife, he recounts his parting with the girl, he discovers the experiential value of what just happened: "Finding someone to whom I could react both as what I was then and what I am now: unity of experience = reality of self" (38).

If the self is the product of the process of cogitation and not the source of it, then one's identity is structured by the events in which one participates rather than by some kind of central intelligence, the ego, which imposes meaning on otherwise "meaningless" reality. Therefore, in the case at hand, the narrator does not structure his past experience from the perspective of the present, that is, in a post hoc manner, but allows the past to unfold itself in his mind without his conscious intervention in the process. This unfolding then merges with the present to produce a truly meaningful experience. This is what Sukenick calls "experiential thinking," a mode which is unpremeditated and, as Charles Olson would put it, post-logical. The reward for not imposing preconceived schemes on reality is "a particular and recurring experience the sum of which is: feeling keenly in harmony with my own impulses and anarchically independent of constrictions which deaden them—an experience essential to the psychology of freedom" (39). It is also, one should say, an experience essential to composition, for it allows the writer to "get it all down as quick as i could while it was alive and i did i hope am doing it because what else is writing for" (40).

The next novella-length story, "The Death of the Novel," takes up many of these same subjects but in an extended form. As its title suggests, it is also a kind of "critifiction" which contains a large number of explicit statements on the poetics of the novel and art in general, taken from the academic notebook of "Professor Sukenick." The best known among them are the first two paragraphs of the story, which begins:

Fiction constitutes a way of looking at the world. Therefore I will begin by considering how the world looks in what I think we may now begin to call the contemporary post-realistic novel. Realistic fiction presupposed chronological time as the medium of a plotted narrative, an irreducible individual psyche as the subject of its characterization, and, above all, the ultimate, concrete reality of things as the object and rationale of its description. In the world of post-realism, all of these absolutes have become absolutely problematic.

The contemporary writer—the writer who is acutely in touch with the life of which he is part—is forced to start from scratch: Reality doesn't exist, time doesn't exist, personality doesn't exist. God was the omniscient author but he died; now no one knows the plot, and since our reality lacks the sanction of a creator, there's no guarantee as to the authenticity of the received version. Time is reduced to presence, the content of a series of discontinuous moments. Time is no longer purposive, and so there is no destiny, only chance. Reality is, simply, our experience, and objectivity is, of course, an illusion. Personality, after passing through a phase of awkward self-consciousness, has become, quite minimally, a mere locus of our experience. In view of these annihilations, it should be no surprise that literature, also, does not exist—how could it? *There is only reading and writing,* which are things we do, like eating and making love, to pass the time, ways of maintaining a considered boredom in face of the abyss. (41, emphasis added)

The last statement is very important for it introduces the performatory aspect of the story: for Sukenick, the story means the activity of writing it, just as for the reader it means reading it. Unlike "Momentum," however, it is only on the story's last pages that we are told that the scene of the telling is a country house in the Connecticut woods and the time is, precisely, January 1968, and that it records a two-week "writing seance" during which the narrator, Ronald Sukenick, has been living, in Jerome Klinkowitz's phrase, "the life of fiction"—"This isn't a story man, this is life" (101). Balancing the past against the present in the act of composition, he is constantly aware that, like a tightrope walker, he cannot pause in the middle of the act but must take his performance to its very end, or he would fall down.

The "act" consists of a series of disjointed recollections of conversations with Professor Sukenick's students at a college near New York (where he had been hired to teach an "advanced honors seminar on The Death of the Novel"), an affair with a New York schoolgirl named Teddy and another affair with his student named Betty, pictures of life on the Lower East Side, quotes from the Professor's notes for the seminar, a recorded telephone conversation, several digressions ("Here's a digression. But that's silly, when there's no plot line there are no digressions" [71]) on subjects as different as birds and fiction writing, a mock-realist "sexploitation" scene ("Or how about a little sex, that's the ticket. That's what this needs. A little sex. Okay, a little sex" [49]), a conversation between Sukenick and his wife, Lynn, about the story being written, and innumerable mundane events registered against the bigger events of the political scene of 1968.

The result is "an unprecedented example of form-lessness" (49) which, though causally and chronologically discontinuous—"Continuity in this piece is like that in the daily comic strips" (75)—is an experiential and artistic whole because the "formless" mass is constantly in motion, one disparate fragment succeeding another in a narrative which flows continually like "a current in a river" (49). The unity of these fragments is provided not on the level of individual episodes but in Ronald Sukenick's imagination in which all this is happening as he is writing the story. "The Death of the Novel" is thus not *about* Sukenick's love affairs, his students, friends and acquaintances, not *about* New York or any other place, not *about* the "reality" of people, places, and things to which the writer makes references in his story ("Reality doesn't exist"!). If anything, it is about something entirely immaterial and inherently amorphous: the "mental atmosphere" of a writer composing his experience into a work of fiction. It is in such an atmosphere that "we improvise our novels as we improvise our lives" (47).

The parallel between fiction (art) and life is very important for Sukenick, for his ideas about the nature of reality provide him with ideas about writing in a most direct way. He says: "If reality exists, it does not do so a priori, but only to be put together. Thus one might say reality is an activity, or process, of which literature is part" (47). If reality is an activity, or process, which does not follow a predetermined course, then literature must also be completely unpremeditated, and it must be constantly in motion—"Keep moving. Where? Nowhere, as fast as possible. Which is just about the state of things chronic and cosmic" (62–63).

Whenever the narrator tries to interfere with the autonomy of the process of composition, the narrative flow is immediately threatened with disruption. For instance, the moment he plans to finish the story at a specific point in time—"Here begins the last hour that I allow myself to finish this performance. Go" (90)—he begins to encounter, one after another, stumbling blocks which interrupt the flowing current of experiential thinking. Like the narrator of "Momentum," he knows that "activity generates energy torpor just dissipates it" (21), so he tries to do "the only thing that matters," which is "to keep going from moment to moment, as quick as fluid and surprising as one moment flowing continuously into the next" (71). When his memory fails him, he knows he can always resort to the imagination to patch the holes in the narrative.

"The Death of the Novel" contains several vignettes scattered throughout the text which are exercises in pure invention and which function as a kind of "filler." Yet, significantly, they have the same experiential value as the other elements of the story—"The world is real because it is imagined" (47), the narrator assures us. Written in the form of mock parables, they tell about several queer "birds," all of whom are incidentally "jays"—one is simply J. J., and others are John Johnson, Jim Jones, Junior Junior, Jr., Joshua Jericho, and Jimmy the Jay. This predilection for Js has no particular significance in this story except to provide a stimulus for Sukenick's improvisatory imagination. For example, early in the story, he is surprised at one point by a very peculiar thought: "Suddenly a letter J. Why J? J is a bird. A bird that mimics other birds. Perhaps because its own voice is so imperious, so demanding, that it would rather deny it. J. J, J, the voice says. It appears to be about three inches above and behind my left ear" (53). This unplanned digression provides the narrator with a direct stimulus to improvise the story of J. J., which clearly is only a pretext to play with "J" a little. Since he cannot predict what sound or word may catch his attention next, he cannot predict his next move. Sometimes the use of a word changes his train of thought abruptly and shatters the continuity of discourse. This in turn frequently leads to new, illuminating digressions.

Such digressive strategies illustrate the principle of indeterminacy at work in Sukenick's fiction—the direction of the narrative flow is utterly unpremeditated and unpredictable, even to the writer. It is only the flowing that matters. The value of this flowing is that it creates an occasion, for the writer and for the reader, to play. True to his assertion made at the very beginning of the story that literature does not exist and "there is only reading and writing," Sukenick never forgets that his performance, in order to be complete, must be witnessed and participated in by the reader. One strategy to encourage this participation is to address the reader directly, as, for example, when he says: "We're at a seance. You the participants, I the medium in face of the total blank nothingness of uncreation" (53). Or, after inserting into the narrative a transcript of a recorded telephone conversation, he asks the reader's opinion about the whole idea and ends up delivering a longer monologue in which he declares: "From now on I'm going to be completely open with you friend, as wide open as the form of this performance" (71). This means not only that he places himself before the reader "nude and defenseless," but also that he literally and literalily reeducates his readers by playing with and ridiculing the conventions of realism, for example "A little sex? Okay. Now let's do a retake of that, with a little more accuracy this time. But first a little background material. Narrative mode" (51).[6] By liberating his writing from the simplifications and falsities of literary convention, he teaches the reader to play freely.

The way to such freely composed experiences is an ongoing process. For the time being, the process temporarily concludes when the time the writer has set for himself to finish the story comes. Since he has planned it in advance and thus violated the principle of indeterminacy of composition, the flow of writing is interfered

with: "Another call. And still another. Three calls in
succession pointing to a financial catastrophe. This is
what happens when you try to finish a story you been
working on for two weeks in one hour. . . . Everything's
blowing up, falling to pieces. Art dissolves back into life.
Chaos. It's not the way I planned it" (100). But, the
writer consoles himself, "I am at my best when everything explodes. I thrive on chaos. I have a feeling for
it, a blues mentality, if you know what I mean" (100–
101). He knows that he has managed somehow to digress
his way through the two-week seance and can now complete his performance by literally walking out from the
scene:

Enough. Saturday, January 20, 1968. Let's take a walk. I
put on my boots. I walk out the door. . . . Where I am headed,
I don't know. I keep walking down the road. . . . In a minute
I'll be out of sight. But before I disappear, I lift my red wool
cap that I bought so the hunters won't blow my head off, a
gesture of goodbye, as if to say, in fact to say, I'm happy folks,
and I wish you luck. I disappear around the bend. So long.
End of story. (101–2)

If "The Death of the Novel" may be called inconclu-
sive, it is so because it was never intended to be otherwise. It fails to "make sense" of the fragments of the
writer's life in a very deliberate manner. If it did not, it
would be just another instance of realistic writing based
on the assumption that reality is logical and describable
and that therefore one can perceive patterns in it that
are meaningful by being rational, or at least rationaliz-
able. Sukenick knows that, as Jerome Klinkowitz puts it,
"where art cannot discover significant relationships, the

best thing is to grab hold of the present experience and call it quits."[7]

A deliberate failure to capture what is called "reality" is turned into an aesthetic creed in the next story, "Roast-beef: A Slice of Life." Written as a documentary record of a very peculiar performance—an actual conversation between the writer and his wife over a dinner tape-recorded in their kitchen—this attempt at what Sukenick calls "concrete literature" or "sonic snapshot" (inspired by George Segal's plaster cast sculptures) produces realism with a vengeance: life recorded in the raw turns out to be most unliterary and, simply, dull. It also proves that there exists a fundamental difference between a living writer and a tape recorder—the latter has no imagination. Therefore, mechanical recording of a physical phenomenon may have only a documentary value. To have an artistic, or aesthetic, value, it must be experienced and registered imaginatively by a human being.

The indispensability of experience in the imaginative act of writing is illustrated by the next story, entitled "What's Your Story." It opens with a static description of Rousseau's painting "The Sleeping Gypsy" and then Leutze's "Washington Crossing the Delaware," but soon this purely visual perception of a static scene, as though recorded by a camera, is transformed into a dynamic interplay of several simultaneous perceptions of several scenes. We soon discover that the narrator of the story is not, as we have expected, in an art gallery watching paintings hanging on walls but is sitting at his ancient desk with a pen in his hand and an open notebook before him, having a fantasy. As a writer, he finds his fantasies (especially that of being victimized by Ruby Geranium, a gangster, and Sergeant GunCannon, a detective) so compelling that he must tell them to somebody (the reader) right away. Sharing one's experience with others is a lifesaving act—"The communication of our experience to others is the elemental act of civilization" (154)—for it "helps you to breathe. Let's not suffocate in our own experience" (154). "What's Your Story" is in this regard what Raymond Federman, referring to Sukenick's writing, calls "a teaching machine,"[8] a simple demonstration, a "how-to" story: "Start with immediate situation. One scene after another, disparate, opaque, absolutely concrete. Later, a fable, a gloss, begins to develop, abstractions appear. End with illuminating formulation. Simple, direct utterance" (154).

Despite its title, the last story of the collection, "The Birds," is predominantly about people, although the image of birds sailing against the blue of the sky repeatedly evokes in the narrator a specific aesthetic experience which, he thinks, a work of fiction should aim at evoking in the reader, too. Unlike people, he observes, birds have a language which does not have to mean—"Bird songs constituted a kind of code which, when correctly deciphered, turned out to have absolutely no meaning" (169). Therefore, it does not matter what they say. "What matters," the narrator says, "is that they carve shapes from nothingness, decorate the silence, make melodious distinctions to distinguish one moment from the next" (161). The language of their flight is "Concrete. Innocent. Beautiful. No meaning" (157), which are qualities that Sukenick wants his writing to possess, too. He declares: "I want to write a story that does a lot of infolding and outfolding" (157), that is, a story which would flow across the blank space of the page transforming itself from moment to moment like the shapes carved by birds riding the sky or like clouds. Consequently, meaning would exist not absolutely in the realm of reference but momentarily in the "blank air silence of page [where] the stream carries mainly on its glassy surface rippled clouds inventing themselves from minute to minute" (155).

Amorphousness and motion are for Sukenick the ideal condition for fiction but not just for purely aesthetic reasons: they are the natural conditon of "things chronic and cosmic," including humanity itself. The acknowledgment of this fact poses a serious problem for a fiction writer of Sukenick's disposition—the problem of character presentation. The realistic novel depended for its coherence on, among other things, a unified presentation of various characters, presented from an unequivocal point of view by a narrator whose identity was fixed and coherent in itself. In the postrealistic novel, no such basis of coherence is possible with the identity of the self now dissolved into a multiplicity of relational selves. The question, then, is, How does one present a character whose identity changes constantly?

In "The Birds," Sukenick illustrates the point by creating such a character, Ero, who constantly undergoes a "bifurcation of personality." After his last encounter with the narrator, Ero assumed the guise of "Spiro the spy, then of the Cardinal, then of George and Nick, and then literally disappeared in a welter of dividing and subdividing identities: Orson, Chet Nexus, the Beach Boy, Madame Lafayette, the Light-fingered Trio, to name just a few" (171). To present such a protean figure Sukenick invents a technique whose aim is "to purposely make characters with characteristics that absolutely [don't] go together, whose names serve as rubrics for totally disparate traits."[9] Although in the course of telling the story the narrator provides the reader with more and more information about the characters, this information does not help in fixing their identities. On the contrary, as the narrator explains: "The principle here is progressive fission as in certain microorganisms. They never catch up with you, whoever you are" (163).

Offering an ironic comment on established techniques of characterization, Sukenick is also aware that his own technique of disparate traits is only provisional, for the whole problem of character presentation is secondary to the question of the meaning of personal identity in our times. Therefore, he seems to suggest, instead of trying to impose our own schemes on reality (for example, by defining personality as a stable unity with identifiable character traits), we should rather concentrate on the process in which writing unfolds. Ideally, Sukenick suggests, this process should be the same one by which Simone Rodia constructed his famous Watts Towers in Los Angeles which was "built entirely without design precedent or orderly planning, created bit by bit on sheer impulse, a natural artist's instinct, and the fantasy of the moment" (163).[10] Through such spontaneous creativity, the artist creates a situation which becomes an occasion for his "I" to present itself as a truly performing self and the work of art as a performance.

5

Up

ESSENTIALLY THE SAME principles of composition as those applied by Sukenick in his stories are in operation, though in an extended form, in his first novel, *Up*. Ostensibly a novel about the life of a group of New York intellectuals and bohemians, it is narrated by one of them, a character named Ronald Sukenick, in a manner which deliberately contradicts the conventions of "good," that is, realistic, storytelling. First of all, the novel has no identifiable plot or story line. Instead of a causal and chronological sequence of events, the reader is presented with what one of the characters, after reading the manuscript of *Up*, calls "a collection of disjointed fragments." He tells Sukenick that his novel lacks any purposive development ("You don't go anywhere at all") and a time structure ("The chronology is completely screwed up.)"[1] Second, the novel does not have a unitary and unequivocal center of narrative mediation, or narrative authority, for the narrator has no stable, definable identity. He presents himself alternately as a young college professor and a not yet successful novelist writing his own biography or as the author of a book about a character named Ronald Sukenick, who is himself writing a novel entitled *The Adventures of Strop Banally*. Fragments of his divided self can also be detected in several other characters appearing in the novel, especially in Ernie Slade, who "always spoke as if he were writing his own biography" (6) and always turned up in the same places as Ron.

Unable to clearly identify himself, the narrator further undercuts his credibility by the way he presents other characters. In his descriptions, they change from one episode to the next so radically that he himself occasionally has trouble recognizing them, as in the following scene:

I was looking for Slade in a bar on Hudson Street where he's asked me to meet him when this nut in an army surplus jacket and a lot of hair comes over and gives me a hug. Jesus, I thought, the queers are getting aggressive in the neighborhood. I really panicked when before I could get away he put his arm around my shoulder and, cursing, started pulling me toward the bar. . . . Suddenly peering at me from behind the drooping mustache and a long dark, curling, messianic beard, there he was. "Ernie Slade." (206)

His method of character presentation is directly questioned by one of the characters, Bernie Marsh, to whom Sukenick recounts a scene he wrote for the novel but then misplaced somewhere. Bernie asks: "Listen, are you sure you're talking about Slade? It doesn't sound like him" (223–24). As it happens, the only stable element in the characterization are the characters' names, but these serve merely as "rubrics for totally disparate traits."

And in the case of Sukenick himself, even that ceases to be an identification. The mailman casually calls him Jim and his chairman stubbornly refuses to get his name right, mispronouncing it as Suchanitch, Subenitch, Suckanitch, and so on.

Faced with the dubiousness of their identities, the individual characters develop idiosyncratic approaches to the question of self-definition. Finch, for example, "submits to chance and the gratifications of the moment" and "desires to be somebody else" (216). Nancy declares that "we're so used to recognizing one another by face and costume that your identity changes completely when you take your clothes off," and so, paradoxically, she hides her "real" self by exposing her body as a model— "Your best friends don't recognize you when they see you nude" (185).

The character most admired by Sukenick, however, is Strop Banally, whose identity is simply what it happens to be at a particular moment with no regard to his earlier personalities, or personas (masks). Sukenick the author of *The Adventures of Strop Banally* says: "The fact is that Strop made up his past as he went along, so that by now it was impossible to separate the truth from the fiction" (4). This way he can feel "at home in heaven or hell," including both the novel of which he is the main hero (*The Adventures of Strop Banally*) and the novel of which his inventor (Sukenick) is the main hero (*Up*). In fact, when Strop and Sukenick meet face-to-face at a party near the end of *Up,* the latter has some good reasons to suspect that the world created by him may be Strop's invention after all.

This comical reversal of the relation between the creator and his creation serves as an effective way of demonstrating the power of self-invention and convinces the reader that there is no sense in trying to separate "the truth" from "the fiction" from "the truth within the fiction" from "the fiction within the truth" and so forth. It is totally irrelevant how many levels of narration, or stories within stories, there are in a novel and how strictly they are separated from or related to one another.

Sukenick makes the point clear when at the very end of *Up* he calls a party to celebrate the end of his novel. Characters whose mode of existence is admittedly purely fictional meet with the writer's real wife, Lynn, and several other persons who are his real friends. At this party, none of the guests is more real or more fictitious than any other. All are fictitious because they appear in a work of fiction; but all are real, too, because Sukenick really put them into his novel. Once readers understand that, they begin to see that behind the stories told by the narrator(s) there is the actual Ronald Sukenick performing a series of acts, both intellectual (imaginative) and physical (manual—writing), sitting there at his desk and, in reality, inventing characters and scenes and putting it all down on paper.

Having such fantasies and writing them down are in fact closer to the writer's experience than what is normally taken to be the reality of day-to-day life. Compared with the fantasy, the content of this reality, which is to a large extent the content of news reports in the mass media, is infinitely abstract and truly detached from our daily experience in the world: "The administration categorically denies Moscow's charge that the American delegation is trying to systematically wreck the tentative negotiations for a preliminary meeting to discuss the possibility of top level talks on a temporary cessation of

the bilateral boycott of the conference to probe re-
sumption of the nuclear moratorium. The time is one
thirteen and a half. Henry Sliesinger reports the news"
(3). This is enough to convince Sukenick that it is not
through the mass media that one establishes a "favorable
rapport with reality"—"Thanks. That lets me know where
I stand. Nowhere. I go back to my cramped and littered
desk" (3). The only way to counteract solipsism and to
make "contact with Outside" is through art, which is
closer to life than, for example, journalism, for it does
more than just discover reality and report on this
discovery.

It should now be clear that *Up* is for Sukenick in the
most literal sense a process in which the writer tries to
get at the truth of his experience by imaginatively recording his thoughts and perceptions occurring during
and because of the composition of his novel. Assuming
invention as his modus operandi, he proceeds in a most
straightforward manner, leaving no doubt about his
strategy. One wild fantasy follows another, but the reader
is not allowed to fall through the words on the page and
suspend disbelief. On the contrary, by employing various
self-reflexive and self-reflective measures, Sukenick
forces the reader to consciously witness the fantasy that
the author was having as he was writing the story.

That the reality of *Up* is ultimately the reality of its
author and its readers, and not of its narrator (whatever
his name) and its characters, is also suggested by Sukenick's reference to facts which exist not within the
closed frame of the narrator's visual imagination but
beyond it, in actuality. At the end of the novel, it is the
reference to Sukenick's wife and friends; earlier, for
example, Sukenick discusses with Bernie Marsh the story

"The Permanent Crisis" (55–56) and refers the reader to the story "The Sleeping Gypsy"—"see *Epoch,* Spring 1959" (174)—which was the real Sukenick's first published work of fiction and which the narrator now calls "my story."

As a writer actually sitting at his desk and composing a novel, Sukenick obviously sees the book he is writing as both an imaginative and a concrete structure. Countering Bernie's charge that he foregoes verisimilitude in *Up,* he answers: "Why should we have to suspend disbelief? It's all words and nothing but words. Are we children reading fairy tales or men trying to work out the essentials of our fate?" (223). He reminds the reader of the materiality of the book on several occasions by using various typographical devices. Apart from its physical, spatial dimension, the novel has of course a temporal structure too. Time in *Up,* however, is not story-time at all but is ultimately a matter of pagination. Time's passage is marked by page numbers which, in the absence of chronology, are the only identifiable reference points throughout the narrative. Thus, for example, in a section called "A Brief Erotic Autobiography," Sukenick first tries to place a story in the novel's (nonexistent) time structure but then finds reference to a specific page a much more convenient solution: "This should actually begin when I was eleven. As a matter of fact it should begin when I was two and a half, with certain gratifying incidents of my naughty nonage which I chuckle to recall. But allow me my few rags of modesty. You remember that on page 69 I let drop how I knew a girl in Manhattan that summer between high school and college 'who was usually good for a lay' " (169).

Time measured by page numbers is in fact time reduced to mere presence, for each page records only the presence of a thought in the writer's mind at the moment of writing it down. Therefore, the entire novel is in the present tense, a series of presences, or an atemporal "collection of disjointed fragments." Reminiscences, fantasies, and improvisations follow one another in an unpremeditated and unpredictable order and merge in a logically discontinuous but experientially and compositionally continuous current, or what Ronnie perceives as "the slow millenarian flow of one thing into another" (289). It has no discursive or logical meaning, but that is exactly what life is like: "No meaning. The opacity of experience" (323). For the unity of experience is wholly a matter of the writer's presence at the scene of "action," at every moment of the going. Echoing Proust, just as he echoed Wordsworth in "Momentum," the narrator states: "Unity of experience equals reality of self" (308). And conversely, by "being totally here," the writer gives his invention the sanction of authenticity. Concluding his three years of work on *Up*, Sukenick confesses:

I'm going to finish this today, the hell with it. I've had enough of this. I'm just playing with words anyway, what did you think I was doing? Just playing with words, ga-ga-ga-ga-ga-ga-goo-goo-gig-geg-gug-gack. I'm thirty-three I've got more important things to attend to, money, career, women, hobbies, vacations, lots of things, really good ones, I got a list somewhere. Nel mezzo del cammin di nostra vita—mi frega niente. I just make it up as I go along, the hell with it, I'm finishing today. Though it's all true what I've written, every word of it, I insist on that. (329)

It is all true because Ronald Sukenick, a real person, really wrote it. And the truth of his novel is exactly the same kind of truth that John Ashbery has in mind when he speaks in *Three Poems* about "the reality which you dreamed and which therefore is real."[2] Simply, the truth is not in *what* the writer says (the story he tells is, after all, a fiction) but in *that* he says it.

When a novel's rationale is not the transmission of some referential meaning but recording the experience of its own composition, the important question is not what it says but how it comes into existence and sustains itself. Part of the answer to this question is already implied in *Up*'s title; as Sukenick explains elsewhere: "*Up* really does go up: it's a flight of the imagination. There is literally a scene in the beginning where an astronaut goes up, and then he comes down again at the end of the book. And the whole novel goes up and down in that curve in a lot of ways."[3]

The metaphor of writing as flight is the most powerfully rendered in the kite-flying episode, where Otis, Finch, Nancy, and Ronnie, after two unsuccessful attempts, finally launch a kite and manage to keep it up in the air for a long while. Kite flying, like nonmimetic writing, is a completely self-contained activity which requires no justification outside itself. It does, however, require certain skills—skills to set the kite in motion and to maintain it in flight for as long as possible. The best results are obtained, Ronnie learns, when the kite flyer, instead of trying to control closely the kite's flight, releases as much string as possible and allows the kite to choose its own way up in the air. Even more, instead of trying to make the kite a "puppet on a string," he should constantly adjust his position in accordance with the kite's movements, which in practice means that he should "run with it." If he stops for a moment, the kite will plunge down immediately. Controlling the kite's flight thus means releasing more string, allowing it more freedom, and only delicately pulling it in so that it can get up even higher after each tug. At the end of this exhilarating experience, however, Ronnie is confronted with the ultimate paradox of kite flying: the act is consummated only when it fails in the end, for no matter how high and for how long the kite flies, it must always eventually come down.

As a metaphor for writing, the image expresses Sukenick's theory of composition as an autonomous and continuous flowing which is not so much governed by the writer as initiated by him and then imaginatively participated in. Like kite flying, writing is an activity whose meaning is the actual performance of this activity and not some goal to be reached by means of this performance and then celebrated after the fact, after the act. Yet, since kite flying "means" only as long as the kite remains up in the air, as long as the pulling of the string makes it fly, the question remains whether a novel, after a successful ascent and a sustained "flight," must also irrevocably end in a nadir. In *Up*, the answer apparently is yes, for the last pages record the ebbing of the experiential flow: "All right, the party is over. I've had enough of this. All I want to do is end the book. If I'm lucky I'll manage it today, that would be nice. Before Friday in any case. Friday is New Year's Eve. Sometime in these five days, by god, I'm going to finish this. Though frankly I'm tired. My eyes are shot. Then there are the interruptions . . ." (328).

For a moment, Sukenick debates continuing the "flight" ("Maybe I better keep it up a while longer, what am I going to do when I'm done?") but instantly decides against it, knowing that he is going to lose the experiential flow anyway: "No, impossible. It's dissolving into words, script on paper. Time to leave my cave, these scenes, the magic paintings on my rocky walls figure in figure, Lascaux, the potent hunters, the bulls dreaming across the centuries. Forget it. Exist, subsist, resist. That's all. That's the plot, the subplot, and the counterplot. End quickly, quietly. Nothing dramatic. I light a pipe ..." (329).

Although Sukenick's invented "kite" 's descent is a natural conclusion of the act, and so it is no cause for despair, the mere fact that it is inevitable must be disturbing to the writer since it violates his assumption that the outcome of composition should be totally unpredictable, indeterminate, and open-ended. On the other hand, however, Sukenick argues that there is nothing wrong about a novel's being a failure of this sort: "The kind of book I most want to write is the kind of book that *fails* back into the experience which it is about. It emerges—and re-merges—with this experience, having added itself to it."[4]

Yet, viewed in this way, *Up* does not fully satisfy the requirement of Sukenick's aesthetics of failure because it moves in a (closed) circle: it emerges as an experience and then folds back into itself. The experience stops when the novel stops. And this is not exactly what Sukenick means by "failing back into experience." He explains: "I'm not interested in creating a book that remains in its own perfect sphere, apart from experience. My work has to cancel itself out to do what it is trying to do. It isn't trying to transcend experience, but is trying to add to experience."[5] Sukenick's second novel, *Out,* is in this respect much more successful, as it literally cancels itself out as it progresses, while the reader is safely transported back into his own reality thanks to an ingenious typographical device employed by the author.

6

Out

IN *OUT,* RONALD SUKENICK invents a formal device which allows him to complete the act of composition not by landing the "kite" on the ground after its upward/downward flight but by releasing the controls completely and allowing his novel to move out from between the book's covers and literally disappear from the page. The novel consists of eleven chapters numbered backwards from 10 to 0, each of which is made up of ten-line blocks of print. The number of lines of printed text in each block corresponds to the chapter's number—in chapter 10 there are ten lines of print per block, in chapter 9 nine lines per block, and so on down to chapter 0, which contains only blank pages. The effect of this typographical layout is that, as the novel progresses, there is visibly less and less of it left before the reader's eyes as the white space expands until the text is no longer there to be seen at all.

This strict arbitrary form plays many roles in the novel, and its expediency can be measured by its appropriateness to or integration with both the discursive content of the book and the experience of writing and reading it. The most immediate is the form's impact on readers: they are constantly reminded of the physicality of the reading act by having to turn the pages of the book at an ever increasing rate corresponding to the acceleration of the pace of the "action" to be finally confronted with eleven blank pages which, although empty, are still there to be turned. As Linda Bergmann observes about *Out,* "The reader is thus literally experiencing the novel after it runs out of words,"[1] which is a clever way of demonstrating that there are experiences beyond words or experiences which need not be expressed in words at all.

More important, however, is the way the form of *Out* is integrated with its content into an inseparable whole. The plot of the novel—and the word "plot" should probably be used here in quotes to indicate the dubiousness of its meaning in the present context—involves the journey of an indefinable character, or a number of characters, across the United States from New York to California. A classic American theme, it might seem, were it not for the indefinability (equally indeterminate are the purpose and the duration of the trip). In effect, the plot develops by an accumulation of causally discontinuous episodes which form random sequences and do not create a meaningful pattern. The only sure thing is the progression from the first line to the last (non-) line across the geography of the book's pages.

The novel starts with two characters, a man named Harrold and a woman named President Nixon, both members of some terrorist group carrying sticks of dynamite as identifications, having a "meet" on a window ledge seven floors up above street level. Harrold explains to the woman several things about the plot in which they are involved. First, he says, "You're either part of the plot or part of the counterplot,"[2] which is the first hint at the cancellation central to this book. Second, he continues, it does not make any difference if one is part of one or the other because, on the one hand, one's identity is never disclosed ("Of course we don't have real names we have aliases"[2]) and, on the other, the plot is not based on any plan or scheme ("It's all chance" [1]). On top of that, Harrold admits that none of what he says is true, a truly Epimenidean confession. His revelations, although addressed to the woman, are also, as will become clear only later, meant as a warning to readers, who at this early point still probably believe that they have just started reading a more or less conventional mystery novel, complete with plotted narrative, well-developed characters, purposive time, causation, and verisimilitude.

Readers are initially encouraged to retain their conventional expectations since early on Sukenick supplies numerous clues promising that an identifiable plot (in both senses of the word) is going to unfold. Thus, chapter 9 begins when the conspirators set their watches and begin the countdown. Two of them, a man and a woman, hurriedly leave the meet and set out on a journey, supposedly a mission of some sort. From then on, things start happening one after another at an ever accelerating pace. The pair go to an apartment, have a quarrel, make love, are assaulted twice in ten minutes by the same man, head for the zoo where the man has a commission, and get lost on their way to the zoo in a street riot; the man manages to get to the zoo, meets his contact there, and together they go to the second man's apartment. The chapter ends in a bizarre episode of the two men being served an alphabet soup by the second man's wife. At the table, they throw dice to find out, by picking an appropriate number of letters from the soup, the meaning of the first man's commission. Their permutations on the letters lead them to the discovery that the message is in a code. But in order to produce the message, the code is not to be deciphered, broken by the intelligence, but simply eaten. In other words, it must be absorbed not mentally but bodily. So they eat it. Then they identify themselves, the husband describing himself as "just a character trying to be a person" (27) and his wife as "not even a character she's an empty hole" (26). Their guest is identified by the stick of dynamite he carries in his pants.

Such a summary is misleading, for it does not suggest how the plot disintegrates into an "alphabet soup" and the expectations of the traditionally minded reader are frustrated one after another. The characters turn out to be pseudofigures who move in and out of the story, merge with one another, come into existence at the drop of their name, and then disappear never to reappear again. Since they change constantly, it is impossible to tell who is who at a given moment and who he or she will be a moment later. The original pair in chapter 9 are Rex and Ova. But soon they become Carl and Velma after they introduce themselves that way to the man who assaults them. Later Velma disappears completely, and Carl meets his contact in the zoo, who introduces himself as Carl. So Carl changes to Donald. The second Carl's wife turns out to be Ova, but she is a different Ova. And so on. Names are changed and exchanged in what Linda

Bergmann has called a "stream of character" with not even one of the characters becoming a stable center of personal reference. As a result, the basis for the unity of action is destroyed completely, as there is no way of telling whether the incidents described occur to the same character(s) or whether they are just "disjointed fragments" of several independent stories put together in a collagelike manner. The story line becomes more and more convoluted, but this does not bring the conspirators or the reader any closer to discovering the purpose of the plot hinted at at the beginning. The chapters that follow proceed essentially in the same manner. The main character, or "stream of character," transforms from Harrold to Carl to Nick to Rex to Ronald Sukenick to Ron to Roland Sycamore to be finally reduced to the minimal R. His itinerary is marked by a series of "meets" with several odd characters. Those random and unpredictable encounters, despite the main character's persistent efforts to figure out their meaning and relevance to his secret commission, do not add up to produce a better understanding of the journey's purpose. Quite the contrary, clues begin to accumulate which suggest that in fact there is not any commission to be carried out, any message to be deciphered, any conspirational action to be unmasked. Questions about the nature of the discontinuous action inevitably pop up every now and then, only to be answered with quips like "Data accumulates obscurity persists" (100), "Connection develops meaning falls away" (128), or "Meaning disintegrates connection proliferates what does that mean" (164).

These comments make it obvious that to ask about the "meaning" of *Out*'s events is to ask the wrong question. The meaning is not *behind* but *in* those events. It is not referential but superficial and, like the alphabet soup, it is not to be interpreted but experienced, not deciphered by the mind but ingested by the body, internalized not via the intellect but via the senses. As the journey progresses, the "stream of character" learns that the only thing to do with his experience, however puzzling it may be, is to use it, that is, to live it in the fullest possible way without asking, as a character named Henry does, about "the meaning of this trip" (88), for one can only hear in reply that the answer is in "a code that when broken is meaningless" (89). Once they embark on their trip, these characters realize that rather than taking it they are being taken by it, pulled along by an overpowering current of events, which gains momentum with every move they make and every word they say.

Keeping up with the flow of experience, the inflow of sensual data or perceptions, requires inexhaustible energy, but as Roland reads in *I Ching (The Book of Changes),* one has little choice if one wants to survive. The *I Ching* says: "It's dangerous to stay still to avoid permanent injury move at once" (175). The movement must be incessant and purposeless, which means also unpremeditated. Harrold learns about this from a sympathetic palmist, Ali Buba, who, answering his question about his destiny, says: "Cultivate the unexpected it's your only chance" and "Hope for surprise welcome the unknown" (34). Keeping track of experience becomes thus an autotelic, "self-contained activity like skating which requires no justification" (41).

The full value of a self-contained sensual approach to the world can be appreciated by Sukenick only when he finds out that it is the chief source of man's imaginative power. He first gets a glimpse of that when, hitching a ride with Empty Fox, an Indian he meets in the Black Hills of South Dakota, he encounters a man who performs a series of impossible acrobatic feats and then disappears. Later, Empty Fox explains the meaning of this episode to his puzzled companion: "Sometimes I have a vision like the vision you saw in the truck just before about the man who flew up the tree that was my vision only I saw it through you" (137). For the time being, Sukenick's puzzlement is not dispelled, but after he learns to transcend the constrictions of rationalistic thinking, he becomes finally able to experience the power of dreaming, or "seeing." His own vision happens to be so overwhelming that Empty Fox must beat him, karate-style, back into reality, warning his apprentice that "if you fly too far you can't come back" (160).

The importance of the lesson that Sukenick learns from Empty Fox can be considered on two planes which at first seem separate but which eventually converge in what turns out to be the chief subject of *Out*. On the level of the story of the main character's journey across the continent, the encounter with the Indian is a turning point both because it marks the middle of the trip and because the main character is finally persuaded of the futility of trying to find out about the purpose and the meaning of his trip. Empty Fox literally opens his eyes to the world, thus allowing him to perceive reality as it really is and use his perception imaginatively instead of rationally. After the Indian disappears, Sukenick finds himself in an admirable condition—"His body feels serious full of its own intelligence his head is peculiarly empty" (161). Having freed himself from the baggage of logical thinking, Sukenick now stops looking for explanations and accepts that there is no plot in which he is involved, no commission to carry out, and that the only purpose of his going is to keep going. With the disintegration of the original plot before the reader's eyes, however, an entirely different "story" is brought to the foreground: the story of Ronald Sukenick the writer composing his novel *Out*.

The relevance of the Empty Fox episode for the metafictional turn of the novel in its middle chapter is most obviously evident in the fact that the name of the main character now *is* Ronald Sukenick. Also, the subject of the conversation between Sukenick and Empty Fox is straightforwardly literary. After introducing themselves to each other, the Indian invites his companion to have a "serious discussion" and asks him about his ambition. Sukenick's answer is that he wants "to write a book like a cloud that changes as it goes," to which Empty Fox replies: "I want to erase all books. My ambition is to unlearn everything I can't read or write that's a start. I want to unlearn till I get to the place where the ocean of the unknown begins where my fathers live" (136). Although it may seem irreconcilable at first, the difference between the two men is quickly resolved and deep affinities become evident. On the one hand, Sukenick's literary concerns are in fact very antiliterary from the point of view of the traditional novel—his writing aims at "unlearning" its tradition and moving toward the "unknown." On the other hand, Empty Fox's hostility to literature is not unconditional. He recites the following brief poem which takes up a familiar metaphor and asserts motion and responsiveness to nature's stimuli as a necessary condition for an (artistic) act to succeed:

Without the wind
The kite is dead
With it everything
Is possible.
(140)

To Sukenick's puzzlement, followed by enlighten-
ment, Empty Fox performs such an act be seeing a vision
"through" his white friend, thus demonstrating to him
the power of dreaming, or fiction making. The most
important thing about the Indian's vision is that it is
verifiably real, for it can be experienced by somebody
else, which is exactly what writing is too: the author's
vision to be really experienced by the reader. Significantly, the value of this experience does not lie in the
content of the vision but in the way this vision is produced and perceived. To be real, or experientially true,
a vision must be "seen" and not merely looked at.

Interestingly, Empty Fox's lesson parallels that which
Juan Matus, an Indian sorcerer, gives to Carlos Castaneda as described by the latter in his Don Juan series.[3]
"Looking" and "seeing," as Don Juan tells Carlos, are
two different kinds of perception: one belongs to the
faculty of the intellect, the other to that of the imagination. The cultivation of the latter allows people to
appropriate the data of their sensual experience not just
in order to describe and explain appearances in logical
terms but to get at, as Castaneda puts it, "the 'essence'
of the things of the world."[4] "Seeing" is thus a way of
acquiring knowledge about the world by imagining things
into reality and experiencing them as real phenomena.
Moreover, the knowledge that comes from this kind of
perception is truly visionary, for it enables one to predict

the future, though neither by deduction nor by induction. Traveling and seeing visions through people, Empty Fox is not guided by ordinary perception and reason. To augment his visionary disposition, he uses "Mr. Peyote's" help. This, he cautions Sukenick after the latter overdoses, must be done considerately, by which he means that one's seeing a vision must be controlled at all points.[5]

Empty Fox's practical philosophy of getting along clearly articulates Ronald Sukenick's own ideas about writing and the role of the imagination developed in his criticism and earlier fiction. Through the Empty Fox episode, they are masterfully incorporated into the narrative structure of the novel, thus turning *Out* into a fully metafictional work, that is, one which examines itself as a fictional system as it proceeds. The outright fictionality of the story told in the first five chapters is suggested by the fact that until the middle chapter, 5, each major episode begins when the main character wakes up from a dream. In effect, a complex structure of dreams-within-dreams (stories-within-stories) is created, each episode taking place on a different fictional level, in a different fictional world. In chapter 5, however, Sukenick suggests that the various events may exist on one level after all, as dreams of one and the same person who simply sees them through the stream of characters (and through the reader too). In fact, the Empty Fox episode itself is introduced as a dream, "Empty Fox's dream or maybe my dream" (135). With this suggestion, the "story" moves to a different level, its protagonist now being the "seer" of the dreams, and the question of his own identity and his own story gradually takes precedence over the meaning of the original "plot."

The character Ronald Sukenick does not enter the scene in chapter 5 as just another member of the "bang gang" trying to find out about the purpose of his commission. Near the end of the preceding chapter, he identifies himself, in first person narration, as the author of the book who invents it as he goes along and plays with his own voice as he speaks it:

It's interesting I'm getting messages ten nine eight seven six five four three two one zero testing testing abcdefghijklmnopqrstuvwxyz ga ga ga gug gek I've said this before can't stop talking we've lost it I've been hit lost and not going to get it back let's start from there I forgot what I was going to say I forgot I forgot I forget I forget thank god at last what now sodium pentathol in the beginning darkness sound of worms crawling through vaseline thung-CHUNG -e-e-e-e-E-E E H A A a a a a h thung CHUNG e e e e E E E H A A A a-a-a-a-h a roaring wind followed by a roaring wind pump a rising wind and then a falling wind pump the worms the pump the wind worms pump wind repeat repeat here we are in the middle of our book speeding along on the breaking crest of the present toward god knows what destination after the first word everything follows anything follows nothing follows the world is pure invention from one minute to the next who said that (117–118)

What this passage illustrates also is what one might call the novel's "never-stop-talking" principle at work: what moves the action are not the various vehicles by which the main character hitches consecutive rides westward as he approaches California but the flowing of words across the pages as the book approaches its conclusion.

When the narrative flow is threatened with a stoppage caused by some disruption in the unfolding of the plot, the novel's progress is saved by the voice of the author which fills the silence with sound just as his hand fills the blank space of the page with letters. The current of words constantly generated by the writer prevents the "kite" from falling to the ground and "pumps" it up so that the "flight" may continue.

The identity of the narrative "I" as a trafficker in words rather than dynamite is in fact hinted at even before he identifies himself directly as the real Ronald Sukenick. For example, at the beginning of the journey, Rex explains to Ova: "All you can do is keep track. You keep track with your head. Your head tells you where your body goes. The important thing is never to stop talking. If you forget the words make sounds make new words. Make words that grunt scream laugh hum sob. The voice is the connection between the body and the head. Silence means you're lost" (11–12). This statement clearly indicates that the important action is going to be that of language and voice and that it is going to take place in the head of the person uttering the words. Then, as the novel approaches its center, the identity of the "stream of character" as an extension of the writer's own personality becomes more and more apparent and the status of the "I" as not just the narrator-hero but the actual inventor of the story is implied—"The land seems wider here opens and flattens out. Wider than what he doesn't know image of a city mountains close hills wide water. I love you. Words in his head. My head . . . " (91).

Finally, the identity of the "I" as the author of *Out* is made obvious in the middle of chapter 6: "Rex lies down to think about it takes notes. What now Rex wonders

what next he closes his notebook his eyes tired of sim-
ulation how did I get into this I allow his mind to wander
play with possibilities he daydreams he's lying I'm lying
in the sun on a chaise inventing stories about himself"
(104–5). So that when chapter 5 begins—"Wake up.
Everything up to here has been a movie" (122)—the
main character, although still vaguely connected with
the "plot," features primarily as the real Ronald Sukenick, who openly declares that he will continue telling the
story of the "plot," or whatever is left of it, but without
pretending any longer that the story preexists the telling
of it. In other words, he tells the readers that he is going
to invent the story right before their eyes and let them
witness not just the product of his performance but the
act of "production" as well.

As Sukenick's novel demonstrates playfully and self-
consciously, the most obvious thing that a writer does
when he writes is that he *writes;* therefore, it is important
to render the experience of writing *as* writing. The emphasis on the mechanics of writing and on the experiential veracity of the intellectual and imaginative act
inevitably leads to a self-reflective mode of composition.
Composing a novel, the writer self-consciously flaunts
the artifice and thus makes the reader aware of both the
concreteness of the medium and of the act of writing
on the one hand and of the fictitious, made-up status of
the story told on the other. Sukenick's strategy in the
second half of the novel, apart from explicit statements
about his intentions, consists chiefly of the technique of
collage linkage by which causally unrelated episodes are
presented as pure fantasies—Roland in the can factory,
Roland leading a crowd out of a canyon attacked by a
cowboy squad, Roland meeting Mr. Derrekker and then

I. Askew, R meeting the Los Angeles area group, and so on—while the unity of the narrative is sustained exclusively by the writer's own voice talking about himself and playing with language. Like Sukenick's earlier works, *Out* is a self-apparent invention whose meaning is not referential or symbolic but primarily experiential. That is, it is not the novel that is supposed to make *sense* but the reader who is given an opportunity to *make* sense. In this connection, Sukenick's ingenious typographical design not only provides a vehicle for moving the action in space from New York to California by means of page turning but also allows the author to leave the novel open-ended. The mystery of the "plot" is not resolved at all, and the novel ends when the action moves beyond its arbitrary frame, when words move out from the page just as the main character, now reduced to R, moves beyond the mainland with Sailor, who sets sail for the Pacific.

Thus, *Out* brings the reader, after an imaginary voyage, to its own end but allows for a continuation of the experience in the reader's own imagination. By then, the reader has been provided with many useful hints about ways to exercise the power of invention. At the same time, heeding Empty Fox's warning that "if you fly too far you can't come back," Sukenick makes sure that both he and the reader are returned safely to reality after this fictional adventure. As for himself, after his appearance in chapter 5, Sukenick declares, "If it's possible I'm getting out of this novel" (164), while the reader is allowed to stay till the very end, where he is told to "wake up" and leave:

this way this way this way this way this way this way this
way out this
way out

(p. 294)

The author's employment of narrative and formal
means to make the reader's experience of the novel continuous with his own experience of creating it serves one
general goal: it makes the reader aware of the fact that
although both writing and reading are activities which
are necessarily matrixed, or framed, a considerable
amount of freedom is left to the participants in the creative process of fiction. To use this freedom imaginatively, one need only become (be made) aware of the
arbitrariness of the space within whose limits experience
unfolds in the course of the writing/reading performance. *Out's* success in reaching this goal marks it as
one of the best metafictional/performatory novels written by an American author in recent years.

The fundamental strategy of metafiction, as Larry
McCaffery observes, can be adequately described by
paraphrasing Colin Turbayne's statement about the "undressing" of metaphors: "First, the detection of the presence of the metaphor; second, the attempt to 'undress'
the metaphor by presenting the literal truth, 'to behold
the deformity of error we need only undress it'; and
third, the restoration of the metaphor, only this time
with awareness of its presence."[6] Since fictions, Mc-
Caffery argues, are very much like metaphors—both
share the tendency to instill themselves as ontological
verities—it is only necessary to replace "metaphor" with
"fiction" in the above statement to get a perfect definition of metafiction making.

What distinguishes *Out* among other recent novels exploring their own status as fictions is that it employs the pattern derived from Turbayne to create a perfectly symmetrical tripartite structure within an arbitrary numerological pattern: the first five chapters present the unfolding of the plot while systematically undercutting its "reality" by studding it with hints about its fictiousness; the middle chapter, 5, lays bare the fictiousness of the story told; and the final five chapters replay the fictions of the novel's first half *as* fictions constructed in front of the reader. By his systematic deconstruction, or "undressing," of the elements of the traditional novel—plot, chronology, causation, characterization, description, and so on—Sukenick exposes the falsities and simplifications of conventional realism and at the same time recovers for the reader what is the most important thing in literature: the experience of fiction making, the sense of active participation in actualizing, and finally generating, the meaning that the novel gives access to.

7

98.6

THE FORMULA INVENTED by Sukenick in *Out*, although aesthetically satisfying, may rightly seem to be morally ambiguous: the novel starts as a journey in search of a meaning and ends as an escape from the now evidently meaningless plight of the main character. In his next novel, *98.6*, Sukenick, apparently aware of this ambiguity, addresses himself to the same issue in a much more direct and unequivocal way. The novel begins when R's companion, Sailor, brings his passenger(s) back to shore at the western edge of the United States, now transformed into a monstrous country called Frankenstein. Their return is in one sense a return to the reality explored in *Out*, but it is also the beginning of a new "trip." While taking up and elaborating on many themes introduced in *Out*, *98.6* clearly shifts the emphasis from artistic self-consciousness toward what Sukenick elsewhere calls a "greater consciousness." Discursively, the novel explores the problems connected with the rise of an ecological consciousness in contemporary society and, more philosophically, the synthesis of imagination and science in postmodern culture. At the same time, although more discursive in content and more orthodox in form, this novel is no less effective in demonstrating that every novel, irrespective of its subject matter, tells primarily the story of its own composition.

The novel's major concerns are introduced in the first of its three parts, called "Frankenstein," which has the form of a series of loosely connected episodes that in a collagelike manner present the decay, disorder, and brutality of life in a modern industrialized society in decline. The unity of the vision conveyed is provided by the voice, or hand, of the author, whose presence is hinted at by the fact that each episode is recounted in the form of a dream, a fantasy, a movie, or some other kind of fiction behind which always lurks the person of the fiction's maker. His identity as the author of *98.6* is implied by the way each episode is featured in the novel—as a dated entry from the writer's notebook, the date of the first entry being Sukenick's birthday. Although these dates are not related to the content of the entries, which are not arranged chronologically anyway, they point to the order in which they were originally conceived in the writer's mind and recorded in his notebook. Thus, the final form of this section of the novel, the arrangement of the particular episodes, is manifestly presented as imposed ex post facto. After all, as Sukenick observes in *Out*, "Form is when you look back and see your footprints in the sand,"[1]—that is, form is a matter of structuring experience after the fact, of discovering patterns and relationships among phenomena which did not exist before they were perceived.

The question of structuring experience, of developing meaningful forms, or simply of getting along, is crucial to one's survival in the world of Frankenstein, where old social, political, and cultural institutions are crumbling, where life is threatened with murder and love with sexual perversity and violence. Illustrating the point with a collage of original newspaper clippings dealing with various murderous practices, Sukenick says that the Manson killings, the Nazi camps, but also simple poltergeists, are all "the consequence of precisely the same phenomenon of life energy in the absence of creative forms turning against itself."[2] Sukenick's view in *98.6* clearly modifies his earlier idea that energy is by its very nature a positive good and that its transmission, in whatever form, should be the ultimate purpose of man's activity, intellectual, artistic, or physical. Loose, or excessive energy, the writer now observes, can be destructive, as is exemplified by the present condition of Frankenstein, a country which is "racing like a wheel out of contact with the ground a loose flywheel spinning faster and faster till it tears the whole machine apart" (9–10). Therefore, after a period of fascination with speed and uncontained energy, which in *Out* brought him dangerously close to losing "contact with the ground," Sukenick now wants to slow down.

He always wanted to be a pilot he no longer wants to be a pilot he doesn't like airplanes anymore. His lust for flight has suddenly evaporated. . . . Still rocking with the motion of the sailboat he's overcome with an appreciation for gravity you might say he falls in love with it. He loves the way it hugs him firm against the ground like a mother. He loves the way he has to press back erect against it his force against its force in balance. He loves the steady pressure of it on the soles of his feet. He dislikes people who are too tall he wants heavy gourd-shaped women squat men who look like squash. People who grow out of the earth and never get too far from it never forget they're going back into it lesson of the pyramids pressing down. (5)

The lesson is also that of Empty Fox, who taught Sukenick that the two most important components of experience are the direct, sensual perception of reality and the imaginative, extraordinary perception of people's relation to it.

The ideal of being at one with nature, both sensually and imaginatively, is represented in the novel by the notion of Ancien Caja, a concept which is never defined but which epitomizes a worldview that is the opposite of the modern rationality responsible for the afflictions of Frankenstein. The Ancien Caja is a condition in which the separation between mind and body, thought and perception, stillness and motion is overcome in the imagination. When used creatively, the imagination is capable of inventing viable forms of social and artistic order in which life's energy is utilized in a beneficial manner. The imagination, and not the intellect, is the right faculty to deal with the chaos and disorder of the present world since it allows people to perceive reality more immediately and it operates in essentially the same nonrational way that nature does. At the same time, being a nonrational faculty, imagination does not shut off consciousness at all, so its operations can not only be monitored and recorded but also controlled to some extent, as the lessons of Empty Fox and Don Juan demonstrate. The interplay between the consciousness and the imagination of a creative mind is thus the central concern of *98.6*, a focal point where all other topics blend into a fully developed theory of artistic creativity continuous with the postmodern ecological and scientific worldview. The crucial role of the imagination in salvaging human experience (including the writing/reading experience) is evident from the very beginning of the novel. Confronted with the reality of Frankenstein, the main character, identified only as "he," rejects the possibility of rationalizing away his own life by openly putting his faith in the extraordinary, or "powers": "He believes in powers meaning the extension of the ordinary to the point of the incredible and he believes that these powers are real though they can't be willed and they belong to everyone who isn't blinded by the negative hallucination of our culture" (11).[3] The remedy that powers offer to counteract the negative hallucination is enchantment which can put two people "in touch" with one another and allows the people who are "in touch" to experience the extraordinary (which, Sukenick says, is in Frankenstein often confused with sex, the result being violent sex).

In a series of disjointed vignettes that make up the first part of 98.6, "he" experiences and sees the extraordinary. His experiences seem to have an ambiguous ontological status at first sight since they are presented both as "movies" or "stories" and also as what "really" happens to "him." Yet the contradiction is only superficial and is a consequence of Sukenick's deliberately ambiguous use of the word "movie." In standard usage, a movie is a motion picture, but here Sukenick is more interested in the motion rather than the picture element of its meaning; he thus implies that a movie, or any kind of fiction, is not a picture of reality to be looked at but is a reality that moves and of which one is a part. Significantly, the movies in *98.6* are "seen" and not watched, for they are fictions which are invented as the main character "sees" visions of the extraordinary from one moment of his life to the next.

This is exactly what all writers of fiction do, inventing their novels from word to word, from one sentence to the next. But since invention is by definition unpremeditated, a writer must constantly counteract the predictability of language which follows from the rules of grammar, syntax, and discourse. The problem with the inventive powers of language is that they are limited a priori by the fact that the use of any known word always refers the reader to what that word designates. An ideal solution would be to communicate in a meaningless language, one in which the meaning does not precede the saying of something. Nature offers multiple examples of languages like that, for instance, "the secret code on the leopard's fur and the tortoise shell" (4) and, though impractical in a work of fiction (which must rely, at least in part, on some discursive, informational content), such codes fascinate Sukenick and his literary alter egos.

Throughout *98.6*, he plays with his own meaningless language called "bjorsq" in which words are made up of letters left over from pangrams that he likes to construct. Such letters sometimes "form interesting words that didn't exist before and that mean nothing but for which meaning develops because they exist" (26). Making meaning a secondary function of language is an act of reversal justified by the current degradation of language as a means of communication. Today's language is so much abused and polluted by what Donald Barthelme has called the "dreck" that its further deterioration can be prevented only by inventing new applications for it. Unfortunately, in the present situation, although "we live in words words are the water in which we swim," we use language chiefly to construct clichés and slogans that "don't mean anything. Or if they mean anything what they mean is incredibly stupid" (25–26) or experientially false.

Perception of the extraordinary through the invention of reality is recognized as a fundamental function of such renewed language in part two of *98.6*, called "Children of Frankenstein," which tells the story of a settlement founded at the western edge of Frankenstein. The outstanding thing about this commune is that, like the novel in which it is described, it is as much a physical as a linguistic reality (if these two are different things), for it is invented by one of its members, Ron, who is trying "to write a novel by recording whatever happens to their group so that they're all characters in his novel including himself. And his novel" (68). Ron's experiential approach to writing has much in common with Sukenick's own conception, and there are many hints suggesting that Ron is another extension of the author's personality. In this novel, however, Sukenick invents a more metafictionally complex strategy than the conventional framework of fiction-within-fiction characteristic of standard metanovels. While apparently distancing himself from Ron by presenting him through third person narration, he reverses the relationship between himself as the creator and Ron as his character. The narrator explains:

Ron is writing a book. He has a novel idea as a matter of fact it's an idea for a novel. His idea is to write a novel by recording whatever happens to their group so that they're all characters in his novel including himself. And his novel. This tends to make Ron dizzy when he thinks about it so he tends not to think about it. . . He feels that novels should be about real life so instead of making up some story he gets a cast of characters and invents a situation for them and he simply writes what happens. What an idea. Only now Ron feels he doesn't need to write the novel. What is happening is the novel. Bjorsq. (68)

What makes Ron and the reader "dizzy" here is that this statement is paradoxical in the best tradition of Zeno. It creates a perfectly self-contained or self-referential system of meaning that makes it impossible to determine the ontological status within any given framework of its elements. For if we assume that Ron is writing a novel about his commune, inventing it, how can he at the same time be a "real" member of it? On the other hand, if we assume that Ron is not writing a novel in the literary sense but is living in the commune and only calling it a novel, how is it possible that the reader is now holding before his eyes a novel which fits in every detail the description of Ron's project? Or is the reader also an invention?

Sukenick's puzzle is designed to demonstrate that the line between reality and fiction is more like a moebius strip than a boundary and that what we call experience comprises indefinite amounts of factual data coming from ordinary perception and fictitious data supplied by the imagination blended into an inseparable whole. Also, it proves that a writer cannot write a successful work of fiction by completely distancing himself from it, though he does not have to be physically present in it.

The moebius strategy employed by Sukenick in *98.6* allows him to focus attention on the novel's metafictional concerns without becoming too narrowly literary or academic. At the same time, although physically absent, the author can make his presence behind the invented world of Ron and his commune so overpowering that the reader, instead of suspending disbelief, unwittingly keeps making comparisons between the real Sukenick and his fictional incarnation. In fact, there are two such incarnations of the author present in *98.6*, Ron/Cloud and a character named Paul, whose new name leaves no doubt about his relation to both Ron/Cloud and Sukenick himself—it is Wind. The two men are the most imaginative members of the commune and although only Ron is admittedly a writer, Paul contributes substantially to the job of imagining their settlement into existence. The basic difference between them is that Ron is more preoccupied with the literariness of his inventions, while Paul invents the life of the commune for purely experiential purposes, in order "to fill the emptiness to fill it with themselves their dreams and nightmares" (84).

The merger of the literary and the experiential is also evident in Ron's attempt "to destroy the English language" (75). Experientially, this attempt represents the general attitude of the communards toward language, which is that "there are better things to do with words than repeat what everyone already knows" (65). Literarily, this means an attempt to destroy the traditional novel and the conventions which compel writers to "repeat what everyone already knows." A language like "bjorsq," which Ron calls a "window language," is of great help here, for it discovers new meanings instead of repeating old ones. By freeing itself from the obligation to represent, a novel in "bjorsq" declares itself a self-apparent invention and thus situates itself in an entirely new relation to reality. No longer a picture of reality, it can itself serve as a kind of model for life by pointing to the general way in which people can make their lives experientially. The way, of course, is invention, which is equally applicable to life as it is to novels, for "life is a lot like a novel you have to make it up" (122). Ron thus believes that true insight does not precede the creative act but is a result of it. By the same token, he recognizes invention as not merely an aesthetic but as an epistemological strategy, thus making his poetic an integral part of his general worldview.

The identity of his approach to life and to fiction by way of the imagination is illustrated by Ron's conception of "psychosynthesis." As the name itself makes clear, psychosynthesis is the opposite of psychoanalysis, a strategy which is the epitome of the modern dualistic and reductive approach to man and nature. Since he sees psychology as "the trademark of a previous era," he molds his companions not as "psychological creatures" but as "creatures of biology and chance" (123). Their biologism shows chiefly in two ways. First, they are all fascinated with animals, which feature prominently in the life of their settlement, particularly birds, but also whales, cows, horses, and the mythical prehistoric creature called the Sasquatch. What attracts them to animals is that animals take their life for what it is without imposing any schemes on it. What Paul, for example, likes particularly about cows is that "they are dumb" (73), while George is obsessed with tracking down the Sasquatch, animals which "couldn't talk about the kind of things we talk about because their voices weren't connected with their brains they were connected with their bodies" (96). The second aspect of the group's biologism has to do with their attempt to restore humankind's natural instincts, especially the sexual impulse, to their proper, natural role. They believe that all problems of their communal life are caused by the mind's censoring of such natural responses which releases a lot of energy that cannot find adequate forms to contain it and so remains loose. Therefore, they devise a way of releasing the resultant pressure by using this energy up in a hedonistic and sexually exuberant orgy called the potlatch.

Their deliberate avoidance of rational patterns of behavior and their orientation toward natural impulses are augmented by their emphasis on the indeterminacy and unpredictability of life. This does not mean, however, that they give themselves up to chance completely and become mere playthings of the universe. By depriving their minds of their authority as decision-making centers, they automatically move away from the modern notion of the self as a rational entity making their personalities equally a function of the body and of the imagination. Yet, despite the importance that they attach to the body, it is the imagination that plays the central role in making the life of the commune an alternative to the reality of Frankenstein. Imagination is regarded by the group as a cure for the problems which make the reality of Frankenstein a nightmare. The commune's standard is "Enough imagination to deal with your particular allotment of biology and chance" (123), though what is "enough" naturally varies from person to person. At one extreme there is Lance, who "has so little imagination he's completely at the mercy of what happens to him" (123) and at the other is Ron/Cloud, who, according to some of his friends, "has too much imagination" (124). But obviously he needs to have more imagination than the others, since he is inventing things not only for him-

self but also for the other communards, as well as for
the potential reader of his novel-in-progress.

Yet the condition that Ron, and through him his fellow
communards, wants to achieve is an ideal that neither
he and his friends nor the communities which surround
their settlement are ready for yet. From the outside, the
commune becomes the object of harassment by a fright-
ening motorcycle gang and local "earthmen," that is,
members of Frankenstein society. From the inside, it is
gradually corroded by the inability of its own members
to free themselves of their old "Is." It turns out that a
change of one's name to a new one is not enough to get
rid of the ego, which eventually resurfaces in the form
of jealousy, possessiveness, or selfish negation of others'
integrity. The new life that the group invents for itself
is not radically new enough, though, at least for the time
being, an impression of healthy normalcy, of being in
agreement with nature (the 98.6, normal body temperature, of the novel's title) is created and maintained. But
this is only an impression, for under the surface the old
diseases are being developed. Just as Valley loses her
child in a miscarriage while her temperature remains
constantly at 98.6, the members of the commune lose
their chance of inventing a new, permanent reality, and
construct instead a ridiculous imitation of what they are
trying to escape.

The eventual failure of the commune is clearly a result
of its members' inability to extricate themselves, both
externally and internally, from the heritage of Frankenstein. But, on a different level, it is also a failure of Ron,
who is unable to invent an adequate form for the energy
generated by his imagination. When things start to disintegrate before his eyes, he tries to prevent a disaster

by literary means: "What chaos. Cloud no longer believes any of this is happening. This is not real life. What was happening is now all over. It lacks credibility. Cloud is writing a novel again. It's almost finished" (147). But it is too late now to withdraw from reality and escape back into a world of pure fiction. Most of Ron's characters have already found a place for themselves in the reality of Frankenstein, that is, outside his invention. The only thing left for him is the experience of having invented a world and lived in it for a while. With no story to be told any longer, he can at last say things just for the mere pleasure of saying them. He can use up the energy leftover from the imperfect form of his novel by producing meaningless words and sentences in "bjorsq," which hide infinite possibilities of new, more successful inventions, as Ron's concluding story of "The Living Buddha" suggests.

In the third part of 98.6, "Palestine," Sukenick replays the novel's major themes in a story of which he is the main character and which tells about a successful commune based on the scientific principles of psychosynthesis. The commune, called The Wave, exists in an ideal country, the "Holy land of the imagination," where people live in "the state of Israel," a state of mind rather than a geographical location in which life's spiritual and physical energies are utilized to bring man to a union with himself, with other people, and with nature. In Palestine, life's energy takes the form of waves which, spiritually, "are the improbabilities of the unknown that one perceives through intuition. Introspection. Empathy. A sense of beauty. Through imagination in other words" (170). On the other hand, "Waves are also the nature of physical life whose cosmic energy moves

through the material of the flesh and leaves it behind"
(172). Artists in Palestine use the waves of spirit, that is,
imagination—"And what is imagination but the waves of
spirit" (171)—for the creation "not only of aesthetic works
but of reality itself" (172), while ordinary people use
the waves of the sea in the ritual activity of surfing. As
Yitzak Fawzi, a renowned astronomer whom Sukenick
meets in The Wave, explains, "Surfing is of the nature
of a sacrament for us it attunes us to the cosmos and
gives every man and woman direct access to that union
with nature" (172). The ideal of union and connection
that waves represent is well grounded in scientific theory,
for, as Fawzi tells Sukenick, the identity of physical and
spiritual realities as temporary manifestations of cosmic
energy in the form of the waves has been proved by
quantum mechanics.

Yet what Sukenick finds the most attractive about science, and atomic physics in particular, is that by em-
phasizing the discontinuity of phenomena, the
inseparability of subject and object and the indispensability of incomplete knowledge as fundamental principles, quantum theory grants new, scientific authority
to Sukenick's own poetic of composition as a wholly dis-
junctive, nondiscursive and self-reflective process. Other
propositions of quantum mechanics which clearly have
implications for Sukenick's literary ideas include the rejection of linear and progressive time ("Can time run
backwards that is the question for today. . . . The physicists say it is not impossible" [178–179]) in favor of
simultaneity ("Maybe everything is happening at once
what then" [179]) and causality in favor of chance ("One
vast coincidence" [179]). But the most important of all
is the renunciation of analysis and the notion of an ab-

solute, that is, objective and rational truth, in favor of synthesis and experience. The significance of experience for scientific discovery was recognized fully by the father of atomic physics, Albert Einstein, who once had the following exchange with Golda Meir, as recounted by her to his interlocutor:

I was questioning his effort to bring the laws that govern atomic particles into line with the general theory of relativity. What good does all this theory do I finally asked him unless we find a way of incorporating it into our experience. My dear skeptic he said. Albert Einstein. He was standing as close as you are to me. My dear skeptic you are perfectly right. Only experience can restore that lost synthesis which analysis has forced us to shatter. Experience alone can decide on truth. (186)

Meir's questions and Einstein's answers acquire special significance in the context of Sukenick's novel, for they concern not just scientific theories but all kinds of human-created systems, whether in the form of mathematical theorems or novels. All such systems are equally fictitious models of reality and their value lies not in their ability to imitate or explain reality but in their ability to be incorporated into our experience of reality. Thus, from the novelist's point of view, experiential veracity has nothing to do with verisimilitude and is in fact the opposite of it. In this connection, Sukenick can be called a true master of failure, for his novel is not only anti-illusionistic but makes of failure a declaration of creed, regarding it as the shortest way to experiential authenticity. *98.6* "fails" by canceling itself on all levels, leaving the reader face-to-face with its actual author sitting at his typewriter and sharing his experience of fiction making with other human beings, truly "a man speaking to men." Since he has to cope with a multitude of thoughts and perceptions at each moment of composition, he resembles "a one man band playing all the instruments" while "stitching together" his novel's "bungled fragments" (187–88).

The novel's last words—"Another failure"—suggest that the novelist's failure is a failure to make sense, to explain why he says this or that, to make connections among the things that are present in his mind as he writes. But this kind of failure is a necessary condition for a novel to present experience as it really is: an ongoing flowing from one moment to the next, from one page to the next.

8

Long Talking Bad Conditions Blues

THE BLUES ANALOGY that Sukenick draws at the end of *98.6* comparing the writing of a novel to "playing the blues letting it go it as it is," is transformed into the central metaphor of writing in his next novel, *Long Talking Bad Conditions Blues*. It was conceived, as Sukenick asserts, not so much as a novel as a traditional "urban blues, a kind of lively lament, you might say, sad, but full of energy and wit, a way of dealing with your troubles."[1] The title of the novel and Sukenick's explanation of the analogy with the blues define both the book's thematic concerns and the mode of presentation. *Long Talking Blues* is an urban novel, its setting a typical modern metropolis going through a period of "bad conditions" which mark its transition to the postindustrial era. The process is characterized by an accelerated dissolution of old social structures and personal relationships which releases energy and puts people under severe strain—hence the energy and the sadness of the blues. Their attempts to adapt to the new situation lead them to acute observations about both the origin and the direction of the current changes in the life of the community and of the individuals that comprise it—hence the wit of the blues. Narratively, the novel is a single utterance, an uninterrupted meditation, or lament, of a voice talking to the reader/listener in rhythmic units indicated in the text not by punctuation but by spacing.

Unlike Sukenick's previous works, *Long Talking Blues* does not feature a writer character, so its metafictional dimension is less obvious. Told by an unidentified voice, the story concerns everyday experiences of a group of friends, sexual partners and rivals, in various configurations, living in a big city and trying to cope with a whole constellation of diverse developments which constitute "the new conditions" of urban life in present-day America. Faced with the "disintegration of phenomena" and "the general disorientation and underlying disquiet you might even say panic the uncertainty about the future and maybe worse about the past,"[2] they develop idiosyncratic responses which are the object of study of one of them, a character named Carl.

Although he is a social scientist of some kind and not a novelist, it is fairly obvious that Carl is another "Sukenick" figure whose project—"to study a kind of personality able to cope with the vicissitudes and complications of the new conditions" (21)—is less sociological than literary in nature. For despite the avowed purpose of his research, Carl does not analyze methodically and interpret collected data but limits himself to simply recording them in his mind. Indeed, he admits that he is more interested in the activity of recording than in its results, being "content to be a camera without film" (6). Thus, he concerns himself with his own verbal response to what happens around him and not with the explanation or interpretation of the meaning of events. His affinity with the whole line of Ronald Sukenick's earlier fictional alter egos is also directly hinted at when it is observed about Carl's methodology that "his only model was clouds their resolution in the sky their subtle transitions from nothing to something in the empty air" (21).

In the Sukenick canon, "cloud" symbolizes the novelist's desire to write a book which affirms change and motion, improvisation and invention, nonmimetism and self-reflexiveness as the chief modes of composition. Part of the "cloud" strategy is also the renunciation of premeditation and strict adherence to principles of logic. Employing these precepts not for literary but for experientially practical purposes, Carl makes the written record of his "field work" comply with Sukenick's novelistic standards. For example, he approaches his subject without any preconception—it is stated at the outset that "one of his ideas or attitudes was that he didn't believe in ideas abstraction went against his nature" (2). Therefore, he shuns generalizations and concentrates instead on the immediate experience of the small facts of life, which impinge upon us directly by their mere occurrence and not by their symbolic or referential significance—"it occurred to him that the crucial thing was detail and that the kind of detail did not much matter" (1). Since he is interested not in some particular kind of detail, but simply in looking and thus "keeping everything company," Carl chooses to explore the neglected side of experience: "who if not he would attend the petty inconography of the quotidian the texture of our days which is their meaning if any which unattended grows

so lonely and forlorn and then turns back on us" (5).
He believes that the true meaning of man's experience
is in "the simple thereness," the presence of even the
most trivial phenomena, for it is this "thereness" which
makes experience possible in the first place.

A further analogy with Sukenick's experiential poetic
of fiction concerns Carl's assertion that the observation
and documentation of the quotidian, however banal it
may be, is always only an occasion for exercising the
power of imagination. He admits that "it was never observation but always invention," so "the documentation
of this very thereness was itself the prophetic act" (6).
By making observation a function of the imagination,
Carl makes the content of observation secondary to the
articulation, or verbalization, of perception. In other
words, he reduces the problem of the perception of
reality to the level of language, where the naming of
what one observes is the crucial thing.

It is ultimately on this linguistic level that Carl's and
Sukenick's approaches dovetail, for, as with Sukenick,
what particularly interests Carl is the "prophetic" aspect
of linguistic action, that is, the inherent ability of language to generate meaning and not just reproduce it.
A significant part of our daily reality, Carl notes, consists
of things which exist only as "quirks of language," things
which, though they may not exist in actuality, can be
articulated, as is the case with, for example, predictions.
As Victor, one of Carl's friends, believes, it does not
matter whether one's predictions turn out to be correct
or not. What is important is simply to make them. Even
if they are never realized in actuality, they may continue
to exist as autonomous and self-referential linguistic objects which testify to the possibilities of language to call

things into being and in this way enrich the quotidian reality of actual things.

Carl's preoccupation with such purely linguistic matters, although apparently incompatible with the original character of his research, is not a matter of arbitrary preference but is based on a sound sociological and psychological observation of the individual person as a "languaged animal." This observation convinces him that language most immediately reflects the current situation of any society and its individuals. This is because humans adapt to reality mainly by appropriating sensual experience through language, which allows us to see language, as Carl does, as "terminal" in both senses of the word: a place where all meaning takes origin and to which it always returns, the ultimate medium through which people become aware of themselves and of the surrounding world. To put it another way, Carl bases his approach on the assumption that consciousness is fundamentally a linguistic consciousness and, therefore, the structure of human psyche can be studied by studying human language. Similarly, by studying the language of mass communication, one can make inferences about the social and political conditions of any given community.

From his general observations of the situation of language at the end of the modern era, Carl concludes that by and large language has stopped functioning as the most powerful system of communication available to human communities. According to Victor, who is the most outspoken on the question of language in contemporary society, language has become an instrument through which "the international super financial intelligence powers [control] one's life down to the most intimate details" (18). The manipulation of language is clearly evident in the media: "mumbling became the style of intentional incoherence discontinuity ending in a virtual celebration of autism whole populations were held incommunicado agents planted in the media discouraged reading encouraged self expression" (18). The result is "lack of commitment fragmented community torpid intellect funny attitudes soggy language" (20). Yet it is not such generalizations as the above one that Carl is after but detail. Thus, he concentrates on examining the way the new—sociolinguistic—conditions are "repeated in each individual separately" (24). Victor's seems to be the most interesting case, since he develops an elaborate and coherent theory and applies it consistently to counteract the current deterioration of language. His approach is particularly appealing to Carl because it offers a truly innovative solution to the demands of the new conditions. The traditional, referential conception of language, it is observed, inevitably leads to "the rigid form of humanistic intelligence known as wisdom which [is] nothing more than information frozen in traditional cliches" (32). It implies a similarly reductive and static conception of humanity according to which human beings are "bits of information in bytes of data mutually incommunicado collectively excommunicated" (11). For Victor, true communication means connection; language has an immense inherent capacity for constituting a true link between individuals since it is capable of flow. Consequently, Victor sees the current atomization of society, the breakup of all kinds of ties or relationships by which communities are held together, chiefly in terms of disruptions in the flow of language. He calls such disruptions "verbal holes," which occur when a person misconstrues the words of another person or when a person is unable to talk with other persons at all.

But the verbal hole is not an isolated phenomenon of a purely linguistic nature, for it is inseparable from other psychic and bodily disorders. Victor invents a whole vocabulary to describe the complex of such disturbances caused by or leading to the emergence of verbal holes. His main premise is that all functions of the human organism are of the nature of flow, that in fact "one [is] precisely one's own flow" (11). In a normal situation, the flow is continuous and uninterrupted, but in a time of crisis—like the emergence of the new conditions which are characterized by an unusually rapid disintegration of phenomena (Victor calls this "accelerated shatter")— the flow of both personal and communal life is constantly threatened with stoppages ("total blockage"). On the personal level, total blockage may be caused by "spasmic flow" ("flow to overflow sooner or later leading to total blockage") or "sector flow" ("a tendency to break down into constituent parts . . . one sector would flow independently of another sector for example visual flow apart from mental flow or emotional flow apart from sexual flow" [11]). On the level of interpersonal relations, total or multiple blockage leads to the breakup of the fundamental social unit called the "carnal whole." This happens when, mostly due to the "sexual impasse," two or more persons are unable to synchronize their individual rhythms of flow. The rhythm of one's own flow is basically the same as the rhythm of the flow of language; therefore, one can avoid blockage by maintaining an uninterrupted flow of discourse synchronized with the other rhythms of the organism—"Keep talking said Drecker if you stop talking you're in trouble" (104).

Carl finds Victor's theory of flow appealing not simply because it is appropriate to the new conditions, which themselves are "fluid atraditional and constantly changing" (32), but because flow is by its very nature atemporal and autotelic. Therefore, it is a perfect metaphor for the kind of life that Carl and his friends are living in the city. They call themselves "confirmed goofoffs," that is, people who have "no aims no expectations no hopes" (13). Their attitude is not simple nihilism but a practical adaptation to the new conditions, whose important aspect is the affirmation of presence, of "living in the moment," and rejection of the notion of the future—"the whole idea of the future was completely passé" (20). The atemporality of the life of the city is in turn a result of its peculiarly insular position: it is located on an island (although the city goes unnamed, its description fits New York in numerous details, both actual and those from Sukenick's earlier works, particularly from *Up*). As such, the city forms a self-contained microcosm which is "thought to be the best area for [Carl's] field study because it manifest[s] the whole complex of circumstances generally referred to as the new conditions" (21). Yet the present condition of the city does not follow so much from its geographical insularity but rather from a temporal one, for the city is also a "time island" characterized by its "alienation . . . from its past insecurity about its future separation from both" (24).

Victor's interpretation of the current social and personal upheavals in the city explains such widespread negative developments as the "lapse and stasis of civic energy" (also described as "energy leak" and "ennervated stasis") and such positive responses as the increasing reliance of some people on chance and natural instincts and the renunciation of rationalized behavior in favor of spontaneity and improvisation. The best example of a person with such an approach is Tony, who rejects thinking as a sure way to stasis and, finding himself "caught up in some kind of flow," decides that the best way to proceed is to keep himself from thinking about it and to concentrate on doing instead. Tony's approach is similar to the strategy of Action Painters, only transplanted into the context of everyday life. Just as "action painting essentialized pure action no painting" (90), Tony assumed that "happening was what it was all about" and thus "he was just following what was happening" (76). Tony's way to a synthesis of thinking and doing through unpremeditated action is greatly admired by Carl, who knows that "direction purpose destination [isn't] important the important thing [is] to keep moving" (48).

Others realize that "to keep moving" depends utterly on the continuous verbalization of experience, as when Drecker says: "keep talking . . . if you stop talking you're in trouble" (104); or more metaphorically, "when the wind stops you're in trouble you have to work up your own wind an interior wind what he liked to call a headwind to start things going again" (109). Drecker's advice has a very obvious implication both for Carl and for all those concerned with studying the nature of the human experience of reality, for it recognizes that experience is equally a function of perception as it is of mentation. The union, or inseparability, of these two faculties is represented by the notion of "headwind" (wind in the head) and by the idea that "living in the city was . . . like living in your own head" (78).

Since thought cannot exist independently of its formulation in words and in fact is often shaped by the very words that express it (the lesson of Wittgenstein), the imperative of experiential veracity imposes on the person trying to record experience an obligation to present his thoughts as emerging from, and not preceding, the process of verbalization. For Carl, whose only recording device is his own mind, this means simply "thinking aloud" or better yet "talking thinking," but for a writer this imperative creates a serious problem of capturing the immediacy of verbalization itself. On the one hand, one's perceptions and their reflection in thoughts are much swifter than the writing down of them, which means that we can never capture them exactly in the form in which they first come to mind. That is, by the time we finish transcribing a thought, it has been rethought many times and its formulation refined in a way which may be more satisfying in the literary sense but not in the experiential one. On the other hand, mechanical recording of the vocal articulation of one's thoughts seems to be a perfect way of getting at the immediacy, or experientiality, of thinking but, as Sukenick observes elsewhere. "It doesn't sound right if you just put precisely the way you talk."[3] The problem for the writer, then, is to get the best of both ways of notation, to render the experience of articulation as inseparable from thinking itself (doing thinking or talking thinking) in a literary, that is, aesthetically satisfying, manner.

Over the years, Sukenick has developed a unique way of composing his novels and short stories in "rhythmic prose" (or prose dominated by the "associative rhythm") in which structure is a matter of recording the rhythm and the sound of natural speech, while style is a matter of the imaginative activity of writing it down.[4] This approach is based on the assumption that "telling it like it is" means not only telling *that* it is—"to begin with not what is but that it is" (111)—but doing so at "the pace of normal speech that depends on the normal silence of the listener" (26).

In Sukenick's rhythmic prose, coherence is often based not just on such conventional syntactic units as sentences, clauses, or paragraphs but, increasingly so, on what he calls "prose measure," a poetic concept reflecting Sukenick's conviction that "the distinction between the long poem or the epic and the novel is beginning to disappear"; hence, "Why can't a novel be like a long poem—or a long song—if it's rhythmic?"[5] What fascinates him about natural speech patterns is that they are essentially agrammatical and repetitive, that is, rhythmic, and do not correspond to conventionalized punctuation at all but develop their own syntactical relations based on rhythm.

Drawing such observations from his work with the tape recorder, Sukenick tries to render this quality of the spoken word in his writing by either abandoning punctuation completely or reducing it significantly and arranging his texts into blocks of a certain specific, though sometimes quite arbitrarily determined, length that forms rhythmic sequences. Already in *Up* (for example, the section on pp. 226–42) and *The Death of the Novel and Other Stories* (for example, "Momentum"), Sukenick used spacing instead of punctuation to indicate rhythm, and in *Out* he extended this method by having the larger spacings of the mathematically determined typographical units interact with the almost uninterrupted (because sparsely, and sometimes quite whimsically, punctuated) flow of language from one sentence into the next. In both *Out* and *98.6*, punctuation is used increasingly to indicate not sentence boundaries but to separate rhythmic units which sometimes comprise a fragment of a sentence and sometimes several sentences. Yet it is only in *Long Talking Blues* that Sukenick makes of his prose measure a completely structural device, fully integrating it with the novel's other elements.

Sukenick accomplishes this in *Long Talking Blues* first of all by abandoning the use of punctuation completely. Thus, formally, the novel consists of one endless sentence which flows continuously from the first word to the last. This form reflects that of a long talking blues, and its lack of a beginning and an end make the novel a truly experiential object whose structure is the structure of experience itself. Appropriately, the last words of *Long Talking Blues* are "things didn't have beginnings and endings in that sense they just start and then they stop" (114). Consequently, the "goingungoing" aspect of the narrative becomes a vehicle of discourse which is reflected in the organization of the text into units whose arrangement corresponds with the unfolding of the novel's thin plot line. The first unit is a twelve-page block of text in which single spaces separate individual words, thus making the movement of the plot visibly (or readably) a function of the flow of language. Then, as the novel progresses, we learn that the flow of both personal and communal life in the city is subject to blockages caused by, among other things, the emergence of an increasing number of verbal holes. Their proliferation is indicated in the text by the introduction of larger spaces between words which constitute verbal holes, blank spots on the printed page, disrupting the continuity of the flow of language across the page (pp. 12–25). The disintegration of phenomena characteristic of "accelerated shatter" leads in turn to the formation of "whole new units" which in the text are represented by blocks of about fifteen lines separated from one another by blocks of blank space of similar length (pp. 26–41).

The middle part of the novel is a description of a car excursion of Carl's friends to Mt. Medwick, which is the only time when all the characters are brought together in a symbolic attempt to counteract collectively the breakup of relationships. Yet, while they drive in the car, they barely talk with one another and are generally uptight about the whole situation. When they reach the summit, the group immediately splits into units of one and two (in fact, as it turns out, the two-person units are not genuine "carnal wholes" and soon they too disintegrate). The nervousness and the tension are reflected in the typographical layout of this section: the text is printed in a vertical column occupying only one-half of the page, so the lines are short and the language is constantly on the brink of being sucked into the precipice of the blank half of the page. Also, the movement of the text in the narrow column corresponds to the ascension of the car up the steep slope of the mountain.

When the peak is reached, both the car and the flow of language across the page stop. Charleen and Carl take a walk together but instead of becoming united into a carnal whole, unable to communicate, they are enveloped by emptiness as it begins to snow—"they were standing in the middle of a blank white space their footprints were covered over almost as soon as they made them visibility whited out at about ten feet it was like nowhere it was like walking into nothing" (56). Similarly, the language "whites out" and the reader is confronted with a perfectly blank space on page 57. When the text reemerges on the next page, the car is already going down the mountainside, taking its passengers back to the city.

Typographically, the second half of the novel is a mirror reflection of the first, which creates a kind of macrorhythmic pattern, as in a blues, of repeating sections. The process of the "thinning out" of the flow of language is reversed and so the novel's last unit again consists of solid blocks of print covering the page. The typographical consolidation of the text reflects Carl's coming to the understanding that one's sense of living in the world depends on the continuity of the articulation, or verbalization, of one's thoughts and perceptions.

Clearly in *Long Talking Blues*, Sukenick has reduced the discursive content to a minimum in order to make the performatory aspect of composition all the more apparent. The most important idea that his novel conveys is that the words one utters are not so much about experience as they are the experiences in question. Consequently, meaning becomes ultimately a matter of linguistic performance which provides a means of, "not imitating but actually entering into the rhythms of the body." Rhythm, he believes, "imparts a certain kind of information" that one can get at "without circulating it through the conscious part of the brain."[6] Of all his novels and short stories, *Long Talking Blues* gets the closest to this ideal by making the vocal articulation of its discursive content a primary act of knowing. Therefore, it may be regarded as a much more fundamentally metafictional work than Sukenick's previous fiction, for it deals with the essentials of writing, which are also the essentials of cognition. It thus becomes Sukenick's most powerful response to the key scientific and philosophical question today: What is the human element in experience.

The development of Sukenick's writing from *Up* through *Long Talking Blues* demonstrates his progressive movement toward that level of abstractness at which fiction becomes expressive only of its own unfolding. Though the process naturally involves the reduction of the importance of discursive content to the minimum and the elimination of such fundamental elements of narrative structure as causal plotting, psychologically credible characterization, and verisimilar description, it does not, as the writer's later works demonstrate particularly clearly, lead to incoherence, shallowness, or simply meaninglessness. On the contrary, by reducing the story to a minimal set of random episodes, by denying his characters personal identity, and by shifting narrative authority to the language of his fiction, Sukenick frees his writing from the traditional obligation to convey ideas, to tell the "truth" about reality, and creates instead situations in which he can concentrate completely on the observation and recording of the process by which his own consciousness structures experience. Writing thus becomes for him a movement into fuller consciousness, for, no longer concerned with particular thoughts, it enables him to get directly into an extension of the process of thinking. This process becomes a prime mode of cognition, offering insights both about the thinking subject's consciousness or psyche and about the world at large.

Sukenick's works explore new ways of understanding what writing is as a form of human activity; by releasing words from their normal contexts and associations and by developing structures which make them available for creative use, Sukenick's fiction ultimately becomes a device for recording his own mental, vocal, and manual performances, which become in their totality a kind of ongoing conversation with himself. Its unique value lies in its ability to suggest a means for readers to develop their own self-consciousness, to free their own imaginations to discover new truths and awarenesses, just as Sukenick has freed his own creative energies.

Part II
Raymond Federman

9

Journey to Chaos: Samuel Beckett's Early Fiction

A S A NOVELIST, Raymond Federman is a relative
latecomer among the group of innovative fiction
writers recognized by Jerome Klinkowitz as the makers
of a "post-contemporary" American literature, writers
who recalled the death-bound novel to a new "life of
fiction" in the late 1960s.[1] Older than most of those
writers (he was born in 1928), Federman had his first
novel published in 1971, while his fellow innovators—
Donald Barthelme, Robert Coover, Steve Katz, Clarence
Major, Ishmael Reed, Gilbert Sorrentino, and Ronald
Sukenick—had by then each at least one major work of
fiction brought out by a commercial publisher. The reasons for Federman's latecoming are largely biographical:
born in France, he lost his immediate family in the Holocaust and came to the United States in 1947 to start a
completely new life at the age of nineteen. After some
years spent in Detroit as a factory worker and amateur

jazz musician, he enlisted in the United States Army and was sent to Japan during the Korean War. Upon his return to America, he enrolled as a student first at Columbia University and then at the university of California at Los Angeles. After getting a doctorate for a dissertation on Samuel Beckett in 1963, he decided to pursue an academic career and, after teaching at the University of California at Santa Barbara, moved to the State University of New York at Buffalo, where he is currently director of the Creative Writing Program.

Federman's academic record prior to the publication of his first novel includes his Ph.D. dissertation, brought out by the University of California Press in 1965 under the title *Journey to Chaos: Samuel Beckett's Early Fiction,* and numerous critical articles and reviews of books by and on Beckett and other French writers published in books and journals in the United States, England, and France.[2] By contrast, during the same period of time, he published only six short fictions, wrote a conventional autobiographical novel entitled *And I Followed My Shadow* (considered by him an unpublishable failure), and began work on *Double or Nothing,* which went to press in 1971. Thus, when this first novel came out, it was a debut not only of a mature man but also of an established scholar, a critic turned novelist who not only had a rich personal experience that he wanted to communicate to his readers but who was also fully aware of the ontological issues involved in the writing of fiction. Thus, even more so than in the case of Ronald Sukenick, Federman's scholarship must be considered before his fiction, since it naturally played a crucial role in the shaping of his views concerning creative writing as he came to practice it in the 1970s.

Journey to Chaos is an important work in part because it is one of the most competent and readable introductions to Beckett's fiction available. But it also powerfully articulates Federman's own views concerning the nature of fiction and its place in our lives and therefore may be rightly considered as his earliest literary manifesto, embodying the nucleus of an innovative poetic of fiction which he was to develop and expand in the late 1960s and the 1970s and then turn into practice in his novels. In a much quoted passage from the book's introductory essay, "The Fiction of Mud," Federman articulates his view of the traditional novel by contrasting the concerns of realistic fiction with those of Beckett's antinovels:

Most works of fiction achieve coherence through a logical accumulation of facts about specific situations and more or less credible characters. In the process of recording, or gradually revealing mental or physical experience organized into aesthetic and ethical form, these works progress toward a definite goal: the discovery of knowledge. The novels of Samuel Beckett seem to advance in exactly the opposite direction, and give the impression of being conscious efforts to reduce or retract all given norms. A Beckett novel progresses by unexpected leaps and bounds, from impasse to impasse, toward apparent chaos and meaninglessness. Whereas a traditional hero performs a series of related actions which inevitably produces a psychological change in his attitude and personality, a change that eventually results in tragic or comic denouement, Beckett's people begin and end their fictional journey at the same place, in the same condition, and without having learned, discovered, or acquired the least knowledge about themselves and the world in which they exist. Theirs is a journey without beginning or end, without purpose or meaning. Though these creatures succeed in creating an illusion of progress, both for themselves and for the reader, they merely occupy time and space—the time it takes for the book to be read, and the space it requires for the story to be told. Ultimately their actions, motions, and verbal contortions are negated by the fact of having been performed or spoken.[3]

What evidently fascinates Federman about Beckett's fiction is the way in which, by defying all norms of realism and rational discourse, the writer turns his total negation of reality into an affirmative gesture by making his epistemological stance, his worldview, positively unequivocal in terms of reality's absence in his fiction. Defining the fundamental principle of Beckett's poetic as "an affirmation of the negative," Federman concentrates in his book on demonstrating how, by his stubborn commitment to an utterly paradoxical creative system, Beckett constructs a fictitious universe "so incongruous, so unrealistic, so chaotic, that one wonders how intelligibility and aesthetic unity are achieved" (ix).

Federman's basic argument is that as much as Beckett's successive works spring from those preceding them, as they inevitably must, they do so in a deliberately undevelopmental and repetitive manner. They unchangeably circle around one and the same theme: the struggle of a mind with itself in an effort to penetrate into its own dark center occupied by that unnameable entity which is pure consciousness transposed into the struggle of an artist with both his imagination and his material in an effort to create an absolute work of art (a pure fiction), one that expresses (articulates) nothing. Thus, if there is any movement in Beckett's works, it is not linearly progressive but circularly ingressive. It is not the movement of a rational mind observing the world from a detached perspective and acquiring knowledge about it by accumulating observed facts, but the movement of a creative imagination turning toward itself, redoubling on itself and retracting all knowledge that originates outside itself. Therefore, as one goes from one Beckett novel to another, whether one begins with *How It Is* or with *Murphy,* one will always find the Beckettian hero taking a journey that is perfectly circular, a journey which is "an epistemological quest whose purpose is not the discovery of some philosophical or psychological truth, but the negation of all concepts formulated by man to rationalize his existence" (58).

The Beckettian quest is, of course, an inherently paradoxical undertaking, and so it excludes the possibility of attaining the condition that his fiction aspires to. For, as Federman observes, "To build novels on such premises is to commit oneself to absurdity and failure" (6). But the kind of failure implicit in Beckett's "journey to chaos," he adds, hides in itself an immense potential for affirmation. Failure, Beckett shows, is intrinsic to all fiction, since every work of fiction is by definition an invention and as such it always fails to tell the truth about the world that it pretends to represent. What Federman finds admirable about Beckett's attitude is that, instead of denying the immanence of this situation by trying to conceal it from the reader, Beckett acknowledges it boldly and turns it to his own advantage. He turns failure into an aesthetic creed and capitalizes on it, as is illustrated by his famous statement that "to be an artist is to fail, as no other dare fail."[4] On the fictional level, he exploits the writer's paradoxical predicament by making his creator-heroes fail artistically and then recognize this failure as an essential element of their existence. As Federman observes, "Like incurable poker players they are committed to their *mise en jeu,* and, win or lose, they cannot withdraw from the game until all cards are played, all the while knowing that the deck of fictional cards can be dealt and redealt endlessly" (202). Thus, though they are aware that they will never win, they also know that they cannot lose either, which provides them with a ground for affirmation in this negative plight, with a rationale for their "fidelity to failure."

Not identifiable characters with physical or psychological features, Beckett's heroes are rather disembodied voices whose existence depends utterly on the words they say, whose existence *is* those words. They thus "improvise their existence on the theme of self, with little respect for human norms. Their fictional progress becomes a dizzying performance which, like jazz improvisations, exploits it own imperfections as it discovers new zones of being. These creatures' shapes, thoughts, words, and actions are as unpredictable as the notes of a jazz musician's instrument, and they achieve coherence by virtue of that unpredictability" (23–24). With verisimilar characters, material reality, and time disappearing from Beckett's universe, reality becomes reduced to a structure of words spoken by a voice in the author's mind and committed by his hand to paper. "What happened," Federman explains, "is that a novel has been written" (12). This reduction (with its implicit rejection of mimetic norms) becomes a powerful epistemological statement, for by exposing the "inadequacy of language, reason and logic to reveal the failure of fiction as a means of apprehending the reality of the world," Beckett also exposes "the failure of intellectual and aesthetic method in the modern world, in modern literature, and . . . thereby directly criticizes Cartesian rationalism" (119). Metaphorically, Beckett turns his heroes' failure (and his own) into a "howling success" by demonstrating that a writer who refuses to compromise himself to the demands of rational thought and conventional discourse succeeds by avoiding having to lie about his experience. Paradoxically, in this way he gets much closer to articulating the meaning of existence (which is anything but rational and purposive) than a writer who imposes artificial systems upon reality and makes them parade as the truth.

This is not to say that Federman has taken the ideas of Beckett at face value—rather, he has studied them critically for their usefulness in working out his own, original and theoretically more advanced, poetic of fiction. The originality, even idiosyncrasy, of his approach to Beckett's work could already be seen in *Journey to Chaos,* where Federman brought into play not only his critical acumen but also his personal experiences—for example, as shown by some of the passages quoted above, his love of jazz and poker—in discussing the novelist's fictional strategies. Therefore, although it is almost always possible to trace a given idea of Federman back to its source in Beckett's fiction, the two are never identical, if only because they appear in different contexts.

Federman describes the way his own work has shared a powerful indebtedness and affinity to Beckett in the following words:

If you read the entire work of Beckett—and it's been over fifty years since he published his first piece of fiction—you'll find only one idea, repeated over and over again. An idea in the form of a question in fact: What the hell am I doing here writing this stuff? This is the essential question, the central idea of Beckett's work—a question that all human beings should ask themselves, the guy in the factory, the guy digging ditches, the guy behind a desk. They all should ask themselves, What the fuck am I doing here in this life? My own writing is always about that.[5]

But admitting that the core of his poetic, the motivation to write fiction in a self-reflexive mode, comes from Beckett, Federman also states: "In a way Beckett in his work gives us the final vision of [his generation's] world. Though Beckett has been going on for years now talking about that dead world, to some extent he closed it for us. After Beckett there is no possibility of writing about the world again, at least not that old dying world."[6] And it is not only impossible to write about that world, but it is also impossible to write in the agonizing way Beckett does. For by erasing "all the junk connected with narrative fiction until by *The Lost Ones* all you have are words totally empty of their story,"[7] Beckett has destroyed the novel as it was known to the modern writer. At the same time, however, he has revived the novel, opening new vistas for his heirs. As Federman puts it, "You *have to tell stories*, Beckett is telling us, don't follow me, I'm leading you on the wrong path, I'm closing the door. That's my life, what I have chosen to follow, but you guys . . . ."[8]

10

Uncollected Criticism

IN THE YEARS that followed his literary appren-
ticeship with Beckett's work, Federman devoted a
substantial amount of time to transforming his scholarly
experience into a practice of fiction. Indeed, the theoretical and practical aspects of his preoccupation with
fiction can hardly be separated, for his critical essays
were usually written either simultaneously with the fictional works or, more frequently, as a posteriori theoretical formulations of problems he first encountered in
the process of creative writing. Significantly, Federman
manages to translate his personal experience as a scholar
and fiction writer into more general terms, so his critical
pieces not only provide the reader of his novels with a
complete account of the theory behind them, but also,
like Sukenick's *In Form*: *Digressions on the Act of Fiction*,
they help define the sources, strategies, and goals of the
whole postmodern movement in American literature.

Aware of the controversial character of his innovative
project, Federman opens his single most important essay,

"Surfiction—Four Propositions in Form of an Introduction," with a definition of fiction that provides a sound basis for his subsequent radical propositions:

Fiction is made of understanding, which for most of us means primarily words—and only words (spoken or written). Therefore, if one admits from the start (at least to oneself) that no meaning pre-exists language, but that language creates meaning as it goes along, that is to say as it is used (spoken or written), as it progresses, then writing (fiction especially) will be a mere process of letting language do its tricks. To write, then, is to *produce* meaning, and not *reproduce* a preexisting meaning. To write is to *progress*, and not to *remain* subjected (by habit or reflexes) to the meaning that supposedly precedes the words. As such, fiction can no longer be reality, or a representation of reality, or an imitation, or even a recreation of reality; it can only be A REALITY—an autonomous reality whose only relation with the real world is to improve that world. To create fiction is, in fact, a way to abolish reality, and especially to abolish the notion that reality is truth.[1]

The crucial thing about Federman's definition is its genuinely performatory character: it practically equates "fiction" with "writing" (the verb) as though they were the same logical and grammatical category. For Federman, fiction is first of all an activity, not the words that are spoken or written but the speaking or writing of those words. Consequently, words are not regarded by him as carriers of information about some reality exterior to fiction but, rather, as cargo, for they acquire meaningful signification not because they convey some meaning antedating their use, but because they are themselves transported into a specific context by the author's thought and voice or hand and thus become agents in the meaning-making process. This in turn means that they cease to be merely a transparent medium and begin to draw attention to themselves as autonomous objects having identifiable physical properties—sounds produced by the voice and shapes written (printed) on the page.

In fiction, which is predominantly written, the topography of the page, the spatial distribution of words as typographical signs, becomes then an important aspect of composition. Recognizing that a work of fiction is first apprehended by the reader through its technological form, as printed text, Federman calls for new ways of utilizing this initial impact of the physical object—which is an aspect of the reading process that traditional fiction ignores completely—by integrating it with the novel's imaginative structure. He asserts: "If we are to make of the novel an art form, we must raise the printed word as the medium, and therefore *where* and *how* it is placed on the printed page makes a difference in what the novel is saying" (*S,* 10). The idea behind raising the printed word as the medium of fiction, Federman points out, is not strange at all as it comes very close to some strategies widely accepted in other areas of creative activity, for example, in abstract painting, which "seek[s] to stress the surface density, or flatness of the painting, in order to acknowledge the literal properties of the painting itself."[2] Like an Action Painting, he suggests, the printed page should be regarded as an opaque surface to which words cling like paint to a canvas and which, instead of an illusion of depth, an image of the real world populated by real people, offers itself as a "shattered white space [in which] the people [are] drawn by the black words from the beginning flattened and disseminated on the white surface of the paper inside the black ink-blood."[3]

All this of course does not mean that fiction's discursive content should be eliminated completely and replaced with pure visual form, that syntax should completely give way to design. Discourse is essential to fiction, but there is an urgent need to redefine its role today; typographical means, Federman argues, are of primary importance in achieving this. First of all, by focusing on the concrete dimension of language as the printed word, a writer can better adapt the medium to the peculiar conditions of fiction as printed text and create situations in which "syntax integrates itself to the constraints of the paper, its format, its dimensions, its margins, its edges, its consistency, its whiteness" (*P,* 109). Second, by typographically pulverizing the page, he destroys the linearity of conventional syntax, a syntax which in traditional fiction "fixes [words] into a place, a space, prescribes an order to them . . . prevents them from wandering" (*P,* 109). This method does not impoverish discourse but in fact enriches it by bringing out those qualities inherent in language which are seldom noticed or made use of by realistic writers and which are brought into play only in the "struggle of word-design against word-syntax." Generally speaking, self-apparent typography effectively helps shift the emphasis from the referential to the non- or self-referential aspects of fiction and thus focuses attention on the autonomy of fiction as an art form, particularly on its own processes and mechanisms.

It should be emphasized that although Federman states that "the essence of a literary discourse . . . is to find its own point of reference, its own rules of organization in itself, and not in the real or imaginary experience on which it rests,"[4] he does not conceive of a literary discourse exclusively, or merely, as the text that is actually written on the page; rather, he places equal emphasis on the role of the reader's performance (both intellectual and physical) in the creation of the work of fiction. His approach is based on the assumption that a literary work is determined not by one center—for example, the text, as the New Critics assumed—but by two centers: the writer and the reader. Moreover, it is the latter that is ultimately given priority over the former under the assumption that, although writing eventually produces meaning, it is reading that actualizes this meaning and gives the work its final shape.

Such a way of defining the writer-text-reader complex differs profoundly from the standard theories of the past upon which the realistic novel based its credibility. In surfiction, which capitalizes on its nonreferentiality, no ready-made meaning is presented to the reader for easy recognition, and so "the whole traditional, conventional, fixed, and boring method of reading" is rendered useless. In his proposition concerning the reading of fiction, Federman argues that new, multiple, and simultaneous ways of reading novels should be devised in order "to give the reader a sense of free participation in the writing/reading process, in order to give the reader an element of choice (active choice) in the ordering of the discourse and the discovery of its meaning" (S, 9). Typographical invention is of great help in giving readers the same freedom that writers have when they write, for, by distorting the linearity of reading, it liberates readers from a fixed relationship with the text and gets them actively involved in "the creation which will give

[them] a sense of having created a meaning and not having simply received, passively, a neatly prearranged meaning" (S, 14).

As has already been noted, typographical variation is not regarded by Federman merely as a device, or gimmick, designed to make actual reading (the physical act) a self-contained activity to be performed and experienced apart from the intellectual or imaginative act. On the contrary, Federman sees typography as a powerful means of uniting the concrete (visual) and the abstract (semantic) aspects of language in fiction. This is most clearly seen in the way the shape of the printed page becomes a visible manifestation of the shape of fiction in general. In Proposition Two of his "Surfiction" manifesto, Federman observes that the shape of traditional fiction was a faithful reflection of the rationalistic way of looking at the world which underlay the very notion of realism. Thus, he points out: "The pseudorealistic novel sought to give a semblance of order to the chaos of life, and did so by relying on the well-made plot (the story line)" (S, 10). It is small wonder, then, that in that type of novel conventional typography and syntax were strictly observed: they so well reflected the spatial and temporal linearity of logical, rational discourse. Today, with the foundations of modern rationality thoroughly shaken and destroyed, "it is no longer necessary to have the events of fiction follow a logical, sequential pattern (in time and in space)" (S, 10). Therefore, Federman argues,

the elements of the new fictitious discourse (words, phrases, sequences, scenes, spaces, etc.) must become digressive from one another—digressive from the element that precedes and the element that follows. In fact, these elements will now occur simultaneously and offer multiple possibilities of rearrangement in the process of reading. The fictitious discourse, no longer progressing from left to right, top to bottom, in a straight line, and along the design of an imposed plot, will follow the contours of the writing itself as it takes shape (unpredictable shape) within the space of the page. It will circle around itself, create new and unexpected movements and figures in the unfolding of the narration, repeating itself, projecting itself backward and forward along the curves of the writing. . . . And consequently, the events related in the narration will also move along this distorted curve. The shape and order of fiction will not result from an imitation of the shape and order of life, but rather from the formal circumvolutions of language as it wells up from the unconscious. (S, 11)

To achieve the desired—aleatory, unpremeditated, and deliberately alogical—shape of fiction, writers must use strategies of composition which will allow them to counteract the predictability inherent in language and discourse (the rules of grammar and logic). Drawing from his personal experience as an amateur jazz musician, Federman points to jazz as a possible source of such strategies, among which he includes improvisation, digression, and the use of arbitrary form. Fiction, then, becomes a game which is not based on some predetermined formula but, rather, on free play, whose rules, which are often the arbitrary rules of typewriting, are no more constricting than the arbitrary rules of playing a musical instrument.

Federman's jazz analogy means not only the freedom of improvisation but also the acceptance of the fact that jazz is a pure process art and so it "also builds itself on a system of wrong chords that the player stumbles upon and then builds from.".[5] Transported into fiction, the rule is that

> when the writer begins his battle against the linearity of syntax with wild strokes, all strokes are recorded, a word carries another word, the writer can always add another, cross it out, repeat it, and thus multiply the network, but the rule of the game forbids him to come back upon what has already been done, a return to zero is not possible, is in fact excluded from the start, the played stroke has to remain played. Undoubtedly it is permitted to do some correcting but corrections are to remain visible: grey chafings, broken lines, crushed, pulverized, multiply into a bundle of hollow and visible furrows! Everything here leaves a mark, but not sign of something, or of something else, but a mark of a multiplicity of events of which none can ever fall back into non-existence! It is a process of self-cancellation that renews itself upon its void, a series, therefore, without possible return, nor corrrection, just words which superimpose themselves upon other words, strokes which reply to other strokes. (*P*, 110)[6]

The emphasis that Federman puts on the mechanics of typewriting and on its improvised character is of course only one way of ensuring the unpredictability of the shape of fiction and the experiential veracity of the process of composition. Apart from that, he contends, composition "should also create, at every step of the story, an element of surprise and the unexpected. . . . The kind of surprise we want in our fiction is not in the action or in the unfolding of events, but in the language. . . . [The] reader no longer wants to know what will happen next; he wants to be surprised by the linguistic ability of the writer, by the incredible feats of the imagination that are going to pop up unexpectedly on the next page."[7]

Although calling attention to the printed page is an effective way of demonstrating, visibly, that, as Federman observes after Jacques Ehrmann, "creating a work of art, or in this case a literary text, is a mere process of transposing language from one space to another" (*IP*, 575), there is much more to fiction than what is visible on the page. As a self-reflexive strategy, typographical play shows that writing fiction is a process of inventing "on the spot" not only the shape but the material of fiction as well, that the act of composition includes both the process and the material to be "processed." In Proposition Three, Federman asserts that in surfiction "there are no limits to the material of fiction" and, consequently, "everything can be said, and must be said, in any possible way" (*S*, 12).

Such an all-embracing notion of the material of fiction may seem dangerously indiscreet but, as novelistic practice demonstrates, writers rarely make a point of pushing the possibilities to extremes (the blank page or doodle). Instead, they should concentrate on the experience that is the most immediately available to them: the experience of writing itself. For "to write a novel is not only to tell a story, it is to confront the very act of writing a novel."[8] The writing act is thus turned into an act of self-reflexion, and since most of such novels have within themselves images of the writer inside the text, it becomes indeed an act of reflection of and on the self. In fact, the writer need not be present in his or her work as its real author at all, for "even the fact of pretending to write a piece of fiction which doesn't reveal the voice of the author is a way of pointing to that voice, or the the absence of that voice."[9] The crucial problem here is that of self-definition, which does not merely involve the question of character presentation and narrative authority but, more generally, the question of the kind of self that writers can inscribe into, and thus define through, their fiction.

As regards the authorial self, it has already been pointed out that in much of postmodern fiction it loses its primacy in relation to the reader, who is now considered as the primary or, rather, definitive maker of meaning. Similarly, the authority of the writer as the original creator of the work itself is apparently depreciated, for, as Federman admits, "by reflecting upon his work, by introspecting the very mechanism of art, the creator discover[s] (with great anguish at times, but also with great laughter) that he [is] no longer supreme, sovereign, no longer a superior, omnipotent being—a prophet-like figure—in full control of his creation, the sole proprietor of it. . . . The ultimate discovery, in our time, is that there are no individual proprietors of language, and therefore, PLAGIARISM is the stuff of literature—PLAGIARISM is not only admissible, it is advisable" (*IP* 571).

The effects of this discovery are clearly visible in much of today's innovative fiction, which "in its self-reflexiveness, is working its way toward nonrepresentation and nonexpression in an effort to rid itself of the authority of its creator and of the burden of originality" (*IP*, 578). This, in turn, automatically leads to a change in the status of the author, who now becomes a medium who is called into existence by language and through whom language then speaks. As Federman puts it, "It is language which creates the author and not the reverse" (*IP*, 574), which is to say that the self is the product of the work and not the source of it. Accordingly, the author is placed in the text on equal footing with the other beings present in his fiction and his ontological status becomes identical with that of purely fictitious creatures; that is, he becomes a character himself.

The disappearance of the author as the omniscient and omnipotent master of the fictitious world means also the dissolution of the character as it is defined in traditional fiction. The notion of the well-made character is thus replaced with a completely new one in which the identity of a character will be determined exclusively by his own substance, that is, language: "Totally free, totally uncommitted to the affairs of the outside world, to the same extent as the fiction in which he will exist (perform, that is), he will participate in the fiction only as a grammatological being" (S, 13). The character's personal identity, in other words, will be created during and through the linguistic performance of the voice of the text as it is made to speak by the writer composing the text and the reader reading it.

Thus, Federman stresses that the crisis of identity suffered by the author and the character in much of contemporary fiction does not mean that the self is to disappear from the novel altogether. It is simply that "post-modern fiction makes use of another Self which can be called a PRESENT-SELF, or perhaps should be called a 'Grammatological Self'—no longer a Self which is a reproduction or a representation of a PAST-SELF, but a self which invents itself in the present of the text, which improvises itself extemporaneously as the text is written."[10] This new self "is usually presented . . . as a disembodied subject which functions as a pure voice (or in some cases as a multivoice which dispersed the centrality of the pronominal Self) and which *performs* the text rather than being *performed* by the text, and thus becomes a Self-performing-Self" (*SVP*, 198).

Two things distinguish the PRESENT-SELF from the PAST-SELF. First, the one is always presented as an invented self (that is, it comes into existence during and because of the creative act), while the other always appears as a remembered self (it is recreated in writing). Second, unlike the PAST-SELF, which can be made credible only "as an extension or a reproduction of how, supposedly, it once existed in the world and in history," the PRESENT-SELF, being a pure voice performing its own presence in the text (performing the text as its own presence, its own self), cannot be exteriorized from this text but can only point to "its own credibility as rhetoric and as linguistic performance" (*PS*, 51–53). Such a notion of self simultaneously emphasizes the performatory aspect of fiction as well as its self-reflexiveness and non-referentiality, or opacity.

As a consequence of the replacement of the PAST-SELF (the well-made character of the realistic novel) with the PRESENT-SELF (the voice of the text in postmodern fiction), the author is situated in a new relation to his work. In traditional fiction, Federman observes, the self is presented usually in a way which makes it appear "more or less distanced from the real being of the author." But in postmodern fiction

the PRESENT-SELF need not only remain nameless, anonymous, and even selfless (in the sense of being characterless), and function as pure disembodied voice. It can also (playfully and ironically) assume the name of its creator. No longer, however, does it need to become an extension or a repro-

duction of that living self. . . . It invents its own reality, its own
unpredictable being, and even its own fictitious past. It may
re-invent its author who then becomes as fictitious as his creation. (*PS*, 52–53)

This reversal of the relationship between the author and
his work may seem to mark the death of the novelist as
a creative artist. But Federman knows perfectly well that
no fiction can call itself into existence of its own accord,
though in the process of writing it may win for itself a
certain degree of autonomy, a point which Federman
dramatizes in *The Voice in the Closet*. He calls not for the
abolition of the author or the literary work as such but
for an entirely new way of looking at literature and art.
He calls for a reinvention both of the status of the standard primary aesthetic categories—the artist, the work
of art, and the audience—and of the meaning of these
categories themselves.

Ultimately, of course, his is a call for a reinvention of
the meaning of meaning itself, for all the propositions
of "Surfiction" discussed so far lead to the two following
questions: How does a work of fiction which lacks the
authority of its creator and which represents only itself
acquire meaning? and, simply, What is the meaning of
such a work? Part of the answer to the first question is
supplied by the proposition concerning the reading of
fiction, where it is stated that meaning is created in the
course of the reading process. But even in the most
radical reader-oriented theories of fiction, it is recognized that though the final meaning is what the reader
creatively actualizes during the act of reading, this meaning (or all the meanings that individual readers of the
work may actualize) is inscribed, as a potentiality, by the

author into his work. Proposition Four of Federman's manifesto considers the question of meaning in relation to the reader as well as the author and the work of fiction from a more general perspective.

In traditional fiction, Federman points out, the notion of meaning was inseparable from the idea that words could somehow represent reality accurately and objectively. What modern philosophers, scientists, and writers did not realize, he observes, is that their knowledge was not absolute at all but was "a mere interpretation—a mere process of making objects coincide with words" (*IP*, 569). Of course, the very idea of interpretation presupposed detached observation as the way of acquiring knowledge, that is, the separation of the observing subject from the observed object, which was the source of all further dualisms. By contrast, in postmodern culture, all forms of duality are negated with far-reaching consequences both in epistemology and aesthetics. Consequently, the notion of absolute knowledge that preexists its discovery and that, once discovered, can be represented by means of a system of logical signs must be rejected today and replaced with the notion of what Federman calls the pursuit of nonknowledge or "the Search of Meaninglessness."[11]

The important shift here seems to be from "knowledge" to "pursuit." Knowledge, or, for that matter, its opposite, no longer interests the contemporary writer for reasons which are fairly obvious: twentieth-century science has effectively demonstrated that life lacks any code that can be discovered and then represented creatively in works of art. The artist can know the world only as much as he can know his own thoughts, which is to say his language, for reality, or our knowledge of it, Federman asserts, is totally a function of language. Explaining his notion of "reality" by referring to a concrete example of a "real" object—the Eiffel Tower—he explains: "The actual object is nothing, an ugly construction, a useless thing. In other words, even if you have seen it, touched it, experienced it, what really counts is what you *say* about it. The Eiffel Tower is *words*, the words we say about it, and as such it's a fiction."[12]

What this example clearly shows is that it does not make much sense to look for meaning in so-called reality, for it can be approached only indirectly through language, that is, *as* language and thus as a fiction. Yet this does not mean that reality is inaccessible, that we are all locked in language or rather locked out by language from the world we live in. Although he uses the word less frequently than Sukenick does, Federman does not depreciate the value of the human *experience* of reality and move toward solipsism. He only recognizes the meaning of experience for what it really is in a work of fiction: the verbalization of the original experience. In fact, he distinguishes three dimensions of experience: the original experience (which is predominantly nonverbal), the mental experience (that which is retained in memory), and the experience of verbalization. It is only the last of the three that can be captured in fiction, which means that even a work of fiction based on the most personal experiences is already twice-removed from reality, by faulty memory and by language; it is always, as Federman likes to say, "a second-hand tale."

The most immediate consequence of adopting such a view is that novelists can no longer regard writing as a way of conveying the truth about the world to the reader, but as an occasion, both for themselves and for the reader, to create a meaning by giving verbal performances of their experience—hence the self-reflexiveness of fiction. The value, or meaning, of this third dimension of experience for the writer lies in that "he begins to understand only in the process of writing." Speaking for himself, Federman explains:

If indeed the process of telling "the" story is an effort on my part to come to terms with a situation which I have really never understood, then I want to keep telling that story so that in the process I might stumble onto the meaning of that story—the right aggregate. . . . The more your write, the more you rewrite (even the same thing over and over again), the better you stand a chance of understanding what you are doing and who you are. . . . Of course, if I knew what the essential was, I wouldn't be looking for it, I wouldn't be trying to write it. In a way, it is because I *can't* find it that I keep looking for it.[13]

In other words, realizing that he does not know what the truth is, that he will never know what it is (was), the writer replaces knowledge with "the act of searching—researching even—within the fiction itself for the meaning of what it means to write fiction" (*FT*, 300). Writing becomes then for him a self-perpetuating act of questioning fiction while writing it and thus also an act of permanent self-discovery and self-creation. As Federman confesses, "In a sense all my fiction is trying to come closer to the truth of my own self by writing myself into existence."[14]

In order to create similar opportunities for readers, to give readers a chance to participate in the creation of a meaning by making sense out of the language of fiction, it is important to liberate them first from whatever preconceptions they might have about (the reading of) fiction and to eclipse the distance between themselves and the fiction they are reading. Therefore, Federman argues, it is necessary to rid fiction of all preexisting meaning, to render it "deliberately illogical, irrational, unrealistic, nonsequitur, and incoherent" (*S*, 13). It is important to prevent any semblance of truth from emerging from the text and establishing itself as *the* truth. Briefly, a writer must constantly disrupt the logic of discourse and all other forms of expectancy, for only then will readers become truly engaged in the fiction by bringing forth their own imaginative powers into play; only then will they experience the work for what it really is: a fiction, a real product of the imagination.

Summing up this outline of Federman's poetic, it should be emphasized that the value of his propositions does not lie so much in the solutions that he offers but in the fact that, by subverting traditional views about fiction, he calls attention to the arbitrariness of all norms and conventions (and not just the inferiority of some and superiority of others). Federman knows that a definitive poetic of fiction is impossible, for in the game of fiction nothing is definitive or ultimate. This is so because, as he observes after Beckett, "Language is both what helps you get where you want to go and at the same time prevents you from getting there."[15] Therefore, whatever one says (affirms) is automatically unmade (negated) by the very act of saying it, by the fact of being said, and so every effort to communicate one's experience in words is abortive and always ends in failure. This kind of failure, however, as Federman knows so well from his reading of Beckett's work, is no cause for despair at all. Quite the contrary, it becomes an occason for self-reflexion, which is the most serious and the most profoundly human act. But it also becomes an occasion for play, which demonstrates that, as Federman assures his readers, all "creation is indeed a laughing matter" (*IP,* 576).

11

Double or Nothing

IN HIS "SURFICTION" MANIFESTO, Federman asserts that "there is some truth in that cliché which says that 'life is fiction,' but not because it happens in the streets, but because as such reality does not exist, or rather exists in its fictionalized version. The experience of life gains meaning only in its recounted form, in its fictionalized version."[1] To get at the underlying mechanisms of the fiction-making process is therefore a crucial issue in writing, for without the proper understanding of how a novel is written, one cannot know what it is and what it does or may do to others— one cannot consciously use it as a medium of communicating experience to others. Though himself a literary scholar and critic, Federman believes that it is not through the retrospective exegesis of the product of composition but through the introspection of the creative act itself that a writer can best approach the question of how experience acquires meaning in the process of fictionalization. Accordingly, in *Double or Nothing*, his first published novel, he turns introspection and questioning into a procedural principle and, while constructing a linguistic structure which is both imaginatively and concretely a self-apparent artifice, submits his own performance, both mental and physical, to close and methodical scrutiny. The novel thus becomes a testing device with which the writer examines the capacity of his own mind and of language to invest experience with meaning and communicate this meaning to the reader. With remarkable inventiveness, he applies an astonishing variety of styles, narrative techniques, and visual designs to transpose the mental process of composition into both the narrative and visual movement of language and thus turn writing into its own powerful metaphor.

The movement of narrative and of language, Federman insists, should be a visible manifestation of the interaction of the four basic forces which are brought into play in the creation of a literary work: memory, imagination, language, and artistic awareness. Recognizing their autonomy and indispensability as elements of composition, he invents in *Double or Nothing* a unique narrative setup in which four separate narrative frames superimposed one upon another are made to converge gradually and merge eventually into a single, multilayered but inseparable structure which asserts both its own autonomy as an aesthetic object and the integrity of the author and the reader as its cocreators.

Since the nucleus of all creative thought is the artist's previous experience retained in his memory, the center of *Double or Nothing*, the innermost frame, is a story about the past: the narrator-hero, a Federman-like character called "the protagonist" and ranked as "the third person" among the novel's dramatis personae, recounts from memory the story of his coming to America shortly after World War II as a nineteen-year-old Jewish immigrant from France who had lost his entire family in the Holocaust and has now to begin a new life in the United States, to learn English, work in a factory, and become a good citizen. Covering approximately one year, the story is composed chiefly of descriptions of the young man's erotic encounters with the new world which offer a hilarious and fresh view of postwar America as seen through the eyes of this Candide of the Holocaust era.

Given the evidently autobiographical content of the story and the straightforwardly realistic style in which it is told, one might expect the overall effect to be that of an authoritative and convincing firsthand account of what really happened in the author's life. However, instead of a conventional autobiography, *Double or Nothing* is a disorderly collection of random episodes which do not fall into a chronological or causal sequence at all. But chaos, Federman tells the reader, is all you get when you try to *remember* the past, for memory is not an orderly and dependable repository of ideas about one's original experience. This is so in part because memory does not retain received information in its totality but selects certain portions of it for retention independently of one's intention or knowledge; in addition, the process of recalling the past to memory is governed by some perverse logic of its own which has nothing to do with the natural logic (or rather unreason) of life or with the conventional logic of rational (realistic) discourse. Therefore, "remembering is always a confusing process. When you remember you don't remember in a straight line"; the narrative consequence of acknowledging this fact is simply that "things don't have to be in C-H-R-O-N-O-L-O-

G-I-C-A-L-O-R-D-E-R."[2] And they never are in the protagonist's story.

But the unreliability of memory resulting from the
sheer impossibility of remembering everything exactly
as it happened is not the only reason why the protagonist
fails to produce a convincing story. The truth of the past
also escapes him because the integrity of his unruly
memory is constantly invaded by an even more tricky
faculty—imagination. Within the narrative frame of the
story told by this third person firsthand, his blatant inventions, or simply lies, can be seen as his subconscious
attempt to compensate for the omissions and distortions
of memory—"the things a guy imagines about himself
when he doesn't know any better" (106)—and their
clumsiness as resulting from his inexperience and un-
skillfulness as a storyteller. However, the failure to re-
strain his exuberant imagination is not only caused by
a character flaw, but it is a structural consequence of the
fact that his account is featured in *Double or Nothing* as
somebody else's fiction, literally a novel (a novel-to-be,
to be precise). This means that the responsibility for the
story's many misrepresentations, exaggerations, and
fabrications automatically devolves upon its official author, a character called "the inventor" and ranked as
"the second person." Despite his superior position in the
narrative hierarchy, a position which, figuratively speaking, is closer in proximity to the source of the story, the
"real" Raymond Federman, this secondary teller is as
unauthoritative and unreliable as the protagonist himself. Described as an "irresponsible paranoiac fellow"
and "inveterate gambler," he alternately claims that the
story he is telling is true because it was told to him by
the young immigrant himself ("that's what he said to me

. . . he was serious about it" [106]) or that it is all a fiction invented by him for the purposes of his literary project ("I insist on this point I am inventing most of this" [114]). The contradictoriness of these declarations speaks in favor of the second possibility: that this narrator is fabricating everything. But the inventor remains double-minded about which of the two versions to stick to because as he proceeds he becomes increasingly aware that, though in a way superior to memory, imagination is not completely autonomous and so it cannot freely exercise its power of invention. Some initial perception of reality (the past), he learns, is a necessary precondition for invention since imagination cannot produce anything unless it is provided by memory with some, however minimal, amount of data to build from. Indeed, it becomes obvious that the story he claims to be inventing is, at least in part, remembered firsthand when it is revealed that, like the protagonist, the inventor is also a Jewish immigrant from France who lost his entire family in a death camp. Characteristically, while persistently denying any connection between himself and the protagonist, he drops numerous hints here and there which suggest that his narrative method combines indefinite amounts of invention *and* remembrance—"One could go on like that for hours REMEMBERING" (45).

This undecidability, or simple confusion of retrospection with invention, is not only typical of the story of the protagonist, whether we assume that it is reported secondhand or remembered (or invented) firsthand by the inventor, but is also typical of an entirely different story that, for some unexplained reason, he feels obliged to tell, a story which explains his current predicament in terms of more recent events which have contributed to it. Thus we learn that he arrived in New York only a few hours before with pockets full of money, some $1200, which he claims to have won in a series of gambling bouts out in the West. Of course, as in other cases, he offers several different and contradictory versions of what supposedly happened, so his lengthy descriptions of the poker game in Los Angeles and the crap game in Las Vegas not only disrupt the narrative flow of the original, primary story but further undermine the credibility of the inventor as a reliable source of information about anything, including his own life. Once again, this time on a different narrative level, the reader is confronted with the bare truth of this man's tale, which is that "it's all an illusion a fiction a lie" (117).

Through this version of the liar's paradox which turns lie, or fiction, into the story's only truth, the inventor acknowledges the failure of memory to capture the past, but at the same time he refuses to accept any responsibility for it by narratively distancing himself from the protagonist and the past. Taking advantage of his narrative superiority over the puppet character created by him, he decides to "jump ahead" right away and

Look into the future so to speak into the conditional rather
But nothing before New York
No past
The Statue of Liberty
Nothing before the boat
All that crap about the War the Farm the Camp the Lampshades excluded (42)

Yet, though he apparently succeeds in escaping the grip of the past by refusing to deal with such unimaginable parts of it as the extermination of the young immigrant's (or his own) family in a death camp and his own survival, he is not allowed to carry out his "irresponsible" plan and get away with it. In the end, it is not the past but the present that catches up with him and takes its toll ruthlessly. His plan is to lock himself in a room for a full year and write a novel telling the story of the young Frenchman's first year in America, but already at this early stage the actual writing of the novel must be postponed infinitely, for the inventor encounters from the beginning a series of obstacles, both objective and subjective, which define his paradoxical predicament of a man trying to write a story (a fiction) about a real life (the truth).

Objectively, his chief problem is that of limited material resources and time—he has only the $1200 to finance his ambitious literary undertaking and, since he is determined to start writing on the following day, he has only a few hours to make all the necessary arrangements (to rent a room, buy enough food, writing material, toilet articles, and so on) to survive a year without having to go out. Aware that he cannot afford to miscalculate—what if, for example, having spent all the money, he runs out of coffee or noodles or typewriter ribbons before the novel is finished?—he gets quite paranoid about working out the minutest details of his survival, to the point of debating the durability of chewing gum or estimating the number of squeezes in a tube of toothpaste and wipes in a roll of toilet paper. This complex double problem is further complicated by the interference of such subjective factors as the man's irresistible memory, extravagant imagination, and paralyzing self-consciousness. While frantically trying to compile a definitive list of supplies to stack in the room, he is repeatedly distracted by the reminiscences of his gambling adventures, by the sexual fantasies of the initiate entering "the belly of America," and by the gnawing doubts about his own competence as a storyteller.

All these are eventually reduced to one general problem, which is not so much how to tell this multilayered story convincingly and truthfully, but how to begin telling it at all. Realizing that he has no writing experience, the inventor devotes an increasing amount of the time left to complete his preparations to considering some theoretical issues involved in fiction making, such as possible ways of structuring a narrative and of presenting psychologically credible characters, the importance of the plot, point of view, and chronology, and so on. He not only wants to know in advance what he will (and will not) tell in his novel but also how he will tell it, so that when he sits down to write no time is wasted on such secondary technical matters. The overall effect is, of course, that his deliberations about "provisional" and literary aspects of writing, along with countless digressions about a variety of unrelated topics ranging from life and work to love and death, progressively push the proper story to be told into the background, thus turning it into a secondary element in the novel's tangled fabric. In fact, this story never gets told as such but only as a by-product of the inventor's rehearsals of various narrative techniques. He never departs from the starting point, for when the preparations seem to be finally completed, he discovers that his underlying assumption— "if the room costs 8 dollars a week then it'll have to be noodles" (1)—may be wrong, in which case all that has been said so far must be cancelled and the calculating must begin anew. The scene is set for another beginning, but this is where the novel ends as it becomes clear that the inventor will never complete his preparations and write the story promised at the outset. By taking up the pen, or indeed by merely planning to do so, the inventor has entrapped himself in a paradoxical system which is open and perfectly circular at the same time, truly a system in which storytelling becomes its own antithesis.

Yet it is the nature of the Beckettian paradox that the negative element is always balanced by the affirmative one. *Double or Nothing* is no exception, and so the negation of reality (the past) as a fiction, or lie, fabricated by imagination superimposed upon memory becomes in this novel an occasion for the affirmation of the (concrete) reality of the imagination itself. The affirmative gesture is not made by the inventor, though, for he loses himself completely while desperately trying to tell a story and thus fails to realize that in the end it is not the story but the telling of it that is important: "The essential difference here whatever that means is not the material as such nor the manner in which you present it nor the message nor the language itself but to do it. What counts is to do it" (80). The inventor never "does it," for, imaginative though it is, his double tale remains purely hypothetical; it exists merely as a potentiality, as something that would or could be realized (become both "real" and "realistic") if he ever managed to tell it. But the unreality of this story, which from beginning to end is told in the conditional tense—"Just think for instance if the room costs 8 dollars a week . . ."—is naturally a matter of practical irrelevance for a person existing outside the fictive space occupied by the inventor. Such a character, significantly called "the first person," is introduced by Federman into the narrative setup of *Double or Nothing* and placed above the other two persons in the established hierarchy of tellers. Described merely as "a rather stubborn and determined middle-aged man," he is given the status of "the *recorder*, the designer, the scribbler as it were of the second person's story" (00), which automatically frees him from any responsibility for the discursive, informational content of the story, for the dubiousness of its truths and the shamelessness of its lies. For him, whatever story there is to tell, real or fictitious, true or false, is merely a pretext for demonstrating his own dexterity in "objectifying" the products of the protagonist's faulty memory and the inventor's vivid but tricky imagination.

Narratively, this first person's presence in the "story" is not detectable since he exists exclusively through what the second person thinks, says, or does and what he then records "to the best of his ability and as objectively as possible" (00). But he conspicuously asserts his presence at that level of discourse which is his proper domain, the space in which the discourse is concretized: the surface of the page. Within that space he works miracles in an effort to have the printed word follow faithfully the convoluted trajectory of the inventor's muddled thoughts. As a result of his conscientiousness, every page of his record becomes a typographical labyrinth, a masterpiece of visual design. The recording as such is not fully abstract in the sense that, for example, an abstract expressionist painting is. For instance, the recorder is able to render concretely the unspeakable truth of the past which both memory (the protagonist) and imagination (the inventor) fail to articulate simply by means of typographical symbols: the parenthetical "(XXXX)" which, more powerfully than any words, conveys the reality of the young survivor's erased past. And of course by making readers suffer the agony of reading the text backward, upward, and in any number of other, even more twisted ways, the recorder allows them to experience the agony of a mind trying to communicate an experience beyond comprehension and description.

However, the words utttered by the protagonist, recounted and reinvented by the inventor and then recorded by the recorder do not constitute the whole text of the novel. Apart from the main section called "Beginning," which is the recorded version of the inventor's performance, there are two other sections, one placed before and the other after it, both written from a point of view external to the story told in the middle section and visibly by a different hand: their typography is relatively more orthodox than that of "Beginning." The first one, entitled "This Is Not the Beginning," is paginated from 0 to 000000000.0 and describes in detail the novel's intramural setup by introducing the three persons involved in the telling of the story and assigning them specific roles and statuses. The third section, "Summary of the Discourse," has the form of a table of contents in which the novel's topics are listed chronologically in a column with exact page reference. Taken together, these three sections form a tripartite structure which is a parody of the form of the traditional novel with its conventional beginning-middle-end sequence. This design powerfully adds to the general effect of spiral circularity without end produced by the novel's paradoxical system based on the principle of duplication (multiplication) and negation (cancellation).

Formulated in the book's title, this principle is operative at all levels of discourse in *Double or Nothing*, and it is responsible for what can be described as an absolute mirror effect: the effect of two, or any number of, mirrors facing or framing one another and multiplying to infinity the nothingness between them. The intentionality of this effect, the conscious creation of the sense of aesthetic unity between the uncommunicable content of the story and the self-cancelling form in which it is presented, cannot of course be attributed to the protagonist, "since the young man (very unsure of himself) has really no voice, at least initially—ultimately he may have a partial voice—in the activities of the second person (but none, that's quite obvious, in the recording of the first person). In other words, he is NOTHING in the double setup, the interplay between the first and second person)" (00000). Similarly, it cannot be attributed to the inventor either, for he is only "organizing (conditionally of course) in his mind . . . the elements of the story" (00); so he cannot even be aware of the textual status that his performance acquires by being recorded by the first person. And the recorder, even if he perceived some artistic order emerging in the recorded story despite or by virtue of the paranoiac condition of the inventor, could not include his perception in the recording without stepping out of his role and violating the rules of the "game" which require that he remain invisible and voiceless. These rules, which are continually broken anyway, are apparently the work of a fourth person. Never identified as the "Raymond Federman" from the title page, this fourth person is called "the author" on the novel's last, unnumbered page which contains a disclaimer that denounces him as "solely responsible" for everything "that the potential READER (commentator or critic) of this discourse may find objectionable."

Given such a view of the role of the author, it is small wonder that his presence "above aside beside and of course underneath the whole set up" only contributes further to the dispersal of the narrative center and the denial of narrative authority to all four tellers. As Welch D. Everman points out, "once this fourth person appears in the fiction, a fifth person is implied. The fifth person, in turn, implies a sixth, and so on. In short, there is a potentially infinite regression of narrative voices which can never reach the reality of Federman or his life."[3] Therefore, no matter how many times, from how many points of view, or in how many different ways this story is told, it will forever remain only a story-within-a-story, infinitely detached from the truth of the writer's original experience. It will always be merely an approximation or a distillation of that experience built from an indefinite amount of remembered and invented facts turned into words and organized into an aesthetic and ethical structure In an a posteriori, hence necessarily false, manner. The infinite regression of narrative frames represents, then, the unbridgeability of the gap between the past and the present, between the writer's life and the recounted story of that life, or simply between reality and fiction. Federman thus shows in *Double or Nothing* that the more words a writer puts into this gap to fill it up, the wider it grows, and no matter how "realistic" he tries to be, his fiction can always be demonstrated to be infinitely detached from the reality that it pretends or aspires to be about.

Taken at face value, the message about the inscrutability of reality implicit in *Double or Nothing* may seem to encourage nihilism or at best solipsism. But what Federman really rejects is not reality at large but rather fictional realism with its conventions which arbitrarily presuppose the existence of some objective and rational laws governing both the material world of things and the spiritual world of people. Renouncing such fundamental tenets of realistic fiction as plot ("I don't give a damn about plots" [100]), representation ("Nothing to do with the outside world" [37]), chronological time ("Things don't have to be in C-H-R-O-N-O-L-O-G-I-C-A-L-O-R-D-E-R" [44]), and psychologically credible characterization ("no psychology everything on the surface" [127]), Federman offers his novel as an open-ended game which has as its only principles invention and flow. Since there are no other a priori rules restricting the imagination's free play with itself, the outcome is totally unpredictable—"Anything can happen here" (114). The idea is to let the imagination loose and allow invention to flow from one moment to the next incessantly—"Most important then is to keep moving" (120). The discourse will shape itself up once the story gets under way, for, after all, "things have to move somewhere . . . you have to go someplace" (56), if only by virtue of the movement of the language from the first to the last word of the discourse.

It might seem that a novel which repudiates such attributes of "good" writing as causation, purposive time, physical and psychological verisimilitude, and, quite simply, logic in favor of free play "on the surface" must inevitably become incoherent and shallow. And surely *Double or Nothing* will appear to be so to a reader narrowly concerned with the minimal story it promises, but then apparently fails, to tell. Through the employment of anti-illusionistic, nonmimetic strategies and devices on every succeeding page of his novel, Federman exposes the arbitrariness and inexpediency of the realistic method and of the expectations that it arouses in the reader. Most notably, playing hide-and-seek with readers, the novel denies them the final satisfaction of locating the author in, or even behind, the text. The rationale behind this denial is stated explicitly in the book itself in a brief critical digression, "Some Reflections on the Novel in Our Time" (inserted between pp. 146 and 147). Its last sentence reads: "Through all the detours that one wishes, the subject who writes will never seize himself in the novel: he will only seize the novel which, by definition, excludes him."

The absence of the writer in his work is indeed an "absent presence," for although the real Raymond Federman is nowhere to be found in the story, elements of his personal identity—his memory, his imagination, his language, and his artistic self-consciousness—manifest themselves at all levels of this "real fictitious discourse." Though structurally separated from each other by the narrative frames within which they are enclosed, these four components of the writing "subject's" personality are made to gradually converge and ultimately merge into a single entity which, however, never acquires a truly referential status and becomes a representation of his own true self. Because of the infinite distancing of the real Federman from his text described earlier, the composite self that emerges through the novel's system of convergence remains a purely textual being, truly the PRESENT-SELF of the text. Accordingly, the story told by the multivoice building on the failure of its tributaries to tell the truth about the writer's past experience becomes the story of its own coming into existence in the course of the discourse's "unfinished movement yet uninterrupted of totalization" (73).

If the methods of *Double or Nothing* implicitly reject realism's false answers, Federman does not at all claim to have new and better answers of his own. Instead, he offers a way of recovering the original questions, a way of learning how to ask those perennial questions in the context of the present world. After all, if we are to maintain the faintest hope of ever getting the right answers, we must first learn how to ask the right questions. Therefore, he suggests, at least for the time being it is better to go on asking questions without trying to answer them. In *Double or Nothing,* he sets an example of how to go about this questioning by writing a novel which is "a huge gigantic questionary full of obsessions" (156), a novel which at all points puzzles its readers and raises questions about what it is doing while doing it, only to immediately deny credibility to whatever answers may suggest themselves in the process. By endlessly duplicating and negating false answers, it forces readers to formulate and ask their own questions ceaselessly.

In the course of this endless interrogation, Federman believes, the readers will not only actively participate in making sense out of the author's personal experience turned into words but hopefully will also ask themselves the one question that the writer wants them to ask: What am I doing here in this life (reading this novel)? The writer knows that the poignancy of his story alone is not enough to stir the reader's imagination and intellect and lead to insights about the sense of it all. For tragic though it is, this story (whether one takes it to be autobiographical or not) would inevitably turn into melodrama were it told in a realistic, logical, and orderly manner. It would thus not only deceive readers by offering another necessarily false version but eventually also prevent them from approaching the essential problem here, which is not what happened but how the experience of that happening is sustained in memory, imagination, and language—ultimately, how any experience gains meaning in the course of mentation. *Double or Nothing* succeeds in placing the latter question in the center of attention by focusing on the very process of verbalization as that activity which generates experience and not merely reproduces preexisting experience. Significantly, by moving the story from the illusionistic depths of "real" life to the linguistic surface of fiction as the stage where writing and reading are performed both mentally and physically, Federman takes readers beyond the cognitive limits of conventional literature and conventionalized thinking and allows them to penetrate the deepest layers of consciousness—which exists, after all, only through the functions of language.

12

Take It or Leave It

THE STORY OF THE protagonist of *Double or Nothing* is continued in Federman's next novel, *Take It or Leave It*,[1] whose narrative goals and strategies are essentially the same as those of the first one. But unlike *Double or Nothing*, which had to repeat its minimal story endlessly in order for the narrative to move forward at all, *Take It or Leave It* does have enough story to carry a conventional novel of average length. Federman is never interested in writing another novel which would merely tell a story, even if it is a story based on the writer's most personal experiences. Therefore, in order to prevent the autobiographical material from becoming the backbone of a plotted narrative, the novelist employs a whole inventory of narrative and formal means to "destorify" the narrative and redirect the reader's attention from its discursive content towards the way it is presented, from the what to the how of the story. *Take It or Leave It* has but only occasional spasms of what the writer calls "typographiphobia." Instead, Federman retards the narrative's unfolding along some story line by discursive means, which is an equally effective method considering the fact that "discursive" also means "digressive" or "desultory."

The basic story of *Take It or Leave It* concerns the adventures of the protagonist, now called Frenchy, some three years after his arrival in the United States as a Holocaust-orphaned Jewish immigrant from France. Drafted into the army during the Korean War, he decides on the spur of the moment to join the paratroopers and is subsequently assigned to the 82nd Airborne Division stationed at Fort Bragg in North Carolina. Although he soon becomes "the Cyrano of the Regiment" writing, quite profitably, love letters for the illiterate hillbillies of the 82nd, he hates being in Fort Bragg and so volunteers to go to the Far East and fight in the war instead. When his orders arrive, he learns that he has thirty days to get to California, where he will embark on the boat for the Far East. Excited, he decides to use the thirty-day vacation to make a trip across country and "investigate the whole lay out explore the East and North the Farwest the whole fucking place—up and down and sideways! Like a pioneer!"

From the outset, however, his plans are interfered with and his expectations (and ours) are regularly frustrated one after another. On the first day of his leave, he learns that all his papers, including his advance pay, have been sent by a bureaucratic error to Camp Drum in upstate New York, where the regiment has gone to practice parachute jumps in the snow.

Instead of waiting for the papers to be redirected to Fort Bragg, he is advised to make a trip up North himself and pick up his money there. This means that he will have to go out of his planned itinerary and make a detour through New England. On his way there, he decides to stop over in New York and see his former lover, Marilyn, but the meeting is a disappointment, since Marilyn's husband makes sure that nothing intimate happens between his wife and their guest. After an uncomfortable night spent on a sofa in the living room, Frenchy decides to continue on his way to Camp Drum without further delay. He works his way through a heavy snowstorm for several hours in his 1947 Buick Special when suddenly, in the middle of the night, his car skids off the road, only to be caught in the middle of its flight into a precipice by the branches of a huge pine tree. At this point, Frenchy must say good-bye to his plan of selling the Buick in New York before setting out for the West. For the time, however, his main concern is to save his own life in the middle of a snow desert.

Incredibly, he is rescued by a gorgeous woman driving alone through the night in a luxurious car. She tells the castaway that her husband happens to be out of town and takes the miserable GI to her house to cure his bruised body and comfort his distressed soul. After a blissful night (or possibly only a blissful dream), without much ado she takes her one-night acquaintance to the nearest railway station and puts him on a train leaving for Camp Drum. Two hours later, Frenchy reunites with his regiment. Arriving at the captain's office, he learns that, in the meantime, his papers and money have been sent back to Fort Bragg. The captain also hands him a telegram from Marilyn in which she tells Frenchy not to get in touch with her again, since her husband has discovered everything about their secret relationship.

Penniless, mistressless, and with several days of his thirty-day leave already wasted, the luckless adventurer goes in a rather dejected mood to his platoon's barrack, where he has to endure the derisive taunts of his companions. The next morning, instead of being offered advice and help, he is ordered by his commander to join his regiment on maneuvers and is forced to make a parachute jump in the snow. He lands on a big rock in the middle of a snow-covered field and breaks both his arms and legs and a considerable number of other bones. After five hours of surgery, his body is fixed up, but the "big trip" is cancelled. Plastered from neck to toes, Frenchy is told that he has rendered himself useless to the military service, and so he is not entitled to a free vacation to be paid for by the United States Army. Thus ends his dream of discovering America.

Although this basic story is told chronologically in a series of episodes described in separate sections, it is hardly presented in a straightforward, orderly, and unified manner. In fact, the importance of chronology is effectively played down by the lack of pagination in the novel, the suggestion being that the various episodes can be read in any order that the reader may wish. The sequence of events does not seem to matter too much since the consecutive incidents do not lead to the expected positive resolution—the initiate's discovery of America and of his own self—but, on the contrary, to the frustration of all expectations and cancellation of all plans. More importantly, the story is not told directly, by Frenchy himself, but indirectly, by a secondhand teller who openly rejects the authority of the primary teller on the grounds that the story was told to him "from the start in a rather dubious manner" and that "there's no way to check no way to make sure to verify to go back to find proofs to back up to fill in that monstrous gap from his mouth to my mouth."

But eventually it is his own irresponsibility as a narrator which prevents Frenchy's story from reaching a level of coherence and plausibility which would allow the reader to identify it as the story of what really happened in the author's life. For instance, the secondary teller originally explains that Frenchy told him his life story not long ago on several occasions with the two sitting under a tree. Later on, however, he says that "it was not under a tree that the story was told to me but truly on the edge of a precipice—if you can imagine that—leaning against the wind," an assertion which is equally questionable in view of his earlier remark that "maybe it was somebody else told me the story as told to him (and so on) and I'm getting the whole thing confused." But the confusion is equally a result of the man's poor memory and of his disorderly imagination. Declaring that his intermediary role requries that he interpret and invent a little, he not only studs his secondhand tale with contradictory comments about the ontological status of his received story but also supplements it with inventions of his own.

The lack of unequivocal narrative mediation is also caused by the fact that the identities of the primary and secondary tellers become hopelessly confounded, so that it is practically impossible to distinguish one from the other despite the fact that their stories are told at two different levels of the novel's fictive reality. From the beginning, it becomes difficult to separate their voices because most of the time the words of the one are quoted verbatim and without quotation marks by the other, with only occasional, and often misleading, parenthetical markers indicating which "I" is whose. Moreover, by a growing number of curious narrative twists and time warps, the protagonist, the secondhand teller, and the secondhand audience step out of their places in the narrative hierarchy and approach one another in ways which are contrary to "the logic of traditional narrative techniques." For example, at one point the listeners to whom the secondary teller is reciting Frenchy's story decide to get a firsthand account of what really happened and, bypassing their speaker, they delegate their own representative to accompany the protagonist in his drive to Vermont. At another point, the reciter disappears for a while, so Frenchy takes over the narration firsthand and addresses the secondhand teller's audience directly as if they were his own listeners. Elsewhere the direction of mediation is reversed completely when the secondary teller transmits his listeners' questions to Frenchy. Such intersecting of different narrative planes naturally makes separating the various narrators not only impossible but also inessential. Their identities lose all personal traits and gradually converge and merge into a single "I."

Admitting that "in fact there is only one I" in the story and anticipating a question about the purpose of employing complex narrative strategies to tell the story of this single, though pluralized, "I," the secondhand teller asks such a question himself: "Thus why not simply tell the tale of the I directly and forget about the I and the HE and the HE and the I and the HE / HE told me, etc. etc. bullshit? Why this fake distanciation, etc., and the double-talk in the midst of an overwise half-way decent recitation?" As always, many different, evasive, contradictory answers are supplied, the most convincing of which is the secondhand teller's argument that Frenchy's story "would be meaningless were it not told (retold over again) second-hand with the kind of reflections superimposed upon it by the voice within the voice which gives it a personal touch of life one might say Yes indeed that story would be boring spoken linearly." This is so because, he explains, "it is by a system of doubletalk that the story rises from its banality to what can be called a level of surfiction."

Since "surfiction" is what Federman defines as "that level of man's activity that reveals life as fiction,"[2] the double-talk used in *Take It or Leave It* prevents the story of the protagonist, which is anything but banal, from being told in a banal way, that is, realistically. By showing little respect for the conventions of rational discourse— narrative authority, characterization, causation, or verisimilitude—double-talk saves this story from falsehood, from being mistaken for what this story (a fiction) is not (reality). Federman's strategy, as Welch Everman observes, "at the outset, places the work at two removes from whatever one might want to think of as the reality beyond words. A tale is not an event in the extralinguistic world, and an exaggerated second-hand tale lacks even the questionable accuracy and immediacy of an eyewitness account. Here, the secondary teller must remember and put into words the remembering and the putting-into-words of the original teller, and so the tale itself is immediately suspect and open to error throughout."[3] Double-talk is thus only seemingly a redundant complication, while in fact it is a convenience and, ultimately, a necessity.

But double-talk is not the only way of transposing the
mental process of displacement into a narrative procedure. The "fake distanciation" accomplished by means
of multileveled narration is further amplified by the di-
gressiveness of the secondhand teller's recitation, a quality which is itself a consequence of double-talk, since
double-talk offers naturally endless possibilities for desultory progression along the story line. Being unsure of
his expertise as a storyteller, the secondary narrator devotes much time and effort to monitoring his own performance and correcting, or at least justifying, his
"distortions, exaggerations, deformations, errors." Of
course, he claims, they are unavoidable in a retold story,
especially when its orginal teller cannot be trusted as a
reliable source of information about his own past. In
moments of "doubts and despair" caused by the fact that
the rules of the game he is playing do not permit him
to present himself in full and in his own name and to
speak of his own adventures as a real person, the orator
inserts himself into the story, diverting it from its course
and inflating his own role out of proportion; he also
believes that, as the responsible and competent secondhand teller he is trying to be, he has the right, and even
duty, to rearrange, explain, interpret and simply improve the story he is telling by borrowing "distorted
material, sub-material, junk material . . . to throw into
the recitation, randomly, to hold together, to enrich, to
thicken what would otherwise be just a simple banal story
of a G.I. who bugs the shit out of us with his illusions!"

Yet not all diversions of the secondhand teller are
willful attempts to assert his own integrity. His recitation
is addressed to a group of hostile listeners who constantly break into his delivery with banter, abuse, critical

remarks, and questions about all kinds of details, not all of which are necessarily directly pertinent. Their interruptions naturally ruffle his countenance and provoke a shower of virulent invectives. His rage is magnified by the fact that his listeners seem to be well trained in literary criticism, particularly in theories developed by the French Tel Quel group, and so they constantly challenge him with practical questions to which, he suspects, they have theoretical answers. Easily taken in by their perfidious queries, he takes agonizing pains to dispel their doubts, venting his anger in foul language and straying from the main topic of his recitation towards subjects which have nothing to do with Frenchy's adventures; frequently he ends up delivering long diatribes on subjects as different as weekend politics, literary theory, and some other fictional versions of the story of the young immigrant's life, such as *Double or Nothing, Amer Eldorado,* and *And I Followed My Shadow.* His digressions leave him so confused that sometimes it takes a good several trials on his part to get the story going again along its proper path.

To make things worse, the secondhand teller is not the only aberrant narrator here. Frenchy himself also tends to depart from his adventures and often reminisces about his premilitary past or anticipates some future events. Similarly, the secondhand teller's listeners become so fed up with the recitations presented to them that on several occasions they decide to quit and pursue their own interests independently of the man on the platform before them.

Though the endless digressions, diversions, aberrations, detours, repetitions, asides, and cancellations do not form a unified narrative, a strong sense of unity is achieved nonetheless, for the narrative constantly circles around one axis, which is the story of the novel's "single unique self" that gradually emerges amidst the narrative and linguistic contortions. This self is neither Frenchy's nor the secondary teller's, but it is the self of the "central voice-text" called MOINOUS (from French: *moi*, "I," and *nous*, "we"). Its emergence makes the reader increasingly aware that, just as the various digressions are meant to push the story off the page, the textual self of *Take It or Leave It* is meant to be not a representation of the authorial self but, rather, a device which serves to dissolve this self into a multiplicity of voices which serve to screen the seemingly voiceless, but necessarily present (if only by his absence), writing subject, the real Federman. In this sense, the textual strategies of *Take It or Leave It* (double-talk, digression) are not merely narrative gimmicks but methods which precisely determine the relationship between the writer and his work. As the novel's critic-in-residence points out in his dissertation about Hombre De La Pluma, his novels "form one endless ESCAPE—a flight, detour digression evasion dodge." The critic explains: "Since Hombre seeks to exlude or cancel himself precisely avoid whatever it is that he is or might be more or less in his mannered speaking and incredible accent (*aigu*) he must escalate the internal space of the novel, disintegrate all forms in a language which cancels itself out at each instant." Analogously, in order to reconcile his internal compulsion to articulate the questions that he has been asking about his own life for so many years with the impossibility of not falsifying the truth of the past by putting it into words, Federman designs *Take It or Leave It* so that it will prevent the story of his life from being told in a way which is necessarily false but which still pretends to offer the truth. Thus, he tells this story in an abortive manner, as a fiction (mis)invented by fictitious beings, voices within other voices, all of them equally fictitious. His primary concern, then, is the erasure of himself as the authoritative source of truth, and this, as Cam Taathaam points out, can only be achieved by the disintegration of all forms which serve the purpose of representing or expressing the writing subject's self as a coherent, fixed, and rational entity. This self, or subjecthood, is obliterated by the escalation of the novel's internal space as the place where the text gets written, where it performs its own self.

With the author dissolving his own identity into a multiplicity of voices-within-voices and his story into a multiplicity of fictions, or lies, and digressions, writing takes center stage in *Take It or Leave It,* which becomes an uninterrupted stream of language which spills over the surface of the page without premeditation, like "a long uninterrupted solo . . . pure improvisation without shape form without order and to tell the truth without meaning." Instead of a metaphorical reflection of the world, the words on the page are a visible manifestation of the totality of phenomena amidst which writing takes place. As the secondhand teller explains, literature really involves

four walls a table a chair paper pencils (or else a typewriter if you compose directly on the typewriter and) (tictac tictac tictac tictac tictac tictac tictac tictac tictac) and after that hours and hours days and nights weeks and months even years and years banging on it (on the damn machine) banging your head against the wall your ass on the chair alone—yes—alone watching the flies fly by picking your nose smoking cigarettes to your death sniffling cutting your nails drumming the table with your fingers doing nothing waiting that something comes into your head asking yourself what the fuck am I doing here! That's where and how literature begins. But that's not all! No—don't imagine that's all I have to say about literature.

And he goes on for several pages listing the activities that writing fiction involves, laughing being one of the central ones.

The identification of the true character of the "story" told in *Take It or Leave It* as the story of its own writing, its own composition, convincingly accounts for the convoluted progress of the narrative, for its digressions, diversions, detours, repetitions, rigmaroles, contradictions, cancellations, and so on. As the constituents of the writing process, these elements turn out to be fully functional. Since the motivation to write fiction should come from the desire to discover what the writer does not know (and not from the desire to express what he knows), he should not concern himself with the contents of his knowledge (the what) but should investigate the processes by which he arrives at knowledge (the how). The only way to proceed, then, is to do it, to start writing right away and keep at it for as long as possible, for only then has the writer a chance of hitting somewhere along the way "on the right aggregate" and discovering something previously unknown to him. That is why, as Federman admits, "there are a lot of wrong things in *Take It or Leave It*,"[4] things which hinder the novel's narrative progress but which at the same time save the continuity of the process of composition.

But when the secondhand teller asserts that "once the story is launched it must go on it must follow its course however crooked it may be even at the risk of crumbling along the way," he does not merely say that the writer's

goal is to set the story in motion and keep it going endlessly no matter what. Writing is always a balancing act
whose success depends on the writer's ability to reconcile
his desire to play freely, to invent and improvise endlessly, with "the cool restraint, the control, the necessary
calculation, the extreme reserve and the cunning that
this game without return presupposes." Necessarily, the
line between the "too much" and the "not enough" that
the writer established by placing the final period on the
novel's last page is always arbitrary, even if the novel is
left, as is the case with *Double or Nothing,* open-ended,
for there are only experiential (and not objective) criteria for judging when the work is finished.

Ultimately, of course, the writer's chief concern is to
maintain the reader's interest from the first to the last
page. And if *Take It or Leave It* succeeds in this respect,
it does so not by creating an artistically polished screen
of illusions which makes the reader forget about himself
and about what he is doing while reading the novel.
Quite the contrary, unlike the secondhand teller, whose
audience departs before the end of his recitation, Federman manages to engage readers actively in the process
of making sense out of the chaos of his novel's language
and thus allows them to experience the joys and frus-
trations of writing, to participate in the struggle of the
writer's mind and hand with the circumstances of writing in their totality. Even if the experience is not always
pleasant (but this depends on the aesthetic preconceptions with which one approaches the book), it is certainly
intense. The kind of reward that Federman offers for
the reader's effort can of course be appreciated only by
readers who are ready to forego conventional expectations, commit themselves as the writer's partner in the

imaginative transaction, and thus experience the work in the fullest way possible.

Finally, it's important to realize that although it makes variation, inconsistency, unpredictability and, eventually, self-cancellation its chief principles of operation, *Take It or Leave It* does offer considerable surface readability.[5] Like *Double or Nothing*, it tells engagingly a hilarious and insightful story of life in the United States viewed by an outsider, a displaced person. It is also an irreverent, though basically good-humored, satire on the academic establishment, particularly the members of the structuralist and deconstructionist schools of literary theory. Yet, it is precisely because of its thematic richness, chiefly of an autobiographical character, that *Take It or Leave It* threatens to desensitize the readers' newly aroused awareness and thus make them unwittingly fall through the words on the page. Realizing this, Federman carefully distributes his quasi-theoretical and critical comments throughout the novel, placing them at pivotal points in order to make sure that the reader will remain conscious of both the physical aspects of composition (typewriting) and reading (scanning and turning the pages) and the psychological mechanisms involved in the writing and reading acts.

The best instance of a self-reflexive moment of this kind, a respite which serves to decondition the reader, is the questionnaire ("courtesy of *Snow White*") inserted in the middle of the novel which is intended "to better situate" the reader in relation to the text. It contains a dozen questions which are central, also literally, to the discourse. Characteristically, the importance of those questions does not lie in the answers that they may possibly elicit, since they are not particularly brilliant or pertinent anyway, but in the fact that they underscore questioning as both art and life's prime mover. This kind of relentless self-questioning and self-reflexivity is particularly valuable, for it unites awareness and performance in a truly exemplary manner. While reading this novel, one realizes that without having to invoke the dubious authority of rationalistic discourse, fiction can still ascertain some truth: the truth of its own presence as a linguistic object, both an abstract and a concrete space in which every imaginative action of the writer and the reader is revealed to be of a genuinely linguistic character as it is rendered concrete in a physical performance with the spoken and/or written word.

13

The Voice in the Closet

I N *DOUBLE OR NOTHING* AND *Take It or Leave It,*
Federman spectacularly subverts the tradition of autobiographical fiction by hopelessly confounding retrospection with invention. Since memory cannot be
separated from imagination, Federman argues, it is then
a matter of simple honesty to keep the reader aware
throughout the whole novel of the dubious truthfulness
of the story told by constantly destroying the illusion
that it is a faithful representation of some supposedly
authentic events from the writer's past. At the same time,
Federman is equally insistent on being honest with himself, too, and so he makes absolutely clear his ambiva-
lence about his own fictional strategies. Indeed, as he
admits in both *Double or Nothing* and *Take It or Leave It,*
as much as these novels satisfy his literary ambitions by
demonstrating the tenacity of his poetic, they nonetheless dramatically fail to answer his profound and personal need to come to terms with his past. In both works,
he makes the story circle endlessly around the central

event of his childhood but never finds a way to speak the truth of what happened on that summer day in 1942 when the Gestapo took his parents and two sisters away to the camps while he, a little boy then, was hiding in a closet just outside the door of the apartment occupied by his family on the third floor of a tenement house in Paris. We get only "(X*X*X*X)" symbolizing the extermination of the boy's family at Auschwitz. And although writing is in itself a powerful symbolic gesture by which Federman metaphorically erases that extermination, he knows that his primal loss cannot be recuperated. His symbolic erasure, therefore, is repeatedly turned into a symbolic evasion, each time leaving the writer with the painful awareness that he has failed again, failed by letting both the truth of the past and the suffering of the present escape him somewhere along the way.

This kind of failure is, of course, intrinsic to all fiction, for it is both the failure of language to articulate the unsayable and the failure of the human mind to understand the incomprehensible. Yet, although as both a survivor and a literary theorist Federman is acutely aware of the cognitive limitations of the mind and of the epistemological limitations of language, he has never fully reconciled himself to the thought that he will never be able to work out the essential of his existence—which was generated by his family's death and his own strange rebirth out of the primordial closet of his childhood.

It is one thing to acknowledge the immanence of the failure of fiction, and it is another thing to accept passively the consequences of acknowledging it. Faithful to Beckett's famous dictum, Federman is determined to "fail as no other dare fail" and thus "make a failure a howling success." Of all his books published so far, the one that comes closest to achieving this goal and becoming a fully successful artistic failure is his bilingual novel *The Voice in the Closet / La Voix dans le Cabinet de Débarras*. This most unusual book, whose text of less than 5,000 words runs for twenty pages only, can indeed be called a novel only in some curiously negatively potential sense. Federman explains about its origin: "In order to produce [the] final twenty pages, I wrote something like four hundred pages. . . . And contained in every page are twenty pages or so of the stuff that has been removed from the text. The process of writing the thing was to write a page as though I was shaking the page—not adding to what I had, but reducing them, taking out the words. The words that were superfluous disappeared."[1] The final result of this procedure is an extremely condensed text which does not even pretend to tell a story, but which, instead, offers the essential of the closet experience turned into pure form. A product of "twenty years [of] banging his head against the wall rattling the old stories,"[2] it powerfully demonstrates that although no words could ever tell the truth about that experience, whether told autobiographically or transposed into the life of a fictitious character, they can still be used to integrate and render concrete the reality of the closet of the past and the reality of the writer's mind struggling with the unspeakable memory as it is given verbal shape in his earlier poetry and fiction.

The first important aspect of the impact of *The Voice in the Closet* on its reader has to do with its most unusual concrete form, meaning the typographical layout of the individual pages as well as the graphic design and the technological form of the book. Typographically, each page of the novel is a perfectly square box of print containing eighteen sixty-eight-character lines of unpunctuated text.[3] There are no hyphenations and all margins are justified, which means that the last letter of each line's last word is always the sixty-eighth character in the line. The text is printed in light grey, thick paper, each page being the shape of a perfect square eight and one-half inches on each side. Between the book's black-and-white covers are included, at the opposite ends, the English and the French versions separated by another text, "Echos à Raymond Federman" by the French writer Maurice Roche. The reader enters the book through a page which has a drawing of a handleless door and after traversing the first twenty pages arrives at a page which has on both sides a drawing of a brick wall. There are also other graphic devices, such as the mirror reflections of Roche's text printed in the inverse (that is, white on black) or the representation of each page's number as a consecutive side of a square (indeed, a square-within-a-square) drawn on the left-hand-side page while the text is printed only on the right-hand-side page, which further intensify the atmosphere of enclosure, impermeability, and impenetrability intrinsic to this book. Visually, then, the pages form a sequence of doors which open onto more doors only to bring the reader to a wall without a door, an effect additionally amplified by the fact that each page is in itself a box in which the words of the text are held captive by the absolutely rigid typographical form.

The visual design of *The Voice in the Closet* creates for readers both a concrete and metaphorical entrance into the closet of Federman's childhood and makes them experience its claustrophobic atmosphere from the inside. Even more so than the joyous freedom of "the wild lines of words . . . cross[ing] the sheets of paper obeying only their own furor"⁴ in *Double or Nothing* and *Take It or Leave It,* the strict discipline of the language of *The Voice in the Closet* makes the reader acutely aware of the reality of its own langauge being painstakingly assembled by the writer into "the carbon design" of its own life.

But these are not the only means through which Federman manages to bridge the distance between the past of his childhood's closet and the present of his writer's closet. Although the book does not tell a story in the usual sense of the word, it creates a curious narrative situation in which the relationships that normally obtain within the framework of fiction are perversely reversed. The protagonist here is the little boy himself speaking to Federman (whose name appears for the first time in his fiction, though, characteristically, it is spelled with a lowercase *f* to make it, as Welch Everman observes, purposely fictive)⁵ directly out of his closet and accusing the writer of having messed up his story in the novels he has written. What we thus have is not the "absent-present" writing subject, the real Federman, remembering the past and turning it into a fiction by shifting narrative authority to a succession of unreliable narrators, as was the case in the previous novels, but the little boy puzzling about what, from his perspective, is his future, the story of his life (to be) written by the grown-up author "after the fact." Taking "federman's" momentary silence as "the signal of a departure in my own voice" (1), he immediately seizes the opportunity to tell "the real story from the other side extricated from the inside roles reversed" (1). But instead of taking full advantage of his unexpected freedom of expression, the narrator-hero immediately engages in violent denunciations of

"federman" for his distortions, misrepresentations, eva-
sions, exaggerations, and cancellations of the boy's story,
for having ruthlessly used and abused his protagonist,
for having turned him into a selfless, voiceless, and
nameless "puppet," all the time showing inexcusable dis-
regard for the truth and integrity of his life.

As the little boy goes on wreaking his anger on his
"creator," the promised story is gradually pushed off the
page, while he himself becomes more and more delirious
with rage and confused. From the beginning, his monologue is a deluge of incoherent language, a stream of
words bearing neither logical nor syntactic relation to
one another. After twenty pages, it predictably ends with
the protagonist still stuck on the opening words: "Here
now again" (20). Like "federman" before him, he talks
himself "into a corner" (a closet) which he never manages to leave in the first place. Assuming the narrative
authority at the outset, he promises "at last a beginning
after so many detours" (1), but twenty pages later he
realizes that he has wasted his only chance to have the
truth of his experience told definitively, once and for
all. Through this deliberate narrative failure, Federman
once again shows that the truth of the past remains
locked in the little boy's closet just as the words he speaks
are locked in the closet of the page.

The curious reversal of roles which allows Federman
to render concrete the experience of the boy in the closet
is also functional at a different narrative plane. There
are actually not one but two interweaving voices speaking in *The Voice in the Closet*. As a matter of fact, the
protagonist's voice is only a voice-within-a-voice, which
explains his failure to live up to his initial promise: he
only thinks that he is speaking in his own voice, while

actually he is himself being spoken by a different teller, who is naturally much more interested in conveying his own story than that of the fictitious character that the protagonist appears to be. Unlike the secondary tellers of *Double or Nothing* and *Take It or Leave It*, however, this teller is not even remotely a credible fictitious human being. His only recognizable human trait is his voice, but this voice is not coming out of a body or a mind but directly from the page of the text voiced, speaking literally through the text from the other side of the pages of the book.

The title's "voice in the closet" is thus not so much the voice of the little boy speaking from the closet of his childhood as it is the voice of Federman's fiction speaking from the closet of the book. Its identity cannot be defined in terms of PAST-SELF, as a representation of the boy's or Federman's self, but only as the PRESENT–SELF of the text in the most literal sense. it is the sum total of all the words of which the novel is composed. In fact, *The Voice in the Closet* is an utterly plagiaristic and intertextual novel, so these words are not the voice's own at all—it is possible to trace virtually every single word spoken by the voice back to its original source in some earlier text, novel or poem, written by Federman. That is to say, the novel as a whole is itself part or prisoner of a larger discourse and, therefore, the knowledge of its "I" cannot possibly exceed that of Federman's other narrator-heroes. Consequently, "the voice in the closet" is doomed to failure right from the beginning: knowing no other words than those which have already been spoken, it can only echo the earlier versions of the same old story ("just heard the first echo of tioli" [2]) and perpetuate the same old lies ("lies again" [1]).

Yet *The Voice in the Closet* is not just another novel in which Federman self-consciously allows himself to be trapped by the language paradox. Through his ingenious narrative strategy (admittedly borrowed from Beckett's *Texts for Nothing*), he demonstrates that although a writer cannot capture his own self in its totality (such a self is always only a sum of one's momentary selves, past and present), he can metaphorically seize himself at the moment of being "excluded" by the novel he is writing. That is, he can seize his most instantly present self as it is being transposed into the PRESENT-SELF of the text in the process of composition. Thanks to the novel's multiple reversals, Federman achieves a "fake distanciation" which allows him to situate himself, along with the reader, in a perspective from which one is offered a view of both the text and the writer writing it. Federman explains:

When you read or write a text you supposedly stand (physically and metaphorically) on this side of the text—by "this side" I mean the side that goes from the eyes to the hands which are holding the text. But somehow *The Voice in the Closet*, if I'm correct about it, forces you to stand (metaphorically speaking) on the other side of the text, as though you've gone right through the story, through the paper itself, and are reading it from the other side.[6]

The page is thus for the reader a door which opens not just into the closet of Federman's past but also the closet of his present, meaning both the room in which he writes and his mind. Looking through the "eyes" of the text— the voice announces: "I see him from the corner of my eye"(1)—the reader can see the writer himself sitting "in his room where everything happens by duplication and repetition" (11), his hands on the keyboard of his selectric typewriter composing the text. As he goes on writing, the voice begins to realize that its autonomy is an illusion because the words it utters are supplied from the outside—"selectricstud makes me speak" (1)—and so the reality of the protagonist's primordial closet gradually "dissolves in verbal articulations" (11) of the man pressing the keys. The story inevitably turns into another "false version" but the reality of Federman's presence at the typewriter solidifies and is concretized as a series of physical acts that are performed by him in the process of composition. Whereas the truth of the past remains locked inside the closet, behind its impenetrable walls, the truth of Federman's telling about it manifests itself visibly on the surface of the page where the words spoken out by the voice are neatly arranged by the "selectricstud" into perfect squares like pieces in a puzzle.

What captures the imagination of the reader of *The Voice in the Closet,* then, is not the story itself—that story, Federman insists, does not sustain interest by itself—but the writerly performance in which the imaginative struggle of the author's mind with the unspeakable memory is transposed into the struggle of his hand (or its mechanical extension, the "selectric" IBM) with words, whose meaning is made a function not so much of semantics but, quite literally, of transcription, or literation. As one reads the book, one is overwhelmed, almost physically, by the intensity of anguish and anxiety of the writer laboriously "search[ing] in his dictionary" (2) for words, words whose appropriateness is in the end determined not by their referential meaning but, quite simply, by the number of letters of which they consist. By his arbitrary use of language as a system of graphic signs which can be counted and arranged into arithmetically determined units, Federman demonstrates that one's past is not a sum of concrete facts and actual experiences but of words that one says about it afterwards. Words, then, eventually put us in touch with the world and make us part of it. As the voice of the text points out near the end of its monologue, reality is itself a "gigantic mythocosm," an "edifice of words" (18) and, therefore, reflexion on the way it is constructed is the most profound act which reveals the true nature of the human experience of reality.

Thus, in *The Voice in the Closet*, the writer creates a self-apparent minimalist verbal structure which becomes a stage on which the drama of his life and of the deaths in this life are presented as a drama of artistic creation. The result is a performance whose aesthetic, ethical, and epistemological cogency is utterly dependent on compositional invention, manual dexterity, auditory and visual keenness, and associative prowess. As for the reader, the first physical contact with the book—turning the first page and taking a look at the black letters boxed into an inescapable form—is enough to precipitate him into the role of the co-operator of the mise-en-scène in which the dramatic speaker is language itself, the medium and the source of knowledge and experience.

14

The Twofold Vibration

WRITTEN IN typographically uniform, character-istically intersticed and yet continuous prose (the only punctuation mark used in the text is the comma), Federman's *The Twofold Vibration* may appear fairly con-ventional by comparison with his earlier, radically in-novative, works. Unlike *Double or Nothing* and *Take It or Leave It,* which are spontaneous outbursts of creative energy unrestrained by any preestablished norms and forms of writing, and *The Voice in the Closet,* which moves in the direction of nondiscursiveness and arbitrary form, *The Twofold Vibration* displays a high degree of surface readability combined with a kind of artistic polish and control rarely aimed at in the earlier novels. Yet, though Federman reaches here a level of accessibility typical of more traditional fiction, *The Twofold Vibration* is as ex-ploratory and, in its own way, as experimental or in-novative as anything that Federman has written so far. Without surpassing the limits of surfiction, it extends the narrative techniques of the first two novels toward the discursiveness of more conventional narrative; and perhaps even more so than *The Voice in the Closet,* it makes questioning and the pursuit of the "meaning of all meanings" the central force behind the creative process. But above all, *The Twofold Vibration* definitively proves that coherence in a novel is a truly performatory category that can be achieved totally as a function of writing.

The narrative situation in *The Twofold Vibration* is typically characterized by an indeterminacy of the relationships that obtain among its multiple narrative planes, which are made to intersect and merge at various points throughout the narrative without any respect for logic or spatiotemporal coherence. The protagonist is an old man who naturally bears some striking resemblances to Federman's other narrator-heroes and to the writer himself. His story is "just a simple moving story" of a Holocaust-orphaned Jewish immigrant from France, an inveterate gambler and lover of women and music who also happens to be the author of obscure poems and surfictionist novels. The time is precisely 31 December 1999, and the place is the antechamber of departure at the spaceport where the old man, who goes unnamed throughout the whole novel, is quietly waiting to embark for the space colonies. In 1999 it is common practice on the planet Earth to dispose of useless people in this simple manner, and the old man seems to be fully reconciled to his fate. But as he sits there quietly with his dog at his feet waiting for the embarkation to begin, his two devoted friends, Namredef (Federman spelled backwards) and Moinous, are desperately trying to avert his deportation. They are convinced that the expulsion decision must be a mistake, for they see no reason why the old man should be considered an undesirable person. They plead with the authorities to change the order, but in vain. They also appeal to the old man to tell them about whatever it is that he has done to cause his selection for removal to the colonies in space, but he refuses to cooperate and tells them to leave him alone.

Yet, Nam and Moi cannot really do anthing to rescue him from expulsion into space, for their possibilities of interfering with his fate are structurally limited: they can hardly become factors in the old man's life, for they are not full-fledged characters at all but merely narrative go-betweens whose proper mission is just to report on the development of the situation to a novelist identified as "Federman," who is writing the story of the old man's life. Outlining his project, he declares that "the subject of this story remains the expulsion of the old man, our central concern will be to find out why"; he adds that as a writer he is "compelled by human compassion, but also by the spirit of creativity, to get to the bottom of this matter, whatever the risks may be."[1]

Unlike Federman's other would-be-writers, who unchangeably get trapped by the Beckettian paradox, "Federman" acknowledges the immanence of the failure of fiction at the outset by refusing to act as "some kind of omnipotent seer," which might seem quite odd to the reader not only because his status of the author naturally entitles him to maintain such a posture, but also because some of his statements about the origins of this story clearly point to its autobiographical character. Still, admitting that his declarations may lead the reader to assume "that this story is autobiographical in the sense that it tells in a sort of camouflaged way the life of the author, namely me disguised as a nameless old man," he insists that such a conclusion would be false because "the writer merely turns experience into words, he displaces, symbolizes, simulates, dissimulates, reinvents, but it's always a betrayal of the original experience, a flagrant falsification" (150–51). Therefore, from the very beginning, he transfers narrative authority to Nam and Moi, modestly assigning himself the status of "an intermediary figure in the telling of this story, a secondhand teller if you wish" (33). He typically secures himself against all responsibility for the possible lies perpetrated by his two narrators by opening his novel in the conditional tense—"If the night passes quietly tomorrow he will have reached the 21st century and be on his way" (2)—so that by its very grammatical form the truth of everything that follows is undermined.

As for the narrating couple, Namredef and Moinous are totally unfit to function as reliable reporters owing to their serious physical defects—Moinous is half-blind and Namredef is half-deaf. Moreover, many of the events they relate to "Federman" were not witnessed or participated in by them at all—"We were not present to witness the scene, it was reported to us years later, more or less as it happened, though undoubtedly some details were omitted" (74)—but are reported by them secondhand on the basis of what they have been told by the old man himself. This narrative distancing is further magnified by the fact that the protagonist, their chief informer, is himself a notorious fiction maker and "a great borrower of words, a thief of language" who has "no scruples in appropriating, misappropriating the words of others" (9). On top of that, "Federman" complains,

Namredef and Moinous have a disorienting way of talking at the same time, interrupting each other, which makes it difficult to keep their stories straight, especially the chronology, sometimes one of them starts relating something, begins to articulate a sentence, and right in the middle of it the other will take over, as if they were one mind, one mouth, often wandering into endless digressions, surprising detours and circumvolutions, in English, in French, doesn't matter, they are both bilingual, they weave in and out of words as though language was for them a rumor transmissible ad infinitum in any direction . . . (44)

Thus, instead of drawing progressively toward some rational explanation of the old man's predicament by accumulating facts about his life, the story related by the handicapped pair gradually turns into a narrative mishmash which is an outright contradiction of all principles of logic and discourse.

Of course, the chaos effected by "Federman's" (and ultimately Federman's) strategy of narrative distancing is a deliberate, artistic contrivance, and as such it is in itself a powerful aesthetic statement. Yet it does not take the reader too long to realize that something greater is at stake here than a purely aesthetic issue, for although his willful failure may be regarded as the prerequisite for a "howling success," it clearly is a secondary consequence of a much more dramatic and total failure intrinsic to this novel. This other kind of failure is "the failure to possess," which unlike "the failure to communicate" (which the old man asserts may be merely comic) has consequences which are ultimately tragic (61). Because of the narrative stratification, this failure is only indirectly experienced by "Federman" and his two narrators, though it is transposed directly into their collective failure to tell the story of the protagonist convincingly.

Charged with the task of unraveling the mystery of the old man's expulsion, Nam and Moi tirelessly pursue him along the meandering path of his rich life as a university professor, surfictionist novelist, womanizer, and gambler and report to their master on his countless adventures and exploits—the old man's arrest during a student riot in Buffalo in the late 1960s and his subsequent love affair with the activist film star June Fanon, his incredible gambling bouts in Europe's major casinos, his miraculous recovery from a deadly illness by means of mad laughter, his emotionally charged visit to the Dachau concentration camp, or his tragicomic attempt to commit suicide, to name just a few. But none of these incidents, facts, and acts, even the most outrageous, seems to be gross enough to justify his deportation to the colonies. In a sense, then, the narrators' failure to explain is not a consequence of their inarticulation but indeed of their failure to acquire, or possess, the knowledge and understanding that "Federman" needs to write his novel in a way which would "reveal for posterity the truth of the old man's predicament . . . the essential of his difficult but interesting experience" (6).

The point, however, is that "Federman" is not merely motivated by "the spirit of creativity" but also, and perhaps predominantly so, by a sense of moral duty or obligation, indeed "a profound and personal need to come to terms with the unexplainable" (5). And what is meant by "the unexplainable" here is not the enigma of the old man's present situation and of his future fate at all, for as is quite predictable in a Federman novel, his deportation is cancelled eventually, though the reasons for that also remain unexplained. The real challenge is not the end of the old man's story but the beginning, specifically the incomprehensible event from his childhood which marked the beginning of his present life and which involved the death of his entire family and his own survival and strange rebirth out of his primordial closet. Nam and Moi rightly feel that the story of the closet may contain the key to the problem they are trying to solve, but despite being free to move in both space and time and visit the old man at various points of his life story, they are never allowed to reach its beginning and produce a firsthand report on what really happened in the closet. They have no way of ascertaining the truth of the closet episode, for all their knowledge in this respect comes from an obscure text written by the old man and entitled *The Voice in the Closet* which, apart from being a secondary source, is admittedly a work of fiction. In fact, even the old man himself has no way of talking directly about his closet experience— all he does when the subject comes up during his friends' visit to his shabby Paris apartment is to give them the book to read and explain how the text functions as a work of fiction. For "Federman," the story of the closet is obviously even further removed from the truth of the old man's past, for he is not even given a chance to read the book but must make do with a secondhand description of its reality as a closet which, in its author's words quoted by the two narrators, "exists only as a sequence of squares, of doors if you prefer, just as the voices in the text exist only as a sequence of cries, the voices can be extended into history, but one can never find the door that leads to the origin or the end of the little boy's story" (118).

The collective failure of the old man, of Nam and Moi, and of "Federman" to tell the truth about the protagonist's troubled existence results not from their inability to communicate this truth but from their failure to discover and understand it. "Federman" indirectly acknowledges this failure when he confesses that the central conern is not solving the mystery of the latter's deportation, and not even describing "the extermination of . . . the old guy's entire family," but "the erasure of that extermination as a central event" (13). He paradoxically succeeds by devising a complex narrative structure which, through the dissolution of the narrative center, becomes a truly Tinguelian device designed to prevent the story from being told. At the same time, however, his artistically successful failure to communicate never quite matches his moral failure to possess, to understand, and to explain his primal loss, which can never be recouped. This in turn leaves him with a sense of guilt which cannot be attenuated by his willful artistic defeat, for the agony of fighting with and being defeated by one's own thoughts and one's own language is, to use the old man's words, "never adequate, it always escape[s] as suffering toward the consciousness of suffering" (9). In the end, "one suffers and one suffers from not suffering enough."(9)

With space reduced to the four walls of the writer's study, time reduced to the present, self reduced to voice, and truth to presence, the reality of *The Twofold Vibration* may seem to shrink dangerously and threaten to disappear into the abstractions of language, its only identifiable locus. But this contraction of reality to a single dimension actually means the writer's liberation from the constrictions of fixed space, linear time, spiritless matter, rational subjecthood, and pragmatic truth. In fact, the novel's verbal space is the sole domain of imagination, and not only is "the reality of imagination . . . more real than reality without imagination" (24), but it is also much greater than the concrete reality of actual things and people; within its limits, the writer is given complete freedom to explore his own mind's capacity for invention. The kind of freedom offered by language is particularly valuable for Federman, for it expresses his own paradoxical predicament of a survivor "condemned for the rest of his life to question relentlessly [his] obscure beginning and never to comprehend how that day he had ceased to be a son and become his own father" (69). The old man makes the point clear in the following explanation of his approach to life offered by him to June Fanon:

I am a survivor, my death is behind me . . . I'm not morbid, I'm happy, can't you see, yes happy to be here with you, but you see the fact of being a survivor, of living with one's death behind, in a way makes you free, free and irresponsible toward your own end, of course you feel a little guilty while you're surviving because there is this thing about your past, your dead past and all that, but you have to get on with things, sustain your excessiveness, so to speak, yes imagine you have this wretched past, so wretched, gruesome, but it's the only past you've got, I mean you're stuck with it, but then they take it away from you, erase it, make typographical symbols out of it, funny little xxxx's on pieces of paper, you're dead as far as they are concerned, nonexistent, I mean how do you live without a past, well you manage to survive anyhow, to fake it, fictitiously, extemporaneously, not as revenant but as devenant, by projecting yourself ahead of yourself . . . you invent yourself as you go along, re-invent what you think really happened, this way you can survive anything, (50–51)

Yet survival is not simply a matter of escaping the horrors of one's actual experience in the world into the realm of fantasy. Imagination, Federman believes, offers something more than a means of stifling remorse by momentarily increasing the suffering manifold. Reconciled to failure on aesthetic grounds, the writer has few doubts about the possibility of ever arriving at an adequate explanation, in rationalistic terms, of the meaning of the Holocaust, but he also knows that, in the absence of such an explanation, man should at least try to prevent atrocities like that from happening again. Therefore, he regards his own imaginative quest for the reinvention of his own past as his contribution to the much more general ongoing project of redefining modern history, indeed modernity as a worldview, in its political, ethical, and also aesthetic dimensions. In one of his numerous digressions, "Federman" speculates: "The Holocaust was a universal affair in which all mankind was implicated and is still implicated, therefore to speak of that sad affair, in life or in fiction, in an effort to come to terms with its incomprehensibility, must also be a collective undertaking" (149). As part of this collective undertaking, he offers in his fiction, not answers to the question "Why did the Holocaust happen?" or, for that matter, "What is the Holocaust?" but a way of asking these questions, which is the adoption of a permanent "what-am-I-doing-here?" stance in life. In his practice of fiction, this means constant introspection of the process of fiction, with preference always given to action over thinking, movement over contemplation, for he believes that only by a self-conscious effort to understand how people transform perception into experience can they glimpse the meaning of human existence. And to arrive at such an understanding, one must first of all "do it," perform his presence in language.

Raymond Federman's writing from *Double or Nothing* through *The Twofold Vibration* impressively proves that the novel conceived on the model of performance offers the best possibilities for carrying out such an investigation of existential fundamentals by means of fiction. In the most generally philosophical sense, by rejecting the aesthetic premises of realism in favor of the postmodern aesthetic of surfiction, it automatically calls into question the epistemological premises of the modern, rationalistic worldview underlying fictional realism. In a more specific experiential sense, a novel constructed according to the performatory principles discussed in this study shows that the quality of living presence, truly the presence of a self, however decentered and indeterminate, can be best conveyed on the performatory level. This performatory voice is an artificial entity, but the writer's staging of the self as a multivoice, a performer of concrete speech acts constituting the identity of this textual self, makes the creative act, writing, both experientially valid for the writer and continuous with another creative act which is naturally different but commensurate with it—reading. In the end, it is this quality of surfiction that makes the voice of the text resound with truly human undertones.

15

Conclusion: The Fiction Writer on Stage

RATHER THAN ATTEMPTING TO develop a general theory of performance as a primary aesthetic category, the present study has tried to demonstrate that the antimimetic disposition of twentieth-century art makes the notion of performance useful in the description and analysis of such diverse art forms as painting and sculpture, the Happening and dance, theater and music, poetry and fiction. For the sake of clarity, it seems expedient to conclude by identifying those features of artistic performance which are shared by most postmodern art and literature. The key features of the emergent performatory model can be arranged in two groups: those which stress the nonmimetism of the work of art (abstractness, opacity, superficiality, self- or nonreferentiality, autonomy, and so on) and those which stress its dynamic character (motion, flow, process, action, enactment, happening, occurrence, and so on). These characteristics allow us to say that a work of art can be its own occurrence, or happening.

Another set of characteristics which logically follows from these key features defines precisely how a work of art occurs or happens. Specifically, a work that consists in an activity or action which does not aim to represent anything outside itself: (1) has an indeterminate and playful character (no preset meaning or premeditation; no direction of development; a reliance on chance, invention, and improvisation; an *a*logical structure or intentional purposelessness); (2) focuses attention on the physical properties of the medium (since the medium is often the sole object of the action performed, the emphasis is on the materials used or on the physical aspects of production with subject matter reduced to the minimum); and (3) has an open form (invites the audience's collaboration in making the work complete). The preceding formulation could thus be restated to read as follows: a work of art can be an open-form event or process in which the medium of a given art form is employed not for the sake of transmitting some prearranged meaning but in order to produce a meaning which could not otherwise be generated and experienced.

Such a definition of nonmimetic art naturally raises the perennial question of aesthetic value, which in traditional aesthetics is very closely tied to that of ethical value. But of course the issue of value is an inherently referential category—according to classic aesthetic theory, a work has value when it tells something meaningful, that is, true, about reality—and thus is of little use in a theory of art based on nonmimetism and nonrepresentational performance. The only kind of truth that a genuinely nonrepresentational work of art conveys is the truth of its own presence or occurrence, the value of which is predominantly a function of experience and not of contemplation and interpretation.

The consequences for aesthetic theory of the revaluation (or indeed devaluation) of value and the attendant loss of authority in postmodern art are fairly obvious: the traditional primary categories either disappear completely or are subordinated to the act of creation. Quite simply, the work of art as object is frequently dispensed with (as in Conceptual Art) or, when a material artifact is present, it becomes an element, often of a secondary character, of the aesthetic experience when it is perceived and acted upon. The primary artist becomes indistinguishable from the performer, for artistic creation consists now primarily in the activity (whether physical or mental) involved. Similarly, in order to make the aesthetic transaction possible, the audience actively engages in the open-ended process of art, thus becoming collaborators in the creative process or performance. The critic is also automatically assigned an entirely new role to play: criticism moves away from evaluation and toward description, while interpretation, to use Jonathan Culler's words, ceases to be "a matter of recovering some meaning which lies behind the work and serves as a center governing its structure; it is rather an attempt to participate in and observe the play of possible meanings to which the [work of art] gives full access."[1]

The work of art can then be said to be a result of the interaction of the activated potentialities of the artist, the performer, the audience (including the critic as a subcategory) and, indispensably, the medium. All have some role to play in the act, all are performers in the theatrical, or one should rather say theatricalized, sense: the artist-performer performs by using the medium in

an aesthetically intentional way ("aesthetically intentional" means increasingly "intentionally purposeless"),
the spectator-critic responds creatively by letting himself
be drawn into the act. Within this interaction the medium (material object, sound, light, environment, langauge) can also be said to perform, for it is being
meaningfully used and responded to by human agents.
Conversely, it shapes the meaning generated in the process of being used by people through the activation, or
actualization, of its own potentialities, principally the
ability to impart information and attract attention to
itself, that is, to be foregrounded.[2]

The idea of art conceived on the model of performance has value also because of its broadly cultural ram-
ifications: it is expressive of the more generalized
tendency in twentieth-century philosophy, science, and
social thought to transcend the dualisms intrinsic to the
modern worldview and move toward the idea of a whole
world by defining reality in terms of process, flow, interaction, play, participation, and performance. According to current theories developed by natural and social
scientists, the physical world exists as long as particles
perform their indeterminate, autotelic operations in the
space-time continuum (quantum physics); people exist
and come to know themselves and other human beings
by participating in the social drama (role theory of personal identity); they come to know and understand nature by entering into communion with it, by joining it
in its flux (the notion of the inseparability of the observer
and the thing observed developed by atomic physics);
their knowledge of the world around them is in turn
concretized, made true, through, as Richard Palmer puts
it, "the loyal articulation, in language, of what *is*";[3] and

language, as J. L. Austin has argued, not only describes but also does things. All this seems enough to justify adopting performance as a metaphor for the dominant mode of much of contemporary art and of postmodern thought and activity in general as well. At the artistic end of the postmodern spectrum, performance articulates the desire, as Herbert Blau contends, "to collapse the painful dualities with which philosophy has struggled from its inception; mind/body, form/content, truth/illusion, spirit/matter, art/life; always, however, keeping a cliff-hanging finger on the critical difference. The potency of performance may almost be measured by the acuity of that perilous act."[4] At the epistemological end, the performatory worldview offers, as Morris Berman observes about Gregory Bateson's approach to the scientific investigation of phenomena, "a non-spiritualist, process-oriented mode of investigation" which will hopefully lead to a situation in which "our science (knowledge of the world) will become artful (artistic)."[5]

In the world of fiction, the work of Ronald Sukenick and Raymond Federman is an impressive proof that there is a common ground where postmodern art and science can become equivalent modes of cognition. By replacing a confidence in realism's ability to respond adequately to the problems and pressures of existence with the awareness of what Federman refers to as "the fiasco of reality and the imposture of history," they thus come closer to the truth of the world today not by imposing the artificial, "violent" order of rational discourse on the chaos of reality but "by confronting the unreality of reality."[6] Like other postmodern novelists, they expose the fictionality of reality by writing novels which reflect upon their own form rather than being reflections of reality. Understandably, their motives in writing this essentialized exploratory fiction as well as the routes by which they pursue their individual goals are idiosyncratic and quite different. Yet, given their academic background as well as their proximity in both space and time, it is not a coincidence that they have come to regard themselves, and be regarded by others, as natural soul mates and spokesmen for the entire surfictionist movement.

Ronald Sukenick's declared goal in writing is to rid fiction of the paraphernalia of traditional narrative art—plot, story, characterization, chronology, description, and so on—and approach his own thinking that occurs in and through writing in its pure, or at least purified, form, including the physical form the text takes as it is written and read. Since, he asserts, "form deals with the structure of experience rather than experience itself," writing naturally becomes "a matter of valuing the process of thinking over any particular idea."[7] In the most general terms, this means that the material processed by thought during composition can be chosen at random from the data of memory, imagination, or perception that are present in the writer's head at the moment of writing.

Unlike Sukenick, Raymond Federman deals in his novels with very carefully selected and very concrete ("almost in the sense of 'cement,' " the writer says) material—the story of his own life—whose basic ontological status seems to be unequivocal and, therefore, independent of what the writer thinks and writes about it *after the fact*. Moreover, because the events of that life are so dramatic and because they are presented by Federman mostly in a realistic manner, they, as he admits, "*can* be viewed as sentimental and even melodramatic."[8] Knowing that appealing to the reader's emotions and intellect by means of melodrama and sentimentality is not only pointless but also fraudulent and hence dishonest, he employs a stunning variety of narrative and formal strategies to show that fiction does not deal with facts but with interpretations of facts and their imaginative transformations into verbal (arti)facts. Making the reader aware of this simple truth, Federman believes, is the duty of every writer who is seriously concerned about what his writing does to his readers, for by exposing the fictionality of fiction he will eventually also expose the fictionality of reality itself. The purpose of this process is not merely "destroying illusions for the sake of destroying illusions."

I'm destroying illusions in order that we may indeed face up to reality, and not what passes for reality. Especially in these days of mass media and television which perpetuate illusions for us and mystify the real and the illusory, it is necessary to clean up the world, push aside the illusions that make this world livable for us. Unless we constantly question what passes for reality, challenge it, defy it, we will always exist in falseness, in a system of twisted facts and glorified illusions, and we quickly become lobotomized by it.[9]

As should be clear from these words, Federman's desire to demystify reality means the repudiation of one of the two traditional goals of literature, namely, sublimation (cognition being the other goal). Such a view may seem to be irreconcilable with his urgent personal compulsion to find a way of coming to terms with his incomprehensible past, of relieving the anxiety caused by this incomprehensibility through writing, and of charging his unspeakable experience with meaning and value in order to make life bearable. But, while often verging on escapism and sentimentality, Federman never lets his novels create a screen of comforting illusions but rather strips his language of the power to create a coherent vision of life. Thus he uses the discursive content of his fiction—the story of his life reduced to a sequence of closets of displacement—much the way that Sukenick uses form in his works. Demystifying his life story as a fiction and his discourse about it as a language, he turns his subject into an element of form, meaning both the abstract form of language and the concrete form of the written and spoken word. His considerations about his own life thus become a means of investigating the ways in which this life is constructed as a story, that is, investigating the ways in which his own mind and language function in the process of appropriating experience.

In this sense, Federman's composition of "real fictitious" discourses represents the same orientation as Sukenick's formal thinking. The message that both writers convey by shifting the reader's attention from the unfolding of the story to the unfolding of the language and composition is that, as Federman puts it, "there is no message, only messengers, and that is the message."[10] In other words, they show that the meaning of fiction, like the meaning of life, is a wholly experiential category: just as life is not about its own sense but is that sense, writing and reading (and, for that matter, any other form of creative activity) are not responses to the meaning of the world but are part of that meaning, are what generate that meaning.

Ronald Sukenick and Raymond Federman are by no means unique in their realization that the postmodern novel, if it is to be made commensurate with postmodern art and culture in general, must no longer be seen as a pretext for the transmission of some preexisting meaning. But these two writers are distinguished from most other contemporary novelists by the acuity of their awareness of what performing the art-perceiving role means today. In their exploration of the problematics of performance, from its narrowly literary aspects, through more broadly aesthetic and cultural areas, to genuinely epistemological dimensions, they have placed themselves on the center stage of postmodern fiction. There, stripped of realism's props, having only language to play with, they engage themselves and their audience in a performance that is both liberating and revelatory.

Notes
Bibliography
Index

Notes

1. Aspects of Performance

1. Hilde Hein, "Performance as an Aesthetic Category," *Journal of Aesthetics and Art Criticism* 28 (1970): 382; F. E. Sparshott, *The Structure of Aesthetics* (Toronto: University of Toronto Press; London: Routledge and Kegan Paul, 1963); Monroe C. Beardsley, *Aesthetics: Problems in the Philosophy of Criticism* (New York: Harcourt, Brace and Co., 1958). Sparshott evades the whole issue on the grounds that "there is no precisely demarcated set of physical things or happenings with which the performance can be unequivocally identified" (36). Beardsley, on the other hand, argues that "the aesthetic object *is* the intention" (22), and he further depreciates the function of performance by subordinating it to production; a production of a work of art, he says, may possess a certain unique aesthetic value, that is, may be an aesthetic object in its own right, whereas a performance, defined by him as merely a playing (one of many more or less similar playings) of a given production, lacks such a value (55–58).
2. Sparshott, 40.
3. See, for example, Karin R. Band–Kuzmany, comp., *Glossary of the Theatre* (Amsterdam: Elsevier Publishing Co., 1969), where "performing art" and "interpretive art" are fully synonymous (entry 543).
4. Hein, 384.
5. Hein, 382.
6. Hein, 382.
7. Beardsley, 319.
8. Beardsley, 18.

9. Harold Rosenberg, *The Tradition of the New* (New York: Horizon Press, 1959), 26–27.

10. Quoted by Robert Creeley, "Introduction," in *Selected Writings of Charles Olson*, ed. Robert Creeley (New York: New Directions, 1966), 7.

11. Harold Rosenberg, *The Anxious Object: Art Today and Its Audience* (New York: Collier Books, 1964), 148; Clement Greenberg, *Art and Culture: Critical Essays* (Boston: Beacon Press, 1965), 195.

12. Rosenberg, *Tradition*, 28.

13. Allan Kaprow, " 'Happenings' in the New York Scene," in *The Modern American Theatre: A Collection of Critical Essays*, ed. Alvin B. Kernan (Englewood Cliffs, N.J.: Prentice-Hall, 1967), 123.

14. Kaprow's words are quoted by Margaret Croyden in her *Lunatics, Lovers and Poets: The Contemporary Experimental Theatre* (New York: Dell, 1975), 82.

15. Kaprow, 123.

16. Susan Sontag, *Against Interpretation and Other Essays* (New York: Farrar, Strauss, & Giroux, 1966), 269.

17. Kaprow, 122.

18. Kaprow, 124.

19. Sontag, 268.

20. Jill Johnston, "The New American Modern Dance," in *The New American Arts*, ed. Richard Kostelanetz (New York: Horizon Press, 1965), 189.

21. John Cage, *Silence* (Middleton, Conn.: Wesleyan University Press, 1961), 13.

22. Cage, 14.

23. Cage, 14.

24. Cage, 14.

25. Cage, 14.

26. Cage, 14–15.

27. Cage, 15.

28. Merce Cunningham, "Space, Time, and Dance," in *Modern Culture and the Arts*, ed. James B. Hall and Barry Ulanov (New York: McGraw-Hill, 1967), 260.

29. Cunningham, 405.

30. Cunningham observes: "A prevalent feeling among many painters that lets them make a space in which anything can happen is a feeling dancers may have too" (402).

31. Johnston, 191.

32. Susan Sontag, "Approaching Artaud," in her *Under the Sign of Saturn* (New York: Farrar, Strauss, Giroux, 1980), 30.

33. Sontag, "Artaud," 31.

34. Sontag observes that "Artaud assimilates all art to dramatic performance" ("Artaud," 29).

35. Artaud's words are quoted by Sontag in "Artaud," 34.

36. Richard Gilman, *The Confusion of Realms* (New York: Vintage Books, 1979), 230.

37. Richard Schechner, *Essays on Performance Theory 1970–1976* (New York: Drama Books Specialists, 1977), 8.

38. Schechner, 18.

39. Schechner, 19.

40. Schechner, 20.

41. Susan Sontag, *Against Interpretation, 10.*

42. Richard Palmer, "Towards a Postmodern Hermeneutics of Performance," in *Performance in Postmodern Culture*, ed. Michel Benamou and Charles Caramello (Madison: Coda Press, 1977), 25.

43. Ludwig Wittgenstein, *Tractatus Logico-Philosophicus*, trans. D. F. Pears and B. F. McGuinness (London: Routledge and Kegan Paul; New York: Humanities Press, 1961), 5.6.

44. Douglas R. Hofstadter, *Gödel, Escher, Bach: An Eternal Golden Braid* (New York: Vintage Books, 1979), 18; Palmer, 28.

45 This statement by Tzvetan Todorov is quoted by Marjorie Perloff in her *The Poetics of Indeterminacy: Rimbaud to Cage* (Princeton: Princeton University Press, 1981), 3.

46. Perloff, *Poetics*, vii.

47. Perloff, *Poetics*, 33–34.

48. Perloff, *Poetics*, 85.

49. Perloff, *Poetics*, 85.

50. Charles Olson, "Projective Verse," in *Selected Writings of Charles Olson*, (New York: New Directions, 1966), 16.

51. Olson, 16.

52. Olson, 24.

53. Olson, 17.

54. Olson, 24.

55. Olson, 25.

56. Olson, 19.

57. Olson, 22.

58. Fred Moramarco, "John Ashbery and Frank O'Hara: The Painterly Poets," *Journal of Modern Literature* 3 (1976): 438; O'Hara's letter is quoted by Marjorie Perloff in her *Frank O'Hara: Poet among Painters* (Austin: University of Texas Press, 1979), 22.

59. O'Hara's words are quoted by Perloff in *O'Hara*, 22.

60. O'Hara's original words, as quoted by Perloff, are: "It is the physical reality of the artist and his activity of expressing it, united with the spiritual reality of the artist in a oneness which

has no need for the mediation of metaphor or symbol. It is Action Painting . . ." (*O'Hara*, 23.)

61. Perloff, *O'Hara*, 116.

62. Jerome Klinkowitz, *The American 1960s: Imaginative Acts in a Decade of Change* (Ames: Iowa State University Press, 1980), 41.

63. Anthony Libby, "O'Hara on the Silver Range," *Contemporary Literature* 2 (1976): 257.

64. John Ashbery, *Three Poems* (Harmondsworth: Penguin Books, 1977), 41.

65. Ashbery, 86.

66. Ashbery, 3.

67. Ashbery, 81, emphasis added.

68. Ashbery, 39.

69. Jackson Mac Low, "Statement," in *The Poetics of the New American Poetry*, ed. Donald Allen and Warren Tallman (New York: Grove Press, 1973), 385.

70. John Cage, *Silence*, 136.

71. Northrop Frye's words from his *The Well-Tempered Critic* are quoted by Perloff in *Poetics*, 42.

72. Frye is quoted by Perloff in *Poetics*, 317.

73. Jerome Rothenberg's statement from his "Pre-Face" to *Revolution of the Word*, reprinted in his *Pre-Faces and Other Writings*, is quoted by Perloff in *Poetics*, 39.

74. Frye is quoted by Perloff in *Poetics*, 42.

75. William Barret, *Time of Need: Forms of Imagination in the Twentieth Century* (New York: Harper and Row, 1972), 11.

76. See Robert Alter, *Partial Magic: The Novel as a Self-Conscious Genre* (Berkeley and Los Angeles: University of California Press, 1975).

77. Raymond Federman, "Life in the Cylinder," *Fiction International* 1 (1973): 114.

78. Richard Poirier, *The Performing Self: Compositions and Decompositions in the Languages of Contemporary Life* (New York: Oxford University Press, 1971), 69.

79. Ihab Hassan, *The Right Promethean Fire: Imagination, Science, and Cultural Change* (Urbana: University of Illinois Press, 1980), 56–57.

80. Tony Tanner, "My Life in American Literature," *TriQuarterly* 30 (1974): 96; Tony Tanner, *City of Words: American Fiction 1950–1970* (London: Jonathan Cape, 1976),

81. Tanner, *City of Words*, 20.

82. Richard Poirier, *A World Elsewhere: The Place of Style in American Literature* (New York: Oxford University Press, 1966), 35; Poirier, *Performing Self*, 86.

83. Poirier, *Performing Self*, 107.
84. Poirier, *Performing Self*, xiii.
85. Poirier, *Performing Self*, 109.
86. Poirier, *Performing Self*, 111.
87. James M. Mellard, *The Exploded Form: The Modernist Novel in America* (Urbana: University of Illinois Press, 1980), 133–34.
88. Mellard, 134.
89. Charles Altieri, *Enlarging the Temple*, quoted in Mellard, 134.
90. Mellard, 135.
91. Mellard, 140.
92. Mellard, 146.
93. Charles Caramello, *Silverless Mirrors: Book, Self and Postmodern American Fiction* (Tallahassee: University Presses of Florida, 1983), 3.
94. Barthes' words quoted by Caramello come from the French critic's book *S/Z*.
95. Caramello, 9; Roland Barthes, *The Pleasure of the Text*, trans. Richard Miller (New York: Hill and Wang, 1975), 9.
96. Caramello, 16; Barthes, 16.
97. Barthes, 66.
98. Barthes, 66.

2. Wallace Stevens: Musing the Obscure

1. Ronald Sukenick, *Wallace Stevens: Musing the Obscure* (New York: New York University Press, 1967). It was originally written as a Ph.D. dissertation entitled "A Wallace Stevens Handbook: A Reading of His Major Poems and an Exposition of His Theory and Practice," Brandeis University, 1962. Subsequent references to the NYU volume are cited in the text. The initial section, "Wallace Stevens: Theory and Practice," is collected in Sukenick's *In Form: Digressions on the Act of Fiction* (Carbondale and Edwardsville: Southern Illinois University Press, 1985), pp. 157–98.
2. Jerome Klinkowitz, *Literary Disruptions: The Making of a Post-Contemporary American Fiction* (Urbana: University of Illinois Press, 1975), 119.
3. One may cite, for example, the famous Stevens-Burnshaw exchange, especially Burnshaw's review of *Ideas of Order* in *New Masses* (1 October, 1935) and Stevens' reply in "Mr. Burnshaw and the Statue," the second poem of "Owl's Clover."

4. Lewis Leary, *American Literature: A Study and Research Guide* (New York: St. Martin's Press, 1976), 124.
5. Wallace Stevens, "Saint John and the Back-Ache," in *The Collected Poems of Wallace Stevens* (New York: Alfred A. Knopf, 1954), 437.
6. Stevens, "An Ordinary Evening in New Haven," in *Collected Poems,* 473.
7. Stevens, "The Man with the Blue Guitar," Section XXII, in *Collected Poems,* 176–77.
8. Wallace Stevens, *Opus Posthumous,* ed. Samuel French Morse (New York: Alfred A. Knopf, 1957), 177.
9. Stevens, "Man Carrying Thing," in *Collected Poems,* 352.

3. In Form: Digressions on the Act of Fiction

1. Ronald Sukenick, *In Form: Digressions on the Act of Fiction* (Carbondale and Edwardsville: Southern Illinois University Press, 1985), 241. Subsequent references are cited in the text.
2. Joe David Bellamy, "The Tape Recorder Records: An Interview with Ronald Sukenick," *The Falcon,* 1971, nos. 2–3:8.

4. The Death of the Novel and Other Stories

1. Jerome Klinkowitz, *Literary Disruptions* (Urbana: University of Illinois Press, 1975), 124.
2. Ronald Sukenick, *Wallace Stevens: Musing the Obscure* (New York: New York University Press, 1967), 12; Ronald Sukenick, *In Form: Digressions on the Act of Fiction* (Carbondale and Edwardsville: Southern Illinois Press, 1985), 171.
3. Sukenick, *Stevens,* 3.
4. Ronald Sukenick, *The Death of the Novel and Other Stories* (New York: Dial Press, 1969), 4. Subsequent references are cited in the text.
5. Joe David Bellamy, "The Tape Recorder Records: An Interview with Ronald Sukenick," *The Falcon,* 1971, nos. 2–3:6.
6. Here is Sukenick mocking the realistic novel's obsession with accurate description: "Meanwhile the glances, the smiles, the smirks, the takes, the winces, the ogles, the sneezes, the grimaces, the eye-flutterings, the nose-pullings, the hiccups, the winks, the nods, the head-shakes, the curl-tossing, the handkerchief-dropping, the posturing, the posing, the deep-breathing exercises, the giggling, the hemming, the hawing, the burping, the nose-

quivering, the eye-rolling, the lip-writhing, the cheek-puffing, the lid-lifting, the head-hanging, the arm-lashing, the gesturing, the gesticulating, the gymnastics, the calisthenics, continued to be directed my way" (51).

7. Klinkowitz, 127.
8. Harry Kirchner, "The Wedding of Dancer and Dance: Fragment No. 1 of an Interview with Raymond Federman" *Cream City Review* 4 (1979): 18.
9. Joe David Bellamy, "Imagination as Perception: An Interview with Ronald Sukenick," *Chicago Review* 23 (1972): 65. Sukenick explains his technique of "disparate traits" in the following way: "You get a character with some name, say Sparrow; and at one point he's described as short and at another he's described as tall. Or, there's a whole episode like that in the novelette in 'The Death of the Novel,' one of those little bits, one of those little stories within a story where the guy is describing his landlord or some guy he thinks might be his landlord. First he describes him as little and then he describes him as big, and then he says he can't remember what he looks like at all" (Charlotte M. Meyer, "An Interview with Ronald Sukenick," *Contemporary Literature* 23 [1982]: 65).
10. Sukenick devotes an entire story to Simone Rodia's Watts Towers—"Endless Short Story: What's Watts," *New Letters* 45 (1979): 177–79.

5. Up

1. Ronald Sukenick, *Up* (New York: Dial Press, 1968), 222.
2. John Ashbery, *Three Poems* (Harmondsworth: Penguin Books, 1977), 86.
3. Larry McCaffery, "An Interview with Ronald Sukenick," in *Anything Can Happen: Interviews with Contemporary American Novelists*, ed. Tom LeClair and Larry McCaffery (Urbana: University of Illinois Press, 1983), 290.
4. McCaffery, 293.
5. McCaffery, 293.

6. Out

1. Linda S. Bergmann, "*Out*: A Novel by Ronald Sukenick," *Chicago Review,* 25, no. 3 (1973):11.

2. Ronald Sukenick, *Out* (Chicago: Swallow Press, 1973), 1. Subsequent references are cited in the text.
3. Sukenick claims that he became aware of Castaneda's work only when he was writing the very last section of *Out*. He says: "At that time I happened to read the first published excerpt from Castaneda's second book, *A Separate Reality,* and I was astonished to find a number of similarities in incident and idea between *Out* and Castaneda's story. The more so that the things in *Out* most parallel to Castaneda's book came out of my dreams, on which I have come to draw heavily in my writing" (Ronald Sukenick, "Upward and Juanward: The Possible Dream," in *Seeing Castaneda: Reactions to the "Don Juan" Writings of Carlos Castaneda,* ed. Daniel Noel [New York: Capricorn Books, 1976], 110).
4. Carlos Castaneda, *A Separate Reality* (Harmondsworth: Penguin Books, 1973), 14.
5. In Castaneda's vocabulary, the notions of "power" and "controlled dreaming" are inseparable. For a discussion of this aspect of the parallel between Sukenick's and Castaneda's works, see Daniel C. Noel, "Tales of Fictive Power: Dreaming and Imagination in Ronald Sukenick's Postmodern Fiction," *Boundary 2* 5 (1976): 117–35.
6. Quoted by Larry McCaffery in *The Metafictional Muse: The Works of Robert Coover, Donald Barthelme, and William H. Gass* (Pittsburgh: University of Pittsburgh Press, 1982), pp. 26–27, from Colin Turbayne's *The Myth of Metaphor.*

7. *98.6*

1. Ronald Sukenick, *Out* (Chicago: Swallow Press, 1973), 164.
2. Ronald Sukenick, *98.6* (New York: Fiction Collective, 1975), 24. Subsequent references are cited in the text.
3. Although the concept of power presented here is practically identical with Castaneda's conception, it is in fact Sukenick's original idea, whose early version can be found in *Out*, where it is described as the extension of the senses. When Roland Sycamore goes to see an optometrist, the latter discovers that his patient reads messages in everything, that is, sees meaningful patterns in the chaos of the surrounding world. He explains this condition in the following way:

This is my diagnosis you're developing what is sometimes called second sight don't get nervous. It happens much more often than you might think usually to people rich in experience who are approaching some kind of maturity as with the poltergeist phenomenon and adolescence it is associated with a certain time of life but usually is censored by the mind even as it is perceived since most people lack the capacity indeed the inclination to contain such powers let alone use them. One sometimes hears of this experience in such terms as the third eye clairvoyance etcetera I prefer to avoid the spectacular it simply means that you can see more than other people. (232–33)

The opposite of power, that is, one's ability to "see," is defined by Sukenick as "negative hallucination," meaning not seeing something that is really there, a much more widespread phenomenon in Frankenstein.

8. Long Talking Bad Conditions Blues

1. Charlotte M. Meyer, "An Interview with Ronald Sukenick," *Contemporary Literature* 23 (1982): 142.
2. Ronald Sukenick, *Long Talking Bad Conditions Blues* (New York: Fiction Collective, 1979), 19. Subsequent references are cited in the text.
3. Joe David Bellamy, "The Tape Recorder Records: An Interview with Ronald Sukenick," *The Falcon,* 1971, nos. 2–3:7.
4. Compare Sukenick's remark that "A style is a way of thinking— and a structure is a way of perceiving" (Bellamy, 12).
5. Larry McCaffery, "An Interview with Ronald Sukenick," in *Anything Can Happen: Interviews with Contemporary American Novelists,* ed. Tom LeClair and Larry McCaffery (Urbana: University of Illinois Press, 1983), 293.
6. Meyer, 138.

9. Journey to Chaos: Samuel Beckett's Early Fiction

1. See Jerome Klinkowitz, *Literary Disruptions* (Urbana: University of Illinois Press, 1975) and Jerome Klinkowitz, *The Life of Fiction,* with graphics by Roy R. Behrens (Urbana: University of Illinois Press, 1977).
2. For a comprehensive bibliography of Federman's works, see Klinkowitz's *Literary Disruptions,* 2nd ed. (Urbana: University of Illinois Press, 1980).

3. Raymond Federman, *Journey to Chaos: Samuel Beckett's Early Fiction* (Berkeley and Los Angeles: University of California Press, 1965), 4. Subsequent references are cited in the text.
4. Beckett's words from "Three Dialogues" are quoted by Federman in *Journey to Chaos*, 204.
5. Larry McCaffery, "An Interview with Raymond Federman," in *Anything Can Happen: Interviews with Contemporary American Novelists*, ed. Tom LeClair and Larry McCaffery (Urbana: University of Illinois Press, 1983), 134.
6. McCaffery, 138.
7. McCaffery, 150.
8. McCaffery, 151.

10. Uncollected Criticism

1. Raymond Federman, "Surfiction—Four Propositions in Form of an Introduction," in *Surfiction: Fiction Now . . . And Tomorrow*, ed. Raymond Federman (Chicago: Swallow Press, 1975), 8. The original version, published as "Surfiction—A Position" in *Partisan Review* 3 (1973): 427–32, contained five propositions. Subsequent references cited in the text are to the revised version appearing in *Surfiction*, with the title of the essay abbreviated as *S*.
2. Raymond Federman, "Self/Voice/Performance," in *Coherence: A Gathering of Experiments in Writing: Towards a New Poetics*, ed. Don Wellman (Cambridge: O.ARS, 1981), 196. Subsequent references are cited in the text as *SVP*.
3. Raymond Federman, "Playgiarism: A Spatial Displacement of Words," *Sub- stance*, 1977, no. 16:112. Subsequent references are cited in the text as *P*. A companion essay, "Imagination as Plagiarism," *New Literary History* 7 (1976): 563–78, is cited as *IP*.
4. Raymond Federman, "What Are Experimental Novels and Why Are There So Many Left Unread?" in *Novel vs. Fiction: The Contemporary Reformation*, ed. Jackson I. Cope and Geoffrey Green (Norman, Okla.: Pilgrim Books, 1981), 30–31. Subsequent references are cited in the text as *WAEN*.
5. Larry McCaffery, "An Interview with Raymond Federman," in *Anything Can Happen: Interviews with Contemporary American Novelists*, ed. Tom LeClair and Larry McCaffery (Urbana: University of Illinois Press, 1983), 131.

6. In order to save space and ensure clarity, the author's original typography has been rearranged, and the text has been punctuated.

7. Raymond Federman and Ronald Sukenick, "The New Innovative Fiction," *Antaeus*, 1976, no. 20:144. Subsequent references are cited in the text as *NIF*.

8. McCaffery, 148.

9. McCaffery, 135.

10. Raymond Federman, "From Past Self to Present Self," *Descant* 24 (1979–80): 52. Subsequent references are cited in the text as *PS*.

11. Raymond Federman, "Fiction Today or the Pursuit of Non-Knowledge," in *Surfiction: Fiction Now . . . And Tomorrow*, 2d ed., ed. Raymond Federman (Chicago: Swallow Press, 1981), 298. Subsequent references are cited in the text as *FT*.

12. McCaffery, 137.

13. McCaffery, 143.

14. McCaffery, 149.

15. McCaffery, 143.

11. Double or Nothing

1. Raymond Federman, "Surfiction—Four Propositions in Form of an Introduction," in *Surfiction: Fiction Now . . . And Tomorrow*, ed. Raymond Federman (Chicago: Swallow Press, 1975), 8.

2. Raymond Federman, *Double or Nothing* (Chicago: Swallow Press, 1971), 44. Subsequent references are cited in the text.

3. Welch D. Everman, "Raymond Federman," in *Dictionary of Literary Biography Yearbook 1982*, ed. Richard Layman (Detroit: Gale Research, 1983), 197.

12. Take It or Leave It

1. While working on *Take It or Leave It* (New York: Fiction Collective, 1976), Federman wrote a shorter version of the same story (he calls it an adaptation, not a translation) in French, published as *Amer Eldorado* (Paris: Editions Stock, 1974). The present study considers only the English text. No page references will be given, since the book is not paginated.

2. Raymond Federman, "Surfiction—Four Propositions in Form of an Introduction," in *Surfiction: Fiction Now . . . And Tomorrow*, ed. Raymond Federman (Chicago: Swallow Press, 1975), 7.
3. Welch D. Everman, "Raymond Federman," in *Dictionary of Literary Biography Yearbook 1982*, ed. Richard Layman (Detroit: Gale Research, 1983), 199.
4. Larry McCaffery, "An Interview with Raymond Federman," in *Anything Can Happen: Interviews with Contemporary American Novelists*, ed. Tom LeClair and Larry McCaffery (Urbana: University of Illinois Press, 1983), 131.
5. It will be remembered that, according to Federman, "readability" is "what guides us back from the text to the world" ("What Are Experimental Novels and Why Are There So Many Left Unread?" in *Novel vs. Fiction: The Contemporary Reformation*, ed. Jackson I. Cope and Geoffrey Green [Norman, Okla.: Pilgrim Books, 1981], 26).

13. The Voice in the Closet

1. Larry McCaffery, "An Interview with Raymond Federman," in *Anything Can Happen: Interviews with Contemporary American Novelists*, ed. Tom LeClair and Larry McCaffery (Urbana: University of Illinois Press, 1983), 145.
2. Raymond Federman, *The Voice in the Closet / La Voix dans le Cabinet de Débarras* (Madison: Coda Press, 1979), 2. Subsequent references are cited in the text.
3. This discussion considers only the English "half" of the book; the figures for the French text are different.
4. Raymond Federman, "Playgiarism: A Spatial Displacement of Words," *Sub-stance*, 1977, no. 16:112.
5. Welch D. Everman, "Raymond Federman," in *Dictionary of Literary Biography Yearbook 1982*, ed. Richard Layman (Detroit: Gale Research, 1983), 199.
6. McCaffery, 146.

14. The Twofold Vibration

1. Raymond Federman, *The Twofold Vibration* (Bloomington: Indiana University Press, 1982), 7. Subsequent references are cited in the text.

15. Conclusion: The Fiction Writer on Stage

1. Jonathan Culler, *Structuralist Poetics: Structuralism, Linguistics, and the Study of Literature* (Ithaca: Cornell University Press, 1975), 247.

2. "Foregrounding" is the accepted translation into English of Jan Mukarovsky's original Czech term "aktualisace," meaning, literally, "actualization."

3. Richard Palmer, "Toward a Postmodern Hermeneutics of Performance," in *Performance in Postmodern Culture,* ed. Michel Benamou and Charles Caramello (Madison: Coda Press, 1977), 28.

4. Herbert Blau, "Letting Be Be Finale of Seem: The Future of an Illusion," in *Performance in Postmodern Culture,* ed. Michel Benamou and Charles Caramello (Madison: Coda Press, 1977), 67.

5. Morris Berman, *The Reenchantment of the World* (Ithaca: Cornell University Press, 1981), 272–73.

6. Raymond Federman, "Fiction in America Today or the Unreality of Reality," *Indian Journal of American Studies* 14 (1984): 16.

7. Ronald Sukenick, "Art and the Underground," *American Book Review* 6 (1984): 2–3; Ronald Sukenick, *In Form: Digressions on the Act of Fiction* (Carbondale and Edwardsville: Southern Illinois University Press, 1985), xvii.

8. Charlotte Meyer, "An Interview with Raymond Federman," *Story Quarterly,* 1982, no. 15–16:41.

9. Larry McCaffery, "An Interview with Raymond Federman," in *Anything Can Happen: Interviews with Contemporary American Novelists,* ed. Tom LeClair and Larry McCaffery (Urbana: University of Illinois Press, 1983), 142.

10. Raymond Federman, "What Are Experimental Novels and Why Are There So Many Left Unread?" in *Novel vs. Fiction: The Contemporary Reformation,* ed. Jackson I. Cope and Geoffrey Green (Norman, Okla.: Pilgrim Books, 1981), 25.

Bibliography

Adams, Timothy Dow. "Obscuring the Muse: The Mock Autobiographies of Ronald Sukenick." *Critique* 20 (1978): 27–39.

————. "Ronald Sukenick," In *Dictionary of Literary Biography Yearbook 1981*, edited by Richard Layman, 251–55. Detroit: Gale Research, 1982.

Allen, Donald, and Warren Tallman, eds. *The Poetics of the New American Poetry.* New York: Grove Press, 1973.

Alter, Robert. *Partial Magic: The Novel as a Self-Conscious Genre.* Berkeley and Los Angeles: University of California Press, 1975.

Altieri, Charles. *Enlarging the Temple: New Directions in American Poetry during the 1960s.* Lewisburg, Pa.: Bucknell University Press, 1979.

————. "A Procedural Definition of Literature." In *What Is Literature?*, edited by Paul Hernadi, 62–78. Bloomington: Indiana University Press, 1978.

Ashbery, John. *Three Poems.* Harmondsworth: Penguin Books, 1977.

Auerbach, Erich. *Mimesis: The Representation of Reality in Western Literature.* Princeton: Princeton University Press, 1953.

Austin, J. L. *How to Do Things with Words.* London: Oxford University Press, 1962.

Barret, William. *Time of Need: Forms of Imagination in the Twentieth Century.* New York: Harper and Row, 1972.

Barthes, Roland. *The Pleasure of the Text.* Translated by Richard Miller. New York: Hill and Wang, 1975.

Beardsley, Monroe C. *Aesthetics: Problems in the Philosophy of Criticism.* New York: Harcourt, Brace and Co., 1958.

Bellamy, Joe David. "Imagination as Perception: An Interview with Ronald Sukenick." *Chicago Review* 23 (1972): 59–72. Reprinted in *The New Fiction: Interviews with Innovative American Writers,* edited by Joe David Bellamy, 55–74. Urbana: University of Illinois Press, 1974.

————. "The Tape Recorder Records: An Interview with Ronald Sukenick." *The Falcon,* 1971, nos. 2–3:5–25.

Benamou, Michel. "Presence and Play." In *Performance in Postmodern Culture,* edited by Michel Benamou and Charles Caramello, 3–7. Madison: Coda Press, 1977.

Benamou, Michel, and Charles Caramello, eds. *Performance in Postmodern Culture.* Madison: Coda Press, 1977.

Bergmann, Linda S. "*Out:* A Novel by Ronald Sukenick." *Chicago Review* 25, no. 3 (1973): 9–12.

Berman, Morris. *The Reenchantment of the World.* Ithaca: Cornell University Press, 1981.

Bigsby, C. W. E. "Metatheatre." *Revue Française D'Etudes Américaines* 5 (1980): 180–97.

Blau, Herbert. "Letting Be Be Finale of Seem: The Future of an Illusion." In *Performance in Postmodern Culture,* edited by Michel Benamou and Charles Caramello, 59–77. Madison: Coda Press, 1977.

Brent, Jonathan, and Peter Gena, eds. "A John Cage Reader in Celebration of his 70th Birthday." *TriQuarterly,* 1982, no. 54:68–232.

Broderick, Vincent A. "Disruptive Participants: Observations of Works by Sukenick and Sorrentino." *Kobe College Studies,* 1978, 39–68.

Brown, Robert L., and Martin Steinmann, Jr. "Native Readers of Fiction: A Speech-Act and Genre-Rule Approach to Defining Literature." In *What Is Literature?*, edited by Paul Hernadi, 141–60. Bloomington: Indiana University Press, 1978.

Cage, John. *Silence*. Middletown, Conn.: Wesleyan University Press, 1961.

Caramello, Charles. "On Styles of Postmodern Writing." In *Performance in Postmodern Culture*, edited by Michel Benamou and Charles Caramello, 221–34. Madison: Coda Press, 1977.

————. Review of *The Voice in the Closet*, by Raymond Federman. *American Book Review* 3 (1981): 10–12.

————. *Silverless Mirrors: Book, Self and Postmodern American Fiction*. Tallahassee: University Presses of Florida, 1983.

Castaneda, Carlos. *A Separate Reality*. Harmondsworth: Penguin Books, 1973.

Cheuse, Alan. "Way Out West: The Exploratory Fiction of 'Ronald Sukenick.' " In *Itinerary: Criticism. Essays on California Writers*, edited by Charles L. Crow, 115–21. Bowling Green, Ohio: Bowling Green University Press, 1978.

Couturier, Maurice, ed. "Representation and Performance in Postmodern Fiction." *Proceedings of the Nice Conference on Postmodern Fiction*, April 1982. Montpellier, France: *Delta*, 1983.

Croyden, Margaret. *Lunatics, Lovers and Poets: The Contemporary Experimental Theatre*. New York: Dell, 1975.

Culler, Jonathan. *Structuralist Poetics: Structuralism, Linguistics and the Study of Literature*. London: Routledge and Kegan Paul; Ithaca: Cornell University Press, 1975.

Cunningham, Merce. "A Collaborative Process between Music and Dance." *TriQuarterly*, 1982, no. 54:173–85.

————. "Space, Time, and Dance." In *Modern Culture and the Arts*, edited by James B. Hall and Barry Ulanov. New York: McGraw-Hill, 1967.

Danto, Arthur C. "Artworks and Real Things." In *Aesthetics Today*, rev. ed., edited by Morris Philipson and Paul J. Gudel, 322–36. New York: New American Library, 1980.

Davidson, Michael. "Languages of Post-Modernism." *Chicago Review* 27 (1975): 11–22.

Dickstein, Morris. *Gates of Eden: American Culture in the Sixties.* New York: Basic Books, 1977.

Dienstfrey, Harris. "The Choice of Inventions." Review of *Double or Nothing*, by Raymond Federman. *Fiction International*, 1974, nos. 2–3:147–50.

Ditsky, John. "The Man on the Quaker Oats Box: Characteristics of Recent Experimental Fiction." *Georgia Review* 26 (1972): 297–313.

Doria, Charles. "Charles Olson: Against the Past." In *American Writing Today*, edited by Richard Kostelanetz, 183–92. Washington, D.C.: United States International Communication Agency, 1982.

Durand, Régis. "The Anxiety of Performance." *New Literary History* 12 (Autumn 1980): 167–76.

————. "Une nouvelle théâtralité: la performance." *Revue Française D'Etudes Américaines* 5 (1980): 199–207.

Eagleton, Terry. *Literary Theory: An Introduction.* Minneapolis: University of Minnesota Press, 1983.

Eaton, Marcia M. "Liars, Ranters, and Dramatic Speakers." In *Aesthetics Today*, rev. ed., edited by Morris Philipson and Paul J. Gudel, 287–304. New York: New American Library, 1980.

Eder, Doris L. "*Surfiction:* Plunging into the Surface." Review of *Surfiction*, ed. by Raymond Federman. *Boundary 2* 5 (1976): 153–65.

Ehrmann, Jacques. "The Death of Literature." In *Surfiction: Fiction Now . . . And Tomorrow*, edited by Raymond Federman, 229–53. Chicago: Swallow Press, 1975.

Ellmann, Richard, and Charles Feidelson, eds. *The Modern Tradition: Backgrounds to Modern Literature*. New York: Oxford University Press, 1965.

Everman, Welch D. "Raymond Federman." In *Dictionary of Literary Biography Yearbook 1982*, edited by Richard Layman, 195–201. Detroit: Gale Research, 1983.

————. Review of *The Twofold Vibration*, by Raymond Federman. *Chicago Tribune*, 26 September 1982.

Federman, Raymond. *Amer Eldorado*. Paris: Editions Stock, 1974.

————. "Beckettian Paradox: Who Is Telling the Truth?" In *Samuel Beckett Now*, edited by Melvin F. Friedman, 103–17. Chicago: University of Chicago Press, 1970.

————. *Double or Nothing*. Chicago: Swallow Press, 1971.

————. "Federman: Voices within Voices." In *Performance in Postmodern Culture*, edited by Michel Benamou and Charles Caramello. 159–98. Madison: Coda Press, 1977.

———— "Fiction in America Today or the Unreality of Reality." *Indian Journal of American Studies* 14 (1984): 5–16.

————. "Fiction Today or the Pursuit of Non-Knowledge." *Humanities in Society* 1 (1978): 115–31. Reprinted in *Surfiction: Fiction Now . . . And Tomorrow*, 2d ed., edited by Raymond Federman, 291–311. Chicago: Swallow Press, 1981.

————. "From Past Self to Present Self." *Descant* 24 (1979–80): 51–53.

————. "Imagination as Plagiarism (An Unfinished Paper)." *New Literary History* 7 (1976): 563–78.

————. "The Impossibility of Saying the Same Old Thing the Same Old Way—Samuel Beckett's Fiction Since *Comment C'est*." *L'Esprit Créateur* 11 (1971): 21–43.

————. "In." Review of *Out*, by Ronald Sukenick. *Partisan Review* 41 (1974): 137–42.

————. "Inside the Thing." *Cream City Review* 5 (1979): 90–94.

———. "An Interview with Stanisław Lem." *Science-Fiction Studies* 10 (1983): 2–14.

———. *Journey to Chaos: Samuel Beckett's Early Fiction*. Berkeley and Los Angeles: University of California Press, 1965.

———. "Life in the Cylinder," Review of *The Lost Ones*, by Samuel Beckett. *Fiction International* 1 (1973)113–17.

———. *Me Too*. Reno: The Westcoast Poetry Press, 1975.

———. "Moinous Dreams." *Polis* 4 (1983):28–30.

———. "Perhaps the Beginning." *Paris Review*, 1978, no. 74:120–21.

———. "Playgiarism: A Spatial Displacement of Words." *Eureka Review* 1 (1975): 1–17. Revised and expanded in *Substance*, 1977, no. 16:107–12.

———. Review of *Company*, by Samuel Beckett. *American Book Review* 3 (1981): 10.

———. "The Rigmarole of Contrariety." In *Moinous and Sucette*. Buffalo: Bolt Court Press, n.d.

———. "Rumor Transmissible Ad Infinitum in Either Direction." Supplement to *Assembling*, 1976, no. 6, n.p.

———. "Self-Plagiaristic Autobiographical Poem in Form of a Letter from Here to Elsewhere." *Oyez Review*, 1977, no. 5:50–55.

———. "Self/Voice/Performance." In *Coherence: A Gathering of Experiments in Writing: Towards a New Poetics*, edited by Don Wellman, 195–99. Cambridge: O.ARS, 1981.

———. "Surfiction—A Position." *Partisan Review* 40 (1973): 427–32.Reprinted in revised form as "Surfiction—Four Propositions in Form of an Introduction." In *Surfiction: Fiction Now . . . And Tomorrow*, edited by Raymond Federman, 5–15. Chicago: Swallow Press, 1975.

———. *Take It or Leave It*. New York: Fiction Collective, 1976.

———. *The Twofold Vibration*. Bloomington: Indiana University Press, 1982.

———. *The Voice in the Closet / La Voix dans le Cabinet de Débarras.* Madison: Coda Press, 1979.

———. "What Are Experimental Novels and Why Are There So Many Left Unread?" In *Novel vs. Fiction: The Contemporary Reformation,* edited by Jackson I. Cope and Geoffrey Green, 23–31. Norman, Okla.: Pilgrim Books, 1981.

———. "Why Maurice Roche." In *Visual Literature Criticism,* edited by Richard Kostelanetz, 129–33. New York: Precisely: 3 4 5, and Reno: West Coast Poetry Review, 1979.

———. ed. *Surfiction: Fiction Now . . . And Tomorrow.* Chicago: Swallow Press, 1975; 2d ed. 1981.

Federman, Raymond, Mas'ud Zavarzadeh, and Joseph Hynes. "Tri(y)log. *Chicago Review* 28 (1976): 93–109.

Federman, Raymond, and Ronald Sukenick. "The New Innovative Fiction." *Antaeus* 20 (1976): 138–49.

Fish, Stanley, *Is There a Text in This Class?: The Authority of Interpretive Communities.* Cambridge: Harvard University Press, 1980.

Fried, Michael. "Art and Objecthood." In *Aesthetics Today,* rev. ed., edited by Morris Philipson and Paul J. Gudel, 214–39. New York: New American Library, 1980.

Friedman, Melvin J. "Dislocations of Setting and Word: Notes on American Fiction Since 1950." *Studies in American Fiction* 5 (1977): 79–98.

Gass, William H. *Fiction and the Figures of Life.* New York: Alfred A. Knopf, 1970.

Gerz, Jochen. "Towards a Language of Doing." In *Surfiction: Fiction Now . . . And Tomorrow,* edited by Raymond Federman, 279–81. Chicago: Swallow Press, 1975.

Gilman, Richard. *The Confusion of Realms.* New York: Vintage Books, 1970.

Glicksberg, Charles I. "Experimental Fiction: Innovation Versus Form." *Centennial Review,* 1974, no. 18:127–50.

Graff, Gerald. *Literature Against Itself: Literary Ideas in Modern Society.* Chicago: University of Chicago Press, 1979.

Greenberg, Clement. *Art and Culture: Critical Essays.* Boston: Beacon Press, 1965.

Greenman, Myron. "Understanding New Fiction." *Modern Fiction Studies* 20 (1974): 307–16.

Guerard, Albert J. "Notes on the Rhetoric of Anti-realist Fiction." *TriQuarterly,* 1974, no. 30:3–50.

Hall, James B., and Barry Ulanov, eds. *Modern Culture and the Arts.* New York: McGraw-Hill, 1967.

Hassan, Ihab. *Contemporary American Literature 1945–1972: An Introduction.* New York: Frederick Ungar, 1973.

———. *The Dismemberment of Orpheus: Toward a Postmodern Literature.* New York: Oxford University Press, 1971.

———. "Joyce, Beckett, and the Postmodern Imagination." *TriQuarterly,* no. 1975, 34:179–200.

———. *Paracriticisms: Seven Speculations of the Times.* Urbana: University of Illinois Press, 1975.

———. "Reading *Out.*" Review of *Out,* by Ronald Sukenick. *Fiction International,* 1973, no. 1:108–9.

———. *The Right Promethean Fire: Imagination, Science, and Cultural Change.* Urbana: University of Illinois Press, 1980.

———. ed. *Liberations: New Essays on the Humanities in Revolution.* Middletown, Conn.: Wesleyan University Press, 1971

Hein, Hilde. "Performance as an Aesthetic Category." *Journal of Aesthetics and Art Criticism* 28 (1970): 381–86.

Hoffman, Daniel, ed. *Harvard Guide to Contemporary American Writing.* Cambridge: Belknap Press—Harvard University Press, 1979.

Hoffmann, Gerhard, Alfred Hornung, and Rüdiger Kunow. "'Modern,' 'Postmodern' and 'Contemporary' as Criteria for the Analysis of 20th Century Literature." *Amerikastudien* 22 (1977): 19–46.

Holland, Norman H. "Literature as Transaction." In *What Is Literature?* edited by Paul Hernadi, 206–18. Bloomington: Indiana University Press, 1978.

Johnston, Jill. "The New American Modern Dance." In *The New American Arts*, edited by Richard Kostelanetz, 162–93. New York: Horizon Press, 1965.

Kaprow, Allan, " 'Happenings' in the New York Scene." In *The Modern American Theater: A Collection of Critical Essays*, edited by Alvin B. Kernan, 121–30. Englewood Cliffs: Prentice-Hall, 1967.

Kellman, Steven G. *The Self-Begetting Novel.* New York: Columbia University Press, 1980.

Kirby, Michael. "Introduction." In *Happenings: An Illustrated Anthology*, edited by Michael Kirby, 9–42. New York: E. P. Dutton, 1965.

————. "The New Theatre." In *The Avant-Garde Tradition in Literature*, edited by Richard Kostelanetz, 324–40. Buffalo: Prometheus Books, 1982.

Kirchner, Harry, "The Wedding of Dancer and Dance: Fragment No. 1 of an Interview with Raymond Federman." *Cream City Review* 4 (1979): 16–21.

Kirili, Alain, and Raymond Federman. "A Conversation About Clyfford Still." *Osiris*, 1980, no. 11:31–38.

Klinkowitz, Jerome. *The American 1960s: Imaginative Acts in a Decade of Change.* Ames: Iowa State University Press, 1980.

————. "Getting Real: Making It (Up) with Ronald Sukenick," *Chicago Review* 23 (1972): 73–82.

————. *The Life of Fiction.* With graphics by Roy R. Behrens. Urbana: University of Illinois Press, 1977.

————. *Literary Disruptions: The Making of a Post-Contemporary American Fiction.* Urbana: University of Illinois Press, 1975; 2d ed., 1980.

————. "A Persuasive Account: Working It Out with Ronald Sukenick." *North American Review*, 258 (1973), 48–52.

————. *The Practice of Fiction in America: Writers from Hawthorne to the Present.* Ames: Iowa State University Press, 1980.

————. "Raymond Federman's Visual Fiction." In *Visual Literature Criticism*, edited by Richard Kostelanetz. New York:

Precisely 3 4 5, and Reno: West Coast Poetry Review, 1979, 123–124.

———. *The Self-Apparent Word: Fiction as Language / Language as Fiction*. Carbondale: Southern Illinois University Press, 1984.

Klinkowitz, Jerome, and Loree Rackstraw. "The American 1970's: Recent Intellectual Trends." *Revue Française D'Etudes Américaines*, no. 8 (1979): 243–54.

Koch, Kenneth. "Frank O'Hara and His Poetry." In *American Writing Today*, edited by Richard Kostelanetz, 249–63. Washington, D.C.: United States International Communication Agency, 1982.

Kostelanetz, Richard. "Introduction: On the New Arts in America." In *The New American Arts*, edited by Richard Kostelanetz, 11–30. New York: Horizon Press, 1965.

———. "The New American Theatre." In *The New American Arts*, edited by Richard Kostelanetz, 50–87. New York: Horizon Press, 1965.

———. "New Fiction in America." In *Surfiction: Fiction Now . . . And Tomorrow*, edited by Raymond Federman, 85–100. Chicago: Swallow Press, 1975.

———. ed. *American Writing Today*. Washington, D.C.: United States International Communication Agency, 1982.

———, ed. *The Avant-Garde Tradition in Literature*. Buffalo: Prometheus Books, 1982.

———, ed. *The New American Arts*. New York: Horizon Press, 1965.

———, ed. *Visual Literature Criticism*. New York: Precisely: 3 4 5, and Reno: West Coast Poetry Review, 1979.

Kozloff, Max. "The New American Painting." In *The New American Arts*, edited by Richard Kostelanetz, 88–116. New York: Horizon Press, 1965.

Kramer, Hilton. "Postmodern: Art and Culture in the 1980s." *The New Criterion* 1 (1982): 36–42.

LeClair, Tom, and Larry McCaffery, eds. *Anything Can Happen: Interviews with Contemporary American Novelists.* Urbana: University of Illinois Press, 1983.

Libby, Anthony. "O'Hara on the Silver Range." *Contemporary Literature* 17 (1976): 240–62.

Lodge, David. *The Modes of Modern Writing: Metaphor, Metonymy, and the Typology of Modern Literature.* London: Arnold, 1977.

Lowenkron, David Henry. "The Metanovel." *College English* 38 (1976): 343–55.

McCaffery, Larry. "An Interview with Raymond Federman." In *Anything Can Happen: Interviews with Contemporary American Novelists,* edited by Tom LeClair and Larry McCaffery, 126–51. Urbana: University of Illinois Press, 1983.

———. "An Interview with Ronald Sukenick." In *Anything Can Happen: Interviews with Contemporary American Novelists,* edited by Tom LeClair and Larry McCaffery, 277–97. Urbana: University of Illinois Press, 1983.

———. "*Literary Disruptions:* Fiction in a 'Post-Contemporary' Age." *Boundary 2,* 1976, no. 4:137–151.

———. *The Metafictional Muse: The Works of Robert Coover, Donald Barthelme, and William H. Gass.* Pittsburgh: University of Pittsburgh Press, 1982.

———. "New Rules of the Game." Review of *Take It or Leave It,* by Raymond Federman. *Chicago Review* 29 (1977): 145–49.

———. "Raymond Federman and the Fiction of Self-Creation: A Critical Mosaic." *par rapport,* 1981, no. 3–4:31–44.

———. "Surfiction." Review of *Surfiction,* ed. Raymond Federman. *Contemporary Literature* 18 (1977): 250–54.

McFadden, George. "'Literature': A Many-Sided Process." In *What Is Literature?* edited by Paul Hernadi, 49–61. Bloomington: Indiana University Press, 1978.

Marcotte, Edward. "Intersticed Prose." *Chicago Review* 26 (1975): 31–36.

Mellard, James M. *The Exploded Form: The Modernist Novel in America.* Urbana: University of Illinois Press, 1980.

Messerli, Douglas. "Experiment and Traditional Forms in Contemporary Literature." *Sun and Moon,* 1980, no. 9–10:3– 25.

Meyer, Charlotte. "An Interview with Raymond Federman." *Story Quarterly,* 1982 no. 15/16:37–52.

————. "An Interview with Ronald Sukenick." *Contemporary Literature* 23 (1982): 129–44.

Moramarco, Fred. "John Ashbery and Frank O'Hara: The Painterly Poets." *Journal of Modern Literature* 5 (1976): 436– 62.

Morawski, Stefan. *Inquiries into the Fundamentals of Aesthetics.* Cambridge: MIT Press, 1978.

Murray, Timothy. Review of *Take It or Leave It,* by Raymond Federman. *Fiction International,* 1976, no. 6–7:164.

Noel, Daniel C. "Tales of Fictive Power: Dreaming and Imagination in Ronald Sukenick's Postmodern Fiction." *Boundary 2* 5 (1976): 117–35.

————, ed. *Seeing Castaneda: Reactions to the "Don Juan" Writings of Carlos Castaneda.* New York: Capricorn Books, 1976.

O'Hara, Frank. *The Selected Poems of Frank O'Hara.* Edited by Donald Allen. New York: Vintage Books. 1974.

Olderman, Raymond M. *Beyond the Waste Land: A Study of the American Novel in the 1960s.* New Haven: Yale University Press, 1972.

Olson, Charles. *Selected Writings.* Edited by Robert Creeley. New York: New Directions, 1966.

Palmer, Richard. "Postmodernity and Hermeneutics." *Boundary 2* 5 (1977): 363–93.

————. "Toward a Postmodern Hermeneutics of Performance." In *Performance in Postmodern Culture,* edited by Michel Benamou and Charles Caramello, 19–32. Madison: Coda Press, 1977.

———. "Toward a Postmodern Interpretive Self-Awareness."
Journal of Religion, 55 (1975): 313–26.

Parker, Hershel. "The Determinacy of the Creative Process
and the 'Authority' of the Author's Textual Decisions." *College Literature* 10 (1983): 99–125.

Pearce, Richard. "Enter the Frame." *TriQuarterly*, 1974, no.
30:71–82. Reprinted in *Surfiction: Fiction Now . . . And Tomorrow*, edited by Raymond Federman, 47–57. Chicago:
Swallow Press.

———. "Riding the Surf: Raymond Federman, Walter Abish,
and Ronald Sukenick." Unpublished.

———. "Where're They at, Where're They Going? Thomas
Pynchon and the American Novel in Motion." Unpublished.

Perloff, Marjorie. *Frank O'Hara: Poet among Painters*. Austin:
University of Texas Press, 1979.

———. *The Poetics of Indeterminacy: Rimbaud to Cage*. Princeton:
Princeton University Press, 1981.

———. " 'Unimpededness and Interpenetration': The Poetic
of John Cage." *TriQuarterly*, 1982, no. 54:76–88.

Philipson, Morris, and Paul J. Gudel, eds. *Aesthetics Today*, rev.
ed. New York: New American Library, 1980.

Poggioli, Renato. *The Theory of the Avant-Garde*. Cambridge:
Harvard University Press, 1981.

Poirier, Richard. *The Performing Self: Compositions and Decompositions in the Languages of Contemporary Life*. New York:
Oxford University Press, 1971.

———. *A World Elsewhere: The Place of Style in American Literature*. New York: Oxford University Press, 1966.

———. "Writing Off the Self." *Raritan* 1 (1981):106–33.

Pütz, Manfred. *The Story of Identity: American Fiction of the Sixties*. Stuttgart: Metzler, 1979.

Quartermain, Peter. "Trusting the Reader." Review of *The
Voice in the Closet*, by Raymond Federman. *Chicago Review*
32 (1980): 65–74.

Riddel, Joseph N. "Wallace Stevens." In *Sixteen Modern American Authors: A Survey of Research and Criticism,* edited by Jackson R. Bryer, 529–71. New York: W. W. Norton, 1973.

Rockwell, John. "Is 'Performance' a New Form of Art?" *New York Times,* 14 August 1983. sec. 2, 1, 13.

Rosenberg, Harold. *The Anxious Object: Art Today and Its Audience.* New York: Collier, 1973.

————. *The De-Definition of Art.* New York: Collier, 1973.

————. *The Tradition of the New.* New York: Horizon Press, 1959.

Rothenberg, Jerome. "New Models, New Visions: Some Notes Toward a Poetics of Performance." In *Performance in Postmodern Culture,* edited by Michel Benamou and Charles Caramello, 11–17. Madison, Coda Press, 1977.

————. *Pre-Faces and Other Writings.* New York: New Directions, 1981.

Russell, Charles. "Individual Voice in the Collective Discourse: Literary Innovation in Postmodern American Fiction." *Substance* no. 27:29–39.

————. "Subversion and Legitimation: The Avant-Garde in Postmodern Culture." *Chicago Review* 23 (1982): 54–59.

————, ed. *The Avant-Garde Today: An International Anthology.* Urbana: University of Illinois Press, 1981.

Sachner, Mark. "How to Tell the Teller from the Told?: Fragment No. 2 of an Interview with Raymond Federman." *Cream City Review* 5 (1979): 76–88.

Said, Edward W. "The Problem of Textuality: Two Exemplary Positions." In *Aesthetics Today,* edited by Morris Philipson and Paul J. Gudel, 87–133. New York: New American Library, 1980.

Salzman, Eric. "The New American Music." In *The New American Arts,* edited by Richard Kostelanetz, 237–64. New York: Horizon Press, 1965.

Sayre, Henry M. "The Object of Performance: Aesthetics in the Seventies." *Georgia Review* 37 (1983): 169–88.

Schechner, Richard. *Essays on Performance Theory 1970–1976.* New York: Drama Books Specialists, 1977.

———. *Public Domain: Essays on Theatre.* New York: Bobbs-Merrill, 1969.

Schmitt, Natalie Cohn. "John Cage, Nature, and Theatre." *TriQuarterly*, 1982, no. 54:89–109.

Scholes, Robert. "The Contributions of Formalism and Structuralism to the Theory of Fiction." In *Towards a Poetics of Fiction,* edited by Mark Spilka, 107–24. Bloomington: Indiana University Press, 1977.

———. *Fabulation and Metafiction.* Urbana: University of Illinois Press, 1979.

———, and Robert Kellog. *The Nature of Narrative.* London: Oxford University Press, 1966.

Siegle, Robert. "The Concept of the Author in Barthes, Foucault, and Fowles." *College Literature* 10 (1983): 126–38.

Smith, Barbara Herrnstein. "Literature, as Performance, Fiction, and Art." *Journal of Philosophy* 67 (1970): 555–63.

Sollers, Philippe. "The Novel and the Experience of Limits." In *Surfiction: Fiction Now . . . And Tomorrow,* edited by Raymond Federman, 59–74. Chicago: Swallow Press, 1975.

Sontag, Susan. *Against Interpretation and Other Essays.* New York: Dell, 1969.

———. *Under the Sign of Saturn.* New York: Farrar, Strauss, Giroux, 1980.

Sparshott, F. E. *The Structure of Aesthetics.* Toronto: University of Toronto Press; London: Routledge and Kegan Paul, 1963.

Stevens, Wallace. *The Collected Poems of Wallace Stevens.* New York: Alfred A. Knopf, 1954.

Stevick, Philip. *Alternative Pleasures: Postrealist Fiction and the Tradition.* Urbana: University of Illinois Press, 1981.

———. "Introduction." In *Anti-Story: An Anthology of Experimental Fiction,* edited by Philip Stevick, ix–xxiii. New York: Free Press, 1971.

Sukenick, Ronald. "Art and the Underground." *American Book Review* 6 (1984): 2–3; Reprinted in *In Form: Digressions on the Act of Fiction.* Carbondale and Edwardsville: Southern Illinois University Press, 1985 (hereafter referred to as *IF*).

———. "At This Very Instant." *Fiction International* 15 (1984): 92–96.

———. Commentary on "The Birds." In *Cutting Edges: Young American Fiction for the '70s,* edited by Jack Hicks, 548. New York: Holt, Rinehart and Winston, 1973.

———. *The Death of the Novel and Other Stories.* New York: Dial Press, 1969.

———. "Eight Digressions on the Politics of Language." *New Literary History* 10 (1979), 467–77; *IF*, pp. 49–65.

———. "The Endless Short Story." *Village Voice,* 6 September 1973.

———. "Endless Short Story (Aziff)." *TriQuarterly,* 1976, no. 35:42.

———. "Endless Short Story: Boxes." *Fiction* 6 (1980):141–51.

———. "The Endless Short Story: Dong Wang." In *Statements 2,* edited by Jonathan Baumbach and Peter Spielberg, 212–17. New York: Fiction Collective, 1977.

———. "Endless Short Story: The Finnegan Digression." *Substance,* 1980, no. 27:3–6; *IF*, pp. 99–103.

———. "Endless Short Story: Five and Ten." *Criss-Cross Art Communications* 6 (1978): 36–41.

———. "The Endless Short Story: Verticals and Horizontals." In *Statements: New Fiction from the Fiction Collective,* edited by Jonathan Baumbach, 184–88. New York: George Braziller, 1975.

———. "Endless Short Story: What's Watts." *New Letters* 45 (1979): 177–79.

———. "Extract from *The Fortune Teller.*" *Trema,* 1977, no. 2:143–46.

———. "Fiction in the Seventies: Ten Digressions on Ten Digressions." *Studies in American Fiction* 5 (1977): 99–108; *IF*, pp. 34–48.

———. "Film Digression. *IF*, pp. 83–98.

———. "From 'The Endless Short Story.'" *Lillabulero*, 1974, no. 14:109–118.

———. *In Form: Digressions on the Act of Fiction.* Carbondale and Edwardsville: Southern Illinois University Press, 1985.

———. "Live and Let Alone on the Lower East Side." *Village Voice*, 13 June 1968.

———. *Long Talking Bad Conditions Blues.* New York: Fiction Collective, 1979.

———. "Misreading Bloom." Review of *Wallace Stevens: The Poems of Our Climate*, by Harold Bloom. *Partisan Review* 45 (1978): 634–36; *IF*, pp. 231–34.

———. "News from Utopia." *Harper's Bookletter*, 18 August 1975.

———. "The New Tradition." *Partisan Review* 39 (1972):580–88. Reprinted in *Surfiction: Fiction Now ... And Tomorrow*, edited by Raymond Federman, 35–45. Chicago: Swallow Press, 1975. *IF*, pp. 201–13.

———. "The Next Part of the Story." *Village Voice*, 13 September 1973.

———. "Nine Digressions on Narrative Authority." *IF*, pp. 66–82.

———. *98.6.* New York: Fiction Collective, 1975.

———. "On the New Cultural Conservatism." *Partisan Review* 39 (1972): 448–51.

———. "On Paul Metcalf." *Lillabulero*, 1973, no. 12:49–50; *IF*, pp. 238–40.

———. "On Reinventing the Novel: Innovative Fiction/Innovative Criteria." *Fiction International*, 1976, no. 2–3:133–34; *IF*, pp. 241–43.

———. *Out.* Chicago: Swallow Press, 1973.

————. "A Postcard from *The Endless Short Story.*" Austin: Cold Mountain Press Poetry Post Card Series Two, 1974.

————. Review of *The Adventures of Mao on the Long March,* by Frederic Tuten. *New York Times Book Review,* 7 November 1971.

————. Review of *The Bonnyclabber,* by George Chambers. *New York Times Book Review,* 3 March 1973.

————. Review of *Double or Nothing,* by Raymond Federman. *New York Times Book Review,* 1 October 1972.

————. Review of *Literature Against Itself,* by Gerald Graff. *American Book Review* 3 (1981):5; *IF,* pp. 234–38.

————. Review of *Was That a Real Poem and Other Essays,* by Robert Creeley. *American Book Review* 3 (1981): 2–3; *IF,* pp. 226–31.

————. "Statement." In *Statements: New Fiction from the Fiction Collective,* edited by Jonathan Baumbach, 7–8. New York: George Braziller, 1975.

————. "Taboo or Not Taboo." *Village Voice,* 3 January 1974.

————. "Thirteen Digressions." *Partisan Review* 43 (1976): 90–101; *IF,* pp. 16–33.

————. "Twelve Digressions Toward a Study of Composition." *New Literary History* 6 (1976): 429–37: *IF,* pp. 3–15.

————. *Up.* New York: Dial Press, 1968.

————. "Upward and Juanward: The Possible Dream." *Village Voice,* 25 January 1973. Reprinted in *Seeing Castaneda: Reactions to the "Don Juan" Writings of Carlos Castaneda,* edited by Daniel C. Noel, 110–20. New York: Capricorn Books, 1976. *IF,* pp. 214–25.

————. *Wallace Stevens: Musing the Obscure.* New York: New York University Press, 1967; first section, "Wallace Stevens: Theory and Practice," collected in *IF,* pp. 157–98.

Sukenick, Ronald, and Raymond Federman. "The New Innovative Fiction." *Antaeus,* 1976, no. 20:138–49.

Suleiman, Susan R., and Inge Crossman, eds. *The Reader in the Text: Essays on Audience and Interpretation.* Princeton: Princeton University Press, 1980.

Tanner, Tony. *City of Words: American Fiction 1950–1970.* London: Jonathan Cape, 1976.

———. "My Life in American Literature." *TriQuarterly,* 1974, no. 30:83–108.

Tatham, Campbell. "Mythotherapy and Postmodern Fictions: Magic Is Afoot." In *Performance in Postmodern Culture,* edited by Michel Benamou and Charles Caramello, 137–57. Madison: Coda Press, 1977.

———. " 'Your Ball' or Performance and Transformance in Postmodern Fiction." *Cream City Review* 5 (1979): 68–75.

Tompkins, Jane, ed. *Reader-Response Criticism: From Formalism to Post-Structuralism.* Baltimore: Johns Hopkins University Press, 1981.

Turner, Victor. *Dramas, Fields, and Metaphors: Symbolic Action in Human Society.* Ithaca: Cornell University Press, 1974.

———. "Frame, Flow and Reflection: Ritual and Drama as Public Liminality." In *Performance in Postmodern Culture,* edited by Michel Benamou and Charles Caramello, 33–55. Madison: Coda Press, 1977.

Vendler, Helen. *Part of Nature, Part of Us: Modern American Poets.* Cambridge: Harvard University Press, 1980.

Wellek, René, and Austin Warren. *Theory of Literature.* New York: Harcourt, Brace and Co., 1949.

Wellman, Don. *Coherence: A Gathering of Experiments in Writing: Towards a New Poetics.* Cambridge: O.ARS, 1981.

Wittgenstein, Ludwig. *Tractatus Logico-Philosophicus.* Translated by D. F. Pears and B. F. McGuinness. London: Routledge and Kegan Paul; New York: Humanities Press, 1961.

Index

Jerzy Kutnik received his Ph.D. from Maria Curie-Sklodowska University, Lublin, Poland, in 1984, where he has taught American history and culture since 1977. In 1984–85, he was a fellow of the American Council of Learned Scoieties at the Center for Twentieth Century Studies, University of Wisconsin-Milwaukee. He has published article on postmodern culture, art, and literature in journals in Poland and in the United States.